THE CODFATHERS

Mr. Williams !

Happy 85th Birthday
from one Maritimer to
another !

JY 12/08

THE Cod

fathers

LESSONS FROM
THE ATLANTIC BUSINESS ELITE

GORDON PITTS

KEY PORTER BOOKS

Library and Archives Canada Cataloguing in Publication

Pitts, Gordon
    The codfathers : lessons from the Atlantic business elite / Gordon Pitts.

Includes index.
ISBN 978-1-55263-718-0 (bound).—ISBN 978-1-55470-089-9 (pbk.)

1. Businesspeople—Atlantic Provinces. 2. Family-owned business enterprises—Atlantic Provinces. I. Title.

HC112.5.A2P57 2005   338.092'2'715   C2005-902770-3

THE CANADA COUNCIL | LE CONSEIL DES ARTS
FOR THE ARTS | DU CANADA
SINCE 1957 | DEPUIS 1957

ONTARIO ARTS COUNCIL
CONSEIL DES ARTS DE L'ONTARIO

The publisher gratefully acknowledges the support of the Canada Council for the Arts and the Ontario Arts Council for its publishing program. We acknowledge the support of the Government of Ontario through the Ontario Media Development Corporation's Ontario Book Initiative.

We acknowledge the financial support of the Government of Canada through the Book Publishing Industry Development Program (BPIDP) for our publishing activities.

Key Porter Books Limited
Six Adelaide Street East, Tenth Floor
Toronto, Ontario
Canada M5C 1H6

www.keyporter.com

Text design: Ingrid Paulson
Electronic formatting: Beth Crane, Heidy Lawrance Associates

Printed and bound in Canada

08 09 10 11 12   5 4 3 2 1

To Gayle and Grant.
This time, more than ever

CONTENTS

PREFACE

I AM NOT A MARITIMER. Salt water does not course through my veins. I have never sailed, nor fished for salmon. I did grow up listening to Don Messer and his Islanders, but that was not by choice. I do not like fiddleheads all that much.

But as a Canadian business journalist for the past 30 years, I've run into a lot of Maritimers. They are everywhere: on Bay Street, in major economic jobs in Ottawa, and running the top companies in the land. I became a specialist in family business, and, lo and behold, the best family-owned companies turned out to be in the Maritimes and Newfoundland. I sensed there was something going on here. Could it be that Atlantic Canadians, sometimes characterized as poverty-stricken, EI-addicted laggards in the economic race, are actually running the country?

I'd meet some captain of industry and he'd tell me of growing up in the upper Saint John River Valley. Bank presidents would want to talk about their first jobs as tellers in St. Stephen or Digby. Then I ran into the McCain brothers, Wallace and Harrison, who actually managed a global french fry empire from Florenceville, New Brunswick—population: 750.

All these titans knew each other. They'd gone to school together, fished or sailed with each other, and done business with each other. So when Harrison McCain died in March 2004, they came out in force to bid final respects to their old comrade. It was a gathering of aging, mostly male chieftains, those who had built huge empires in the Maritimes and those who went away to make their names. It was like a solemn gathering of dons at some Mafia capo's funeral.

So when I wrote a story for the *Globe and Mail* on this generation of Atlantic leaders, it seemed only natural that Frank McKenna, the former premier of New Brunswick, would say jokingly he is part of a "Maritime Mafia," a tightly knit, loyal network of owners and professionals. Others noted that there was a Newfoundland Mafia too, but it was quite different in style. I figured that if there are such mafias, Wallace McCain, Arthur and James Irving, Ron Joyce, Richard Currie, and Donald and David Sobey must be among the godfathers—or, perhaps more appropriately, the "Codfathers." Shortly after my story ran, Wallace McCain told me of being approached by a woman who had read the article and was curious about his Mafia connections. She just didn't know that sort of thing went on in the Maritimes.

Publisher Anna Porter saw the story too, and she approached me about writing a book about this little-known managerial and entrepreneurial elite. Of course, I wasn't a Maritimer or a Newfoundlander, but I felt that only an Upper Canadian could appreciate the wider power and influence of this group. I might not know the mean streets of the south end of Saint John, but I know the meaner streets of King and Bay in Toronto, where Maritimers are also a force to be reckoned with.

Besides, I had grown up listening to Don, Charlie, and Marg, I laughed with Stompin' Tom and consider Stan Rogers to be a Canadian treasure. I too came from the East—rural Eastern Ontario, another region marginalized by the huge, sprawling mass of Toronto. I am a country boy with a background similar to the self-made plutocrats who dominate the

Maritime Mafia. I understand that of all the Atlantic Canada icons, the cod fishery is perhaps the oldest symbol of pride and resilience. Now, with that fishery facing an increasingly uncertain future, this region needs new icons of hope. These bosses of blueberries, scallops, cable TV, oil, french fries, beer, and airlines, whose stories are told in this book, are truly the Codfathers for the 21st century.

THERE ARE MANY PEOPLE to acknowledge for helping bring this book to life. Much thanks to John Stackhouse and Cathryn Motherwell, my editors at the *Globe and Mail*'s *Report on Business*; to a former editor, Mike Babad; and to my colleagues, especially my pod-mates past and present, Greg, John, Keith, Marina, Marian, Richard, Catherine, Haris, and Bruce.

I am indebted to all the people who sat down for interviews, including: Trevor Adey, George Armoyan, Dan Barker, Jon Barry, Mark Binns, John Bragg, Lee Bragg, Lino Celeste, John Chamard, Purdy Crawford, John Crosbie, Brian Lee Crowley, Richard Currie, Sir Graham Day, Craig Dobbin, Mark Dobbin, Phil Dowd, Trudy Eagan, Tom Eisenhauer, Geoff Flood, Kevin Francis, Bryana Ganong, David Ganong, Gary Gorman, Julie Gossen, Buzz Hargrove, Lawson Hunter, Bernard Imbeault, Peter Jelley, Laura McCain Jensen, Ron Joyce, Colin Latham, Brian Levitt, Dean MacDonald, John MacDonald, Judith Maxwell, Allison McCain, Wallace McCain, Michael McCain, Frank McKenna, John McLennan, Derek Oland, Giles Oland, Steve Parker, Ches Penney, Gerry Pond, Sean Riley, John Risley, Cedric Ritchie, Derrick Rowe, Ken Rowe, Donald Savoie, Katherine Scott, Allan Shaw, Robert Shea, Richard Simms, Irwin Simon, David Sobey, Donald Sobey, Frank Sobey, Paul Sobey, Rob Sobey, John Steele, Rob Steele, Annette Verschuren, Rod White, Vic Young, and Robert Zildjian.

I want to acknowledge books that I found helpful: *Citizens Irving* by John DeMont; *A House Divided* by Paul Waldie; *The Edible Man* by Ann Kingston; *Pulling Against Gravity* by Donald Savoie; *Tales from Under the Rim* by Ron Buist; *Frank* by Philip Lee; *The Right Fight* by Jacques Poitras; *Rockbound* by Frank Parker Day; *Open Ice* by Doug Hunter; *Frank Sobey* by Harry Bruce; *Rare Ambition* by Michael Harris; and of course, *Please Kill Me: The Uncensored Oral History of Punk,* compiled by Legs McNeill and Gillian McCain.

For special help, inspiration, and hospitality, I want to thank Bob Blunden, Scott McCain, Ruth McCrea, Jennifer Henderson and Costas Halavrezos, Gary O'Meara, Dave Pyette, Sarah and Charles, John DeMont and, for beer and talk, the denizens of The Ship pub and The Rose and Thistle in St. John's.

As always, I am deeply in debt to my family, Elaine, Martha, and Katie, my co-conspirators; Mum, for making me watch Don Messer; Jayne; Scott and Doris; Lib and Steve; and the nieces and nephews. Gayle and Grant were there for me, with their house and unconditional support. My agent Dean Cooke was, as usual, a rock.

Special thanks to the people at Key Porter, led by Anna Porter, who had the idea; Jordan Fenn, who supported that vision; and Meg Taylor, my superb editor and true friend who brought the Talisker. Finally, to Molly, who sat beside me through yet another book.

FRANK'S PARTY

IT IS A SUNNY AUGUST afternoon on the rugged shores of the Northumberland Strait in northern Nova Scotia. Sleek cars deliver prosperous-looking men and women to the luxury golf course built by Tim Hortons doughnut tycoon Ron Joyce. The landing strip nearby is a constant blur of activity as executive planes roar in from London, England, and from Toronto and Saint John. As they emerge from their cars and private planes, visitors take in the softly rolling greens, big blue sky, rustic-style luxury condos, and the coast of Prince Edward Island twinkling on the horizon.

Who are these impressive, affluent people who have landed in the heart of the Atlantic provinces, reputed to be an economic backwater? They are the region's far-flung economic elite, including many of Canada's, and the world's, leading business titans. They have come together at the invitation of Moncton lawyer and former New Brunswick premier Frank McKenna to attend his fourth annual Maritimes business summit, held for the second year at the Nova Scotia golf course of Fox Harb'r.

They gather from near and far. From just down the road in Stellarton, there are the Sobey grocery titans, led by the current patriarchs, Donald and David; David's son Paul, the leader of the next generation; Donald's son Robert; and their nephew, Frank, namesake of the company's late, great empire-builder. There are the reclusive brothers Arthur and James Irving, the most powerful businessmen in the Maritimes, and their children, including Kenneth, the tall, coolly handsome boss of Irving Oil, and Jim Jr., the hulking leader of the Irving forestry interests. From the canyons of Bay Street, there is Purdy Crawford, the wise Buddha who advises many of these people, and his friend and sparring partner, John Bragg, the world's blueberry king from nearby Oxford, Nova Scotia. From Calgary, millionaire oilman Grant Bartlett has come to see his friend Ron Joyce and drop in on his family in Nova Scotia. Derek Oland, from one of the oldest business clans in the Maritimes, and Bernard Imbeault, from one of its newest, have come in from New Brunswick. There is the gregarious host, Ron Joyce, the former cop who teamed up with NHL hockey star Tim Horton to create what became an $800-million fortune from doughnuts and coffee. And there is food magnate Wallace McCain, and his sons Scott and Michael, all tall and rangy like Gary Cooper striding in from central casting for some western movie.

But there is one titan who is not present, Wallace's older brother, Harrison, a dominant figure in this Maritime business class until very recently. Many of these same people had gathered five months earlier in a small white church in Florenceville on the Saint John River to pay their last respects to Harrison McCain, who died after a long battle with heart disease and related ailments. His absence leaves a huge void because he was a kinetic force, larger than life, even in his early seventies when he was ailing. With Wallace, he had built a global french fry empire, then the two men feuded over succession, and Wallace emigrated to Toronto. Toward the end of Harrison's life, they had reached a rapprochement. For the aging patriarchs of Maritime business, it is a touching reminder of the passage of time and generations, and of the heavy burdens of succession.

On this August day in 2004, they have also come to see Bill Clinton, the former U.S. president, who has taken time off from a busy book tour to make a detour to Fox Harb'r, for a rumoured six-figure fee, which is being picked up by McKenna's corporate sponsors, including his law firm McInnes Cooper. The former president is noticeably tired and wan, showing signs of the heart problems that, a few weeks later, landed him in hospital for a bypass operation. But on this evening, he would be electric, delivering a stunning summary of the world's geopolitical landscape. The 150 men and women assembled in Fox Harb'r's health club for the evening speech are mightily impressed. "I sat on the edge of my chair," John Bragg says later. "It was like he was lecturing to a group of doctoral students about world affairs." Wallace McCain likens Clinton to a racehorse who canters listlessly to the starting gate and then when he hears the crowd clapping, he really gets into it and comes alive, despite his obvious fatigue.

These men and women appreciate Clinton for another reason: the former Arkansas governor was a politician from a desperately poor and backward part of his country—an area dismissed as a lightweight economic power—who rose to national importance, who brought respect and recognition to his home state. "The man from Hope" was held up as a role model for Frank McKenna, the former New Brunswick premier who became a major national figure by drawing investment and jobs to his hard-scrabble province. "I have always been high on him," McKenna muses. "I, too, was trying to punch above my weight." In fact, Clinton is a model

for all the men and women in the room, who wield an influence and power that belies the economic weakness of the
region that spawned them. After all, Arkansas has bred not
only the smartest U.S. politician of his era but also world-class
companies, such as Wal-Mart, the world's largest retailer, and
Tyson Foods, the chicken empire, that wield power dispro-
portionate to the income and size of their state. Maritimers
see themselves in the same mould.

It shows that being poor and thinly populated can actually be a competitive advantage, giving this area the tightest
and most influential business network in the country. It has
created a paradox, in fact. This regional financial weakling,
considered a quaint, rustic but impoverished vacation spot
—the home of Anne of Green Gables, Anne Murray, and
Stompin' Tom Connors—is a subtle powerhouse in the world
economy, turning out some of the most innovative and
powerful business leaders. Think of all the superlatives of
Atlantic Canada: it holds the country's biggest oil refinery;
the world's largest french fry producer; the world's major
blueberry producer; the country's major scallop supplier, to
name a few. But these men and women tell another story: In
parallel with blue-collar Atlantic Canadians who have "gone
down the road," well-educated Maritime managers and owners
have often outgrown their roots in the East to find careers in
Central and Western Canada, the United States, and the rest
of the world. There is the example of corporate lawyer Purdy
Crawford, the kid from Five Islands, Nova Scotia, just south
of Fox Harb'r, who plays the role of the conscience of
Corporate Canada, or Richard Currie, the son of a Saint
John machinist, who became the finest manager of his generation as he helped build Loblaws into the country's leading
grocery empire.

This export of entrepreneurial and managerial talent is Canada's worst-kept secret. Both expatriate and home-based branches of the Maritime Mafia, the tight network at the heart of this economic power, operate so quietly and subtly, you can hardly hear the loonies jingling in their ample pockets. But anyone who operates in Bay Street or Calgary's oil patch knows that the Mafia is all pervasive and very loyal to its origins.

Critics might argue that these people are just part of the East Coast disease of poverty and dependency, that they have to leave home to find opportunity, thus contributing to the managerial and human-talent deficit in these traditionally have-not provinces. That observation is valid but the reality is more complex. More than any group of expatriate managers, Maritimers, as well as their Newfoundland cousins, retain a sense of place, of the land and sea that produced them. They keep second homes and cottages on the East Coast; some even commute to Toronto and Montreal on a weekly basis. Or they stay rooted close to home, working for the powerful family companies that form the foundation of the Maritime establishment. This fierce loyalty is, in fact, the Maritimes' single biggest competitive advantage, the one characteristic that gives this region a fighting chance in the global economic wars.

It is an elite that is small and compact enough that you can hold it in your hands, which is another source of its effectiveness. In Toronto, there is a Bay Street elite, a Chinese-Canadian business elite, an Italian property elite, a former European tradesman elite—but in the Maritimes, there is just the Maritime Mafia. It is the McCains, Irvings, Sobeys, and their friends and advisers, plus a trove of expatriates doing business in other parts of the world. (It is the same pattern with Newfoundlanders, who have experienced a large diaspora of managerial and technical talent.) The Maritimers went to school together in the East Coast universities; they work in the capital campaigns of the universities and hospitals; meet regularly on the boards of the Sobey family's two public companies, of Wallace McCain's Maple Leaf Foods or shell-fish entrepreneur John Risley's Clearwater Seafoods. They do business with the Maritimes' elite law firm Stewart McKelvey Stirling Scales, or McInnes Cooper, Frank McKenna's old law firm. They are members of the Atlantic Institute for Market Studies, the subversively free-market think-tank run by Brian Lee Crowley, a transplanted Vancouverite who preaches cold turkey from handouts in a region that, in the view of many outsiders, mainlines grants and unemployment benefits. Many have been members of the Atlantic chapter of the Young Presidents' Organization. They play together, sailing on week-ends or, in New Brunswick, taking off to a fishing lodge on the Miramichi or Restigouche rivers—and recently they have been meeting at Fox Harb'r.

This is not the only region that exerts such a powerful hold on its departed sons and daughters—the eastern Quebec area of the Beauce produces legions of entrepreneurs who do very well in Montreal. Saskatchewan has created a genera-tion of oilmen who have made fortunes in Calgary. But as Purdy Crawford slyly points out, his friends from Saskat-chewan don't seem to have that urge to go back to their home province whenever they can. This is the age of the Maritime Mafia, when the ranks of Canadian business are replete with folks who frankly would prefer to be sailing off Lunenburg or Digby or Saint John rather than fighting the morning rush hour in Toronto. But the poor economic prospects at home have turned many of them into affluent émigrés, forced to live and work away from the land they love.

As they move away, Maritimers take with them a style of management that is distinct and influential. Rather than becoming Upper Canadians or New Yorkers, they quietly infiltrate the business cultures of their new homes and introduce their own Maritime ways to their new colleagues. They tend to be strong in operations, in running manufacturing and processing functions, in watching their income statements with the sharp eyes of a swooping seagull. They are not financial engineers who play with balance sheets and asset numbers, and they leave the marketing to others. They believe if you build a sound company, watch your pennies, and keep your people happy, the other stuff will look after itself. This inclination sometimes limits Maritimers to certain industries, such as manufacturing and food processing. The one Achilles heel of Atlantic business people is the danger of insularity from new ideas. But the good ones are wise enough to reach out to other talents. One master of this is Richard Currie, who skillfully tapped the marketing and financial minds of his managers in building a grocery colossus.

Maritimers are often blunt, no-nonsense communicators who despise what they call the "bullshit" of Toronto's Bay Street. They'd prefer to seal a deal with a handshake rather than a lawyer's letter. They operate on a first-name basis— in McCain Foods, the owners were always "Wallace" and "Harrison." The forestry Irvings are James and Jim Jr., or, J.K. and J.D, respectively. This informality is not so much a Maritime trait but a rural Canadian characteristic, and the best Maritime companies are rural in home and culture: the McCains from Florenceville, the Sobeys from Stellarton, and even the Irvings, whose headquarters is Saint John but whose soul resides in the original titan K.C. Irving's birthplace of Bouctouche, New Brunswick.

There is another aspect to this openness and candour— most of these tycoons cuss like the sailors they often are on the weekends. The air turns blue with expletives. The McCains are legendary for their swearing, and some Sobeys have to tone it down in front of outsiders. Michael McCain, Wallace's son, once said that if you took all the cuss words out of his father's and uncle's vocabulary they would become functionally illiterate.

History and geography have made many Maritimers more comfortable doing business with New Englanders than with Central Canadians. The East Coast's modern commercial history began in the 1600s and 1700s as one corner of a trading triangle with Britain and the Caribbean, and in the 19th century, New England began to replace Old England as the focus. In pre-Confederation days, the U.S. market was always part of the home market for these children of United Empire Loyalists, Acadians and Scottish, English and Irish immigrants. The major lines of commerce ran north-south. It was only with Confederation and the building of the railroads that the Maritimes began to look west, first to Montreal and then to Toronto. Maritimers often felt that trade-off, which brought a measure of economic security, robbed them of their heritage and their great potential, as they slid into relative poverty compared with their new central Canadian compatriots. But the people migrations continued to be north-south, and sports affections remained tied to the Bruins and Red Sox, not the teams of Toronto and Montreal. Now, in the 21st century, free trade has restored the north-south axis and Maritimers are revelling again in their natural ties to the "Boston states."

Like Richard Currie, they see themselves as meritocrats, who believe it is possible to rise from poverty to great wealth. There is old money in the Atlantic region, and the traditional Halifax elite in particular was a bastion of privileged closed society. The old family companies still dominate huge swaths of the region. But it is possible to get to the top in one generation. Two of the bumptious arrivistes are Ron Joyce, the unschooled son of a working-class widow, and John Risley, who once had his phone ripped off the wall by the telephone company when he couldn't pay his bills.

But there are not many women at Fox Harb'r, for the Maritime Mafia is still a testosterone-drenched culture. The aging chieftains of the big family businesses, with some exceptions, have designated sons to inherit their businesses. Yet there is hope among the daughters, who in many cases have forged their own impressive careers—such as Mary Jean and Judy Irving, successful daughters of James Irving; and Laura McCain Jensen, the wine-making daughter of Harrison McCain, and her sister Gillian, an accomplished New York poet. Others are taking bigger roles inside the family business, such as chocolate heiress Bryana Ganong; and Julie Gossen, who runs CanJet Airlines, one arm of the Halifax aviation empire built by her father, Ken Rowe. But it's also striking that there are not many new Canadians among this elite, a reflection of the closed culture and the inability to attract and keep a dynamic immigrant entrepreneurial cadre.

Still, Maritimers do exhibit a handy flexibility in one area: the ability to cross easily between public and private sectors, which perhaps reflects the nature of business in the region. A number of core industries, including fisheries and agribusiness, mix private ownership with a heavy government hand. The gang from St. Francis Xavier University seems particularly adept—witness the government-business careers of Frank McKenna and former prime minister Brian Mulroney, both St. FX grads. But the most striking example is Peter Nicholson, son of a Nova Scotia provincial finance minister and a brilliant strategic thinker whose career often seems like a flurry of movement between the corridors of corporate power and the halls of government. Once part of a federal fisheries task force and a key adviser at the Bank of Nova Scotia and telecom giant BCE, he recently moved from the Organisation for Economic Co-operation and Development in Paris to the office of Prime Minister Paul Martin. Another Maritimer comfortable in private and public enterprise is Judith Maxwell, one of Canada's economic thought leaders and Nicholson's high school classmate in Annapolis Royal, Nova Scotia. Maxwell, an Anglican minister's daughter whose career has been as sparkling as Nicholson's, says there is no formal network of Maritimers in Ottawa, but "there is a very special warmth in knowing that those other people grew up in those small towns in the East. There is a kinship."

As Maritimers expand their influence, their management traits become the ruling characteristics of Canadian executives: In the world economy, Canadians are known to be adaptable, practical, no-nonsense, meritocratic, and possessing the ability to adapt gracefully to public and private enterprise. Like Maritimers, they remain hopelessly devoted to the physical environment they grew up in. For Maritimers, the tug of the sea and the soil is powerful, plus there is the view that it isn't "right" that their region has evolved in the 20th and 21st centuries as the sad sack of Canada. So they come home with hope and the expectation that they can actually change things.

These homing instincts are most evident in August, when there are hundreds of family gatherings as the cousins and the children make their annual visits "from away." This is sacred time for the Mafia as they replenish their spirit, and their closeness to the land and sea. And Fox Harb'r is the central networking event, where the old and new elites come together to play golf, drink wine, do business, and listen to some high-powered celebrity speaker—such as Clinton, Paul Martin, John Major, or George Bush Sr. When Frank McKenna was trying to persuade Bill Clinton to come to Fox Harb'r, his ace in the hole was the presence of a native New Brunswicker on Clinton's personal staff. The Mafia extends into a surprisingly broad territory.

It is appropriate that Frank McKenna is holding this event, because as premier, he was the most masterful player in this network, whether scoring a new call centre for Saint John through an old university contact or getting to the bottom of a labour dispute. When there was union trouble, he knew he could call Basil (Buzz) Hargrove, born in Bath, New Brunswick, but now boss of the powerful Canadian Auto Workers union. "I'd call Buzz and curse at him, and say, 'Listen, you're going to close this goddam place down.' There's a brotherhood where we can do that."

Indeed, the story of the Maritimes can be told through the Hargroves of tiny Mineral, New Brunswick, who came to Canada from England in the 18th–19th centuries and became hard-scrabble farmers along the Saint John Valley. And look what's happened to them: Norton Hargrove is a senior executive in Sabian Cymbals, a musical instrument company in Meductic, New Brunswick, that makes percussion instruments for a global music market. Second cousin Basil is the top executive for McCain Foods in Australia, leading that company's bold expansion into China. And his namesake and cousin, also named Basil but better known as Buzz, is nothing less than the most powerful union leader in Canada. Buzz, the labour leader, is proud of his cousins and siblings, who rose from poverty in the New Brunswick backwoods to become leaders in Canadian labour and capital. But he admires none of them more than his brother Nevil, who stayed home, built a fine Petro-Can service station and repair business in Hartland, New Brunswick, and is now the town's mayor. That, too, represents success. Through the Hargroves, the historical journey and the modern reach of this Maritime Mafia become clear.

CHAPTER 1

ONE WORLD, ONE FRY

MICHAEL McCAIN, the president of food giant Maple Leaf Foods, is a classic Maritimer, from his friendly handshake and straight way of talking to the down-home demeanour that even a Central Canadian business education and a decade in Toronto have not entirely erased. The conversation is sprinkled with the occasional "shit" or "hell," which he is trying to control by deputizing a colleague to tell him every time he lapses into expletive overkill. The lean, good-looking McCain, now 48, has the genes too. He is the son of Wallace McCain, co-founder of New Brunswick's McCain Foods, and Margaret Norrie McCain, a philanthropic powerhouse who hails from Truro, Nova Scotia. These two aspects— hard-nosed entrepreneurial instinct and caring social ethic —represent two deep strains in the Maritimes psyche.

For Michael, being a Maritimer is not a geographical thing: He hasn't actually lived on the East Coast for 20 years. He moved to Chicago in the mid-80s and never went back to rural New Brunswick, except to visit his and his wife's families. He is living in Toronto now, and for him, his wife, and their five children, this is home. He vacations on Georgian Bay, not on the seacoast of Nova Scotia, like his mother and father. He isn't into buying New Brunswick hockey teams like his even taller, easy-going older brother Scott, who is a Maple Leaf vice-president. He feels comfortable doing business on Bay Street or St. Clair Avenue, the mid-town street that runs outside his offices.

For him, the Maritimes is not so much a geographical entity but a state of mind that he and his family bring to their social and business relationships. It means disdain for pomp, process and hierarchy, and all the bureaucracy associated with large corporations, even though he runs a national food giant. "It's about focusing people on the task at hand, about being genuine and real, about getting things done, not just the perception," McCain says. "It affects communications, and relationships, which are open and genuine and candid and direct, as opposed to being more political."

To clinch his argument, he grabs a list of the leadership values that he, Wallace, and Scott are trying to instill into Maple Leaf, a company with roots that extend back 140 years and that is Canada's largest pork-processing company, and a major corporate baker. He lists the objectives: doing what is right; treating people with respect; being doers, not talkers; and candid, direct communications. These values, he says, have their roots in Maritime culture or, more generally, rural culture. "People who come to this company find it overwhelmingly refreshing in informality, candour, and openness," he says.

Actually, it sounds a lot like what any company, anywhere, would hope to instill in its workforce—genuineness, honesty, directness. But Maritimers believe these qualities are what make them special. It gives them a sense of solidarity as they sail forth on the sea of international business, with its cast of phonies, wannabes, and egotists. It is not that the mythology is true or false—what matters is that Maritimers believe in their hearts it represents a way of doing business that is truly Atlantic Canadian. It means when you meet Easterners in a boardroom or on a plane, you know instantly what they are all about. You know the town they come from, the high school they went to, the university they attended, and you probably know their uncle and aunt back home. In fact, you'll drop in to see them next summer and tell them how their niece or nephew is doing in the big bad business world. Michael smiles as he recounts how a young man dropped by his house the other night to take his daughter to the spring prom. It turned out the kid was studying in Toronto but hailed from Cape Breton Island, and soon everybody was sitting around talking about home.

The conversation with Michael McCain takes place in the boardroom of Maple Leaf Foods, on the 15th floor of an office building at St. Clair and Yonge. This is action central of the Maritime Mafia in Toronto. The Wallace McCain family has managed to create an enclave of East Coast values in the centre of Upper Canada. Wallace, Michael, and Scott are important business leaders; Margaret McCain is a formidable philanthropic figure in Toronto. They have become a quietly subversive force in the Central Canadian business elite, with the support of others in their circle, such as banker Cedric Ritchie, lawyer Purdy Crawford, retailer and corporate director Richard Currie, lawyer and ex-premier Frank McKenna, and Home Depot boss Annette Verschuren.

It has all happened so quickly that the McCains practically pinch themselves. Fifty years ago, Harrison and Wallace McCain were two brothers from an enterprising Saint John Valley farming and seed-potato exporting family. But then they went to work for the Irving family, Harrison on the oil side, Wallace as a manager in the hardware business. They dreamed of going into business for themselves, and, with the help of their brothers, Robert and Andrew, they hit on the audacious idea of mass-processing frozen french fries, whereas in the past fries were consumed fresh and unfrozen.

They quit the Irvings and built a plant in Florenceville, where they had grown up. The young entrepreneurs were keen to make their presence known, so they hit on the scheme of one week paying all their workers in $2 bills. Lawson Hunter, the son of a storekeeper in Florenceville and now a prominent Ottawa corporate lawyer, remembers the family shop being inundated one day with $2 bills. It was a powerful sign to the merchants in town that the McCains had arrived: They were now a force in the village.

Fearless in pursuing international markets, the brothers hopped on the bandwagon of two-income families, fast food, and convenience, a movement that swept the world in the last half of the 20th century. They created a whole new industry. Today, a third of all the commercial french fries consumed globally are McCain fries, and McCain Foods is a $6-billion company. The McCain motto of One World, One Fry sounds delusionally grandiose but it reflects a commercial reality.

Their success was built on Maritime pluck and the help of a friendly banker, Cedric Ritchie, a boy from Upper Kent, New Brunswick, just up the road from Florenceville, who rose to the upper echelons of the Bank of Nova Scotia as CEO and chairman. Ritchie was part of a generation of senior bankers from the Maritimes. Without a university degree, these men rose from branch tellers to vice-presidents and CEOs. His old Saint John Valley pals Harrison and Wallace knew what to do when they needed to make an investment. "Harrison and Wallace's financial strategy was 1-800-CALL-CEDRIC," Michael McCain says, laughing.

Ritchie had joined the bank in Bath, New Brunswick, as a teller and worked his way up to general manager in the early 1970s and eventually to CEO, a job he held for almost two decades, continually defying journalists who kept speculating on his would-be successors. In fact, he survived most of the contenders. He kept in touch with his Maritime roots, and he helped the McCains, Irvings, Sobeys, and Braggs become internationally active entrepreneurs. At the same time, he was keenly aware of the Maritime reliance on employment insurance and other government handouts. But today he sees both enterprise and dependency as flowing from the same wellspring, the closeness to the sea. The ocean has created a buccaneering mentality, a sense of constantly battling the elements, ignoring boundaries, and taking what you can when it's available. "You have to admire a guy who goes out every day into rough water and doesn't know what he is going to come back with," says Ritchie, a craggy-faced warrior now in his late 70s. "He has to be a bit of a gambler. There is probably a greater awareness of the elements that are stacked against you." There is, he says, a drive to "take what you can," and in an industry like fishing that offers only seasonal employment, that attitude was not only sensible but necessary. That basic economic fact has helped shape the regional mentality of pragmatism, he argues. In the same way, the Canada–U.S. border is a hypothetical thing to many Maritimers. "It is tailor-made for a game of 'Can you smuggle something across?'"

The McCain boys didn't smuggle but they were roving businessmen who treated nearby Maine as just another source of potatoes for their global processing machine. Borders were just a minor inconvenience for two guys with a couple of planes parked on the tarmac behind their homes. The McCain brothers always contended they were not great financial types, but Wallace's son, Michael, describes that as "bullshit." They did not spend much time with the balance sheet but could quote income-statement figures to five decimal places.

That was the Maritime way—it was all about making money first.

But in the early 1990s, the two brothers began to argue about succession and specifically about whether Wallace's younger son Michael would eventually succeed them. Wallace backed Michael; Harrison opposed him. That dispute triggered angry words, lawsuits, and a painful split, as Wallace in 1995 bought Toronto-based Maple Leaf, while retaining one-third ownership of McCain Foods.

The brothers' feud was like a thunderbolt in the tightly knit Maritime elite, whose members discovered they had to choose sides or skillfully walk the tightrope between the two. It came as a complete shock, possibly even to the McCains. One former McCain Foods employee told me that when he left the company in the mid-1980s, he was taken aside by each McCain brother to wish him well. Harrison reminded the man that the company he was leaving McCain Foods for had been torn by a family dispute in the past. "Are you sure that is behind them?" Harrison asked, adding firmly that "Wallace and I will never fight over the business." Within a decade, they were facing each other in court.

Today, members of the family feel it is not a question of who was right or wrong—it just happened, and it is time to move on.

For Wallace, the decision to buy Maple Leaf just made a lot of sense. "I could see that things were not going well for me in New Brunswick," he says with wry understatement. "I didn't want to retire, and I had two sons who were both businessmen with good potential; I wanted to do something and they wanted to do something."

The McCains decided that the ideal situation would be to find a business to run in Canada and if not Canada, they were willing to go to Chicago, a city they liked and where Michael had lived for almost a decade. They found Chicago friendlier, more down-to-earth, more Maritime in nature, than Toronto. And if Chicago yielded nothing, they knew of a company in Australia they could buy. Margaret McCain put only one condition on the family move: She and Wallace would have to maintain a second home in Nova Scotia. "She said we've got to spend two or three months in Nova Scotia for the rest of our lives," Wallace says.

They found out about Maple Leaf Foods, a giant in Canada's corporate history, once known as Canada Packers but now a faded icon that had suffered mightily from absentee ownership in Britain. The deal was brought to Wallace by an investment banker, and the McCains also found a deep-pocketed co-investor, the Ontario Teachers' Pension Plan. But the transaction was completed much more quickly than Wallace would have liked. "We started on the basis that we had a couple of months of due diligence but it turned out we had six or eight hours." Basically all the work was done in one marathon weekend: Talks started on Friday night and the deal was signed on Sunday. "There was no due diligence," Wallace said. "We just read statements for the last five years." In fact they didn't find out the real problems until they got inside and saw the results of years of neglect of systems, people, and plants. Pork turned out to be a far tougher business than french fries because it was a mature business that was not growing in traditional geographical markets. Harrison and Wallace had experienced the thrill of starting an entire food category, frozen fries, from scratch.

After a decade of turning around Maple Leaf Foods, Wallace insists he is happy with how things turned out. "I'm a strong Canadian and my wife is a strong Canadian and our first choice was to stay in Canada." But it was not without mixed emotions. One Atlantic entrepreneur recalls riding down the elevator at Maple Leaf Foods with Wallace, who had just moved to Toronto. Wallace tends to focus intensely on the issue at hand, and on this particular day he was fuming about the frustrations of moving to Toronto. The elevator stopped at every floor and people were getting on, but Wallace was oblivious: His language kept getting saltier and saltier. The elevator stopped at the bottom floor. The lobby was full of people, and Wallace looked at the other man and shouted, "What the fuck am I doing here anyway?" Then he stormed out of the elevator.

Part of this adjustment involved severing ties with the Bank of Nova Scotia, which had served him for 40 years. But Scotiabank was McCain Foods' main banker and Wallace was buying another food company. Richard Thomson, the chairman of the Toronto Dominion Bank, zealously wooed the Maple Leaf account. Wallace said he explained to him that "Dick, I don't know anything about finance, but I do know how to run a company. All I know about finance is that I had two telephone numbers, I had Cedric Ritchie's office and his house. When I needed money, if I were in Hong Kong or in Sydney or in Frankfurt, I would get a hold of Cedric and say I need X dollars, send it to such and such a bank, and that was the end of it." Eventually, Thomson said, "Now I want to be your Cedric Ritchie."

And so the family settled into the Toronto life. Wallace marvels that from his house in affluent Rosedale he can still be in the office in seven or eight minutes, about the time it took him to wind his way down from his home on the hill over the Saint John River to the office in Florenceville. It's not too bad, this Toronto life. He might just get used to it.

LIKE MANY SUCCESSFUL MARITIMERS, Wallace McCain's accomplishments are grounded in street smarts, not a lot of fancy degrees. He did get a degree from Mount Allison, but it was the third school he attended, after Acadia and University of

New Brunswick. "At Acadia I didn't do any work; it was a Baptist school and I was in trouble all the time," he says. After Wallace's second year, his father called up the principal to inquire about his son's somewhat isolated dormitory placement for the next fall. After the conversation, in which the principal chronicled Wallace's grisly escapades, there was a general agreement that Wallace should perhaps move on to another school for the following September. He didn't settle down much at University of New Brunswick either, but at Mount A, he was able to get some work done.

If university held limited appeal for young Wallace, he did get a great business grounding in his first job as a sales manager for the Irvings' hardware business. The McCains' relationship with the Irvings was always complex, a mixture of mutual admiration and fierce antagonism. Both Harrison and Wallace started out working for Irving companies, and Wallace was close to the wealthy Saint John family, particularly to Arthur, the middle son of hard-driving company-builder K.C. Irving. Wallace also paints a picture of the Irving siblings that defies the popular image of severe Calvinist prigs. "Art and I used to run around together a lot, visit the odd girl," Wallace smiles. "We were both single and raised a little hell and we were at the Irving house a lot. We'd be out somewhere in the day and I'd stay at the house; K.C. was a nice man, very polite, but tough and straight."

Despite the Irving reputation for being hard on managers, Wallace found them great people to work for. "I never found they pushed people, but you could get so wrapped up in your work that you didn't pay attention." Under the Irvings, Wallace and Harrison hit their stride, and became about as obsessed and hard-working as their employers. When the McCains struck out on their own, the relationship clearly shifted. They became competitors, if not directly, at least in

the hunt for government financial support and local brag-
ging rights.

In the upper Saint John Valley the McCains were supreme
and the Irvings were outsiders. In Saint John and other parts
of the province, the Irvings held sway. Generally the two ruling
families co-existed, until the voracious Irvings moved into the
McCains' chosen turf. In 1980 the Irvings went into the french
fry business with their own Cavendish Farms brand. They also
built a transport business to rival the McCains' trucking firm,
Day & Ross. The daughter of a long-time McCain manager
told me that her father ordered that all things Irving be banned
from the household—gasoline, heating oil, french fries,
anything that could be traced back to the Irvings.

The simmering rivalry blew up in the early 1990s when
the Irvings proposed to build a $72-million french fry plant
in Prince Edward Island with $40 million of federal govern-
ment support. The McCains proceeded to pledge their own
new P.E.I. plant without government support—although they
were often the beneficiaries of government programs. The
announcements set off a round of ferocious lobbying and
negotiating that led to both companies expanding operations
but with Ottawa dropping support for the Irvings' new plant.
The relationship drifted back into a kind of uneasy truce—
friendly on a personal level but intensely competitive in business.

To outsiders, it seems amazing that New Brunswick, with
its 730,000 people, has spawned two corporate empires with
annual sales in the multi-billions of dollars. But that's not all:
It has forged a number of niche businesses with international
reputations, such as Moosehead Breweries, Ganong chocolates, and New Brunswick Telephone, which, in the 1990s,
before it was swallowed by a regional corporate merger, was
considered the most innovative phone company in the country,
perhaps in North America.

"New Brunswickers are more driven," says John MacDonald, a Cape Breton-born engineer who was president of NB Tel in its glory years before getting on the well-travelled expressway to Central Canada to join corporate cousin Bell Canada. He believes that drive comes from the challenges of doing business there: the small population and large distances, the bilingual market, the lack of any large urban concentration, the income disparities. That means a company has to throw out all the formulae that work everywhere else. He found, for example, that what played at Bell Canada didn't play in New Brunswick. But the New Brunswick drive and improvisation travels very well: The province has produced British media titan Lord Beaverbrook, finance and steel magnate Sir James Dunn, Wallace and Harrison McCain, K.C. Irving, and Mr. MacDonald himself, notwithstanding his Nova Scotia childhood.

It was perhaps inevitable that the McCains and Irvings could not be intimate—the province is barely big enough for the two of them. But while Wallace's friendship with Arthur Irving cooled, he was able to forge another partnership that was much more important to his life. As a senior at Mount Allison, he got to know a young freshman named Margaret Norrie, the daughter of a fine old Nova Scotia Liberal family. When he became a rising young manager for the Irving hardware operations, Wallace happened to be passing through the Truro area. So he called up Margaret Norrie, who agreed to go out for a coffee that Sunday night. The rest is history. The two married and raised four children, two boys, Scott and Michael, and two girls, Martha and Eleanor, and formed one of the most formidable marital partnerships in the Canadian elite.

It is possible that many Canadians do not know Wallace McCain but are familiar with Margaret Norrie McCain, whose activism has become a mainstay of the social-policy and philanthropy scene. "I like to think that his commercial impact is absolutely matched by her philanthropic impact," says their son Michael. He explains that while Wallace spent much of his adult life building a business, often passing 140 days a year on the road, his mother was focused on the family. But when the family was grown, she stated firmly that she now intended to make her own mark outside the home.

A lot of that effort went into her alma mater, Mount Allison, where her involvement was so all-encompassing, the university is known as "Mount Margaret" around the McCain house. She began to focus increasingly on the critical importance of early childhood education and has helped form Canadian public policy in this area. In 1994, she became the first woman named as lieutenant-governor of New Brunswick. She helped establish a foundation that promotes public education and research into family violence.

Margaret always had strong ties to Toronto, where she attended high school at Havergal College and, after Mount A, got a degree in social work at the University of Toronto. Recently, she has directed her considerable energy to the National Ballet of Canada and helped spearhead the fundraising for the $90-million new National Ballet School in downtown Toronto. That campaign relied heavily on the giving and fundraising of the entire McCain family, including Wallace, who donated $5 million. Margaret also rounded up $15 million from a single secret donor. Wallace's other significant contribution was applying his sales skills to attracting donations. For him, fundraising is essentially the same as landing a sale in business: You get in the door, you make your pitch, and you get some wins and some losses.

As a french fry salesman, Wallace had a reputation for boldness and persistence. He was the guy who camped on your doorstep and just wouldn't give up, and those skills have been transferred to his new avocation. He likes to team up with a colleague, like the well-connected Purdy Crawford, who might know the person who is being pitched. Crawford says that "Wallace was the world's best french fry salesman and also the best fundraiser. He has a unique style. He is one of few guys I've met who can tell the person he's asking for money, 'I don't want to take a cheque for $200,000, I want half a million.'" And sometimes, he gets it.

The ballet school campaign is Wallace and Margaret's statement that they are a Toronto power couple, not showy or pompous, but social-minded and quietly effective with their own networks in their new hometown.

THE NIGHT OF MARCH 16. 2004, was like any other for Allison McCain, the son of Wallace and Harrison's late brother Andrew. He finished work and, as he often did, drove up the big hill from the McCain Foods headquarters to his uncle Harrison's Cape Cod-style house overlooking the Saint John Valley. Allison, at 53, was the chairman of McCain Foods, the hand-picked successor to Harrison, who in failing health had stepped back to become "founding chairman," but still had huge influence in the organization. The two men, who were very close, had a drink together and started to talk shop. They had a slight difference of opinion on some aspect of McCain Foods, and Allison said, "Okay, I don't agree but I'll think about it and come back tomorrow night and see you." He never spoke to Harrison again. The older man collapsed the next morning, was flown to Boston's elite Lahey Clinic, and died the following day. "I miss him because he was a lot of fun," Allison said a year later. His love for his dynamic uncle is profound. "I think people in general miss him because he was a larger-than-life personality. He was a mentor to me, no question."

The death of the charismatic Harrison was a flashpoint in the transition of the McCain food empire, as it moves from being a New Brunswick company to a national force. By the time Harrison died, Wallace had been in Toronto for nine years—although he was occasionally coming home to see his once-estranged brother. McCain Foods' chief executive officer, a non-McCain, was located in Toronto's towering BCE Place. And now with the death of Harrison, the geographical centre of this wealthy, enterprising, and powerful family seemed to be shifting more decisively to Central Canada.

For a while Harrison had served as a kind of ballast—as long as he was living in Florenceville, the soul of the company resided there too. But increasingly, Florenceville is seen as a national headquarters, with some global operations, while Toronto is the worldwide head office.

Nothing spoke louder than the two houses built side-by-side by these remarkable entrepreneurs, on the big hill overlooking the Saint John River and the french fry factory complex. In early 2005, both houses stood hauntingly empty, testimony to the ravages of family succession disputes and globalization. But the airstrip behind the houses was still busy, just as it was in the 1970s and 80s, when Harrison and Wallace used to fly to Australia, France, Manitoba, and Chicago, all outposts of a french fry empire that had grown to desserts, snacks, and pizzas. Now a McCain Foods corporate jet runs a scheduled service three times a week to Toronto, the nerve centre of a global empire. And McCain Foods' new CEO is a North Dakota farm boy named Dale Morrison, whose CV includes a stint as president of U.S. multinational Campbell Soup.

With Harrison gone, Allison McCain sees himself as the bridge between the business, run by Morrison, and the increasingly far-flung family. Even Allison's three sisters are now living in Toronto, leaving him and two brothers in New Brunswick. Ownership has become more diverse: Harrison's four surviving children—a son, Peter, died in 1997—control a third of the company; Wallace and his family a third; the late Andrew's family, including Allison, a sixth; and the late Robert's family, another sixth. "Dale runs the company—I do miscellaneous things," Allison explains. "I am involved in some things in the company and some in the family, and I try to link the family and business together." He also admits his role is to worry about the company's place in Florenceville and in the Maritimes. As testimony to that concern, he became chair of the University of New Brunswick fundraising campaign at the invitation of Richard Currie, the new chancellor and the chairman of telecommunications holding company BCE. It's a small world: More than 30 years ago, Dick Currie, fresh out of Harvard Business School, turned down a job offer from McCain Foods.

Allison lacks the high-voltage personality of Harrison, Wallace, and Michael McCain. But he seems sincere and smart, in a low-key way that befits his engineering training. As a young man, he made it known that he absolutely didn't want to work in the family business. He took engineering at the University of New Brunswick and joined the flood of UNB engineering grads who went to NB Tel after graduation. But after just three years he left because, he says now, he hated the restrictions of such a highly regulated industry and didn't like the life of an engineer with the phone company. He took some time, travelled in Europe, and on the way home dropped into London, where he had lunch with Uncle Harrison and his British lieutenant, Mac McCarthy.

It was fortuitous timing because, in the mid-1970s, McCain Foods was making a big move in Britain. It had just opened a new factory in Whittlesey, north of London, and Harrison suggested that Allison take a look at the new venture. Allison spent a day there and then travelled up to McCain Foods' British headquarters in Yorkshire, in the seaside town of Scarborough. He liked what he saw: "I just said this is the kind of environment I want to work in, young guys excited about what they were doing."

He went home to Florenceville, where he told Harrison that he'd like a job, and ended up in the engineering department. But he made it clear he wanted to travel the world. After several years, he went off to work in Australia, one of McCain Foods' prime new targets. After a short stint there, he moved to Britain, where he worked closely with McCarthy. In all, he stayed away from Canada for 19 years, until the Wallace-Harrison split brought him home and Harrison designated him as his successor.

As McCain Foods expanded internationally, it liked to put local people in the major roles. After all, they understood the market and the society. But in the first few years in any country, as local people were trained, the McCains sent many of their Canadian managers abroad, and they were often Maritimers. "They seem to travel well," Allison says, because they came from small towns and were quite happy living in the rural centres where McCain Foods ran french fry plants. To live in Scarborough, Yorkshire, was a big step up for a young Maritimer, who might have grown up in Hartland, Bath, or Woodstock, New Brunswick. In time these Maritimers often came back home to Canada, but some stayed abroad and became part of their adopted societies. In a sense, that's what happened to Allison. "We didn't send people and have them live like transients; we wanted them to become part of a community," he says.

The pattern of sending in McCain people to teach the ropes continued in 1997, when the company bought the

Ore-Ida snack business in the United States, which more than doubled operations south of the border. "We sent a fair number of people from around the world," Allison says. "We have a particular style and expertise, a culture that is important to get established."

Allison, the father of two children, worries a lot about whether McCain Foods can maintain its core functions in Florenceville. When he came back to Canada from Britain, he could see that the Maritimes were much better off than when he left 20 years earlier. "But I'm not sure relative to the rest of Canada that we've closed the gap; I don't think so in a material way, and that is something that has to be addressed. I live there and I'd like to live in a better community."

But he also knows that there is a tremendous magnetic pull to Central Canada, in its location, its infrastructure of finance and marketing, and sheer population numbers. But like many Maritime nationalists, Allison wants to defy gravity. One of the big challenges is getting executives to move east. "It's important that we not allow it to be a situation where everybody can choose which place they want to be, because the drift would be toward Toronto." In Florenceville, "it is a little bit more difficult to hire there, but every time you hire one it is slightly easier to hire the next one."

McCain Foods is particularly proud of its record in setting up its worldwide information systems operations in Florenceville, which is two hours northwest of Fredericton on the Trans-Canada Highway. To solve the severe skills shortage, it has been an active immigration sponsor, attracting technicians from countries like India, Pakistan, Cuba, and the United States. Altogether, the IS operations employ about 230 people in a village with a population of only 750. The company estimates there are about 25 different cultures represented in the workforce. But will they stay here? "I think so," Allison says, quoting his vice-president of information systems, a native East Indian, who says turnover is exceedingly low. The Florenceville influx of new Canadians is seen as a role model for what can be accomplished in the immigration-starved Maritimes.

Wallace McCain also admires the cultural diversity but he says it will be tricky to keep immigrants in Florenceville after their work permits of three years run out. Florenceville may have a lot of cultures represented, but it is not a big population centre for any of them. If you're an Indian immigrant, you may find a dozen similar families around Florenceville but there are many thousands in Toronto. "Are you going to stay where there is a dozen? I think they are going to have their hands full to keep them here."

His skepticism underlines the challenge of attracting new entrepreneurial blood to a region where the establishment often seems closed, tight, and, except for pockets, universally white. In the best of situations, the technicians who settle in Florenceville and put down roots would stay and build new companies, creating clusters of innovation similar to those in Burnaby, British Columbia, or Markham, Ontario. But there is no evidence yet that will happen. The sad irony is that even the new generations of the grand old Maritime family companies, like the McCains, are drifting away to Central Canada, Western Canada, or the United States. The McCain story highlights the challenges of building entrepreneurs far away from the centres of new economic dynamism, which tend to be urban and multicultural, not rural and Anglo-Irish-Scottish.

The mourners who attended the funeral of Harrison McCain also underlined this dichotomy: The economic and industrial elite of the Maritimes was represented. The pallbearers who hoisted Harrison's casket were a white, aging group of men. They were the people who went to school with Harrison and sold their potatoes to his factories. But they are not the people who must succeed now if the Maritimes is to dig itself out of its economic hole.

The need for new blood is reinforced by the knowledge that McCain Foods faces some huge economic and business challenges. It has been a challenging decade for the french fry itself, which has come under attack by the anti-carb, anti-fat movement. But McCain Foods has fought back by reducing levels of trans fats in its core fried potato product. It has also found new areas of growth, moving into Third World countries where the Atkins diet is just a cruel rumour. In 2005, the company was building its first factory in China, having built up the market by importing french fries and feeding the burgeoning fast food giants such as McDonald's and Kentucky Fried Chicken. The head of the China offensive is Basil Hargrove, the man from Bath who runs the Australian operations where he has been based for 26 years.

McCain Foods is a fine company, a powerhouse in the global french fry business, but it is a mere piffle beside the multinational diversified food giants, such as Nestlé, Unilever, ConAgra, and others. The industry is consolidating rapidly, sweeping up small to medium-sized players of the size and narrow product range of McCain. A giant multinational owner would surely gut the Florenccville operations, moving all decision-making to larger centres. But there is another solution that is readily available. Why not merge McCain Foods and Maple Leaf Foods, Canada's two largest independent food companies, into a Canadian powerhouse with more than $12 billion in annual sales? It would create economies of scale in marketing, administration, and general overhead. There would be very little product overlap and, therefore, no major plant closings. (Of course, the problem is there are not that many synergies either.) Most important, the Wallace McCain family is a major shareholder in both companies, with a third of McCain Foods and 40 per cent voting interest in Maple Leaf Foods. With Harrison gone, the personality barriers impeding a merger of McCain-owned companies seem less imposing.

New Brunswick chocolate king David Ganong believes that the merger may be both inevitable but also potentially just as damaging to New Brunswick as a foreign owner would be. "Nobody I ever talked to agrees with me, but I would anticipate a Maple Leaf Foods acquisition of McCain Foods is in the works. Why wouldn't you? Wallace owns a third [of McCain Foods] anyway, and Harrison's kids have it divided up. Wouldn't you like a big cheque to do with it what you want?" He worries that even with Wallace and Michael at the helm, the new merged company might gut the upper Saint John Valley of head office operations. "It would hurt the province," Ganong says.

When asked about that prospect, Wallace McCain is quick to respond that while the combined operations would be a good-sized food company, the transaction isn't on the radar screen. His nephew Allison seconds that motion: The merger is not in the cards. But surely McCain Foods will go public, in order to finance the acquisitions that will allow it to get bigger and remain independent? Allison says he doesn't know if this will happen, although he gets calls from investment bankers all the time. He feels that through debt financing, McCain Foods can acquire just about anything it needs. If it requires more funds than available through debt financing, the company has to ask whether it has the management depth to take it on. The result could be a takeover by the acquired company's managers.

Another major reason family companies go public is to provide investment options for family members as the generations unfold and interests diverge. In the post–Harrison world, there will be more and more McCains who own shares but don't work in the company. Their personal financial interests will begin to supercede their aspirations for the family company. Consider Harrison's own children's career paths: While Mark is a McCain Foods manager, Laura and her husband own wineries in Ontario and Nova Scotia, Gillian is a poet in New York City, and Ann is active in the family foundations. Yet Allison says providing a marketplace for family shares is not a problem in the current generation.

Still, Michael McCain leaves no doubt that it is an issue now, as far as his family branch is concerned. He adamantly supports the idea of McCain Foods going public soon. Michael likes what is happening at McCain Foods and admires new CEO Dale Morrison, who has "great vision and a drive for success." But Michael says that in any family enterprise, it is important that the individuals have freedom of choice to own as much of the company as they want, independent from the interests of the majority.

In early 2005, the Wallace McCain branch was locked into a 33 per cent minority interest in privately owned McCain Foods, which probably could not be sold to anyone but other family members. Wallace's family would like to reduce its interest because it feels it has too much financial exposure to McCain Foods, but it would not sell out altogether. "It is good common sense to sell it down a little bit and rebalance the portfolio," Michael says. In fact, this will become a more pressing issue in the future because, Michael says, "the McCains aren't what they used to be. They are not all aligned."

Going public does two important things, Michael points out. It provides a basic discipline for the company, whose decisions are subject daily to a stock-market judgment. At Maple Leaf, there are some days when Michael may resent those disciplines, but he recognizes that they are important for the long-term health of the company.

Second, going public gives the disparate group of share-holders the freedom to sell down their interests, or not. "I want the freedom to choose without going hat in hand to someone who represents the majority." The irony, he says, is that when you provide family members more freedom of choice, history suggests that they will be more determined to stay invested in the company. It takes away the resentment that comes with being locked in.

But Michael also feels that in the future, McCain Foods will require the financing oomph of public equity markets. It may feel like a big company to Canadians, but it is small in the new world order where both rivals and customers are getting a lot bigger. The company, he concludes, "is small in the scheme of things in a world that is valuing bigger every day. That has to be a concern."

These days, though, Michael's prime preoccupation is with Maple Leaf Foods, which after 10 years of McCain ownership, is almost in the shape the family wants. Michael sees it as a "lump of coal" that has been transformed into something much more glittering. In 2004, it completed the takeover of Schneider Foods, another major Ontario-based pork processor, which it bought from U.S. pork giant Smithfield Foods. Now that Maple Leaf has solidified its platform in Canada, Michael is going to push it out into the wider world, just as his father and uncle did with french fries in the 1960s and 1970s.

When the McCains took over Maple Leaf, only 3 per cent of its assets were outside Canada. That percentage rose to 17 per cent before the Schneider takeover, which cut it back to 12 to 13 per cent. Now, the target is to raise that number to 25 per cent by 2010. Michael sees an interesting paradox: McCain Foods does 80 per cent of its business outside Canada, but with a tight product line focus on potatoes; Maple Leaf does more than 80 per cent inside Canada, but with a broad range of products.

Now he plans to take that product array to other countries, through both acquisitions and start-ups. When I talked to Michael in early 2005, he had just opened Maple Leaf-owned Canada Bread's largest bagel bakery, in Rotherham, England, which turns out 48,000 bagels an hour. Maple Leaf is already the largest bagel baker in North America and sees huge potential in Britain, where bagel consumption is growing, even though it is only one-eighth of per-capita North American levels. Now fast food operators are introducing bagels as breakfast breads, which will drive the growth in the market.

Becoming a mass-market pioneer for bagels in Britain signals how far the McCains have come from the seed-potato exporting business that Wallace and Harrison's father, A.D., ran out of Florenceville. But if the McCains have come a long way in two generations, they will probably travel even farther. Perhaps no one better represents that journey than two of Harrison's daughters: Gillian, the poet, is also the unofficial historian of the punk music movement in New York, as co-editor of *Please Kill Me: The Uncensored Oral History of Punk*; and her wine-making sister Laura is co-owner with her husband of Creekside Winery in the Niagara Region and Blomidon Estate Winery in Canning, Nova Scotia.

Laura is probably the most entrepreneurial of her father's children, a chip off the old block with energy and charisma to burn. "I love to start things," says Laura, a slim dark-haired 45-year-old, admitting that she prefers to delegate daily management when a business gets to be a certain size. Having worked in the french fry business from age 13, she got a commerce degree from Dalhousie and was within a term of graduating with an MBA from Northeastern University in Boston, when she caught the entrepreneurial bug. She bought a Halifax fish business in her mid-20s and spent 13 years in that tough game, shipping lobsters and salt cod into European markets. Her father wanted her to join McCain Foods, but she was a single woman in business, and Halifax was a better place to be than Florenceville. She became a rare woman joining the Young Presidents Organization, where she mingled with the likes of Paul Sobey and John Risley.

She also exhibited a McCain-like fearlessness that got her in and out of some very tight corners. At one point, she hit upon what she thought was a terrific idea to take advantage of price up-ticks in the volatile global lobster markets. She trucked 50,000 pounds of live lobsters into a pound at Plum Point, Newfoundland, keeping them in crates, watching and waiting for prices to rise, at which point she would ship them by air into Europe. But a parasite got into the pound's water, and she lost two-thirds of her lobsters. It was a crushing blow, and Harrison, who supported her ventures, was not happy, but she survived.

In the mid-90s, her mother, Billie, was dying, and the Americans were making a big move into the European lobster market with flexible credit conditions for buyers. She sold the business and went back to Florenceville, stayed with Harrison after Billie's death, and started doing some work for McCain Foods. But she met a wine company manager named Peter Jensen and the two became romantically and entrepreneurially involved. They got married, went into the wine business, and Laura, after age 38, had two children. She and Peter built Creekside Winery, which, she claims, makes the best wine in Ontario. She went into the wine business with golfer Mike Weir and bought Blomidon in Nova Scotia. By mid-2005, the couple had a dream—to assemble the first nation-wide vintner, making wine from Nova Scotia to British Columbia's Okanagan Valley, where they hoped to buy something.

Meanwhile, as Laura and Peter build their wine company, she remains committed to McCain Foods, saying there is no inclination in her branch of the family to dilute their father's one-third interest in the company. And the Harrison McCain children go home regularly, mainly to the family retreat at St. Andrews by-the-Sea in southern New Brunswick. "I gravitate to people from the Maritimes," Laura says. "I just can't help it."

They all remain very much Maritimers, whose art and craft are informed by the McCain family's tortuous journey of the past 50 years. Even New York-based Gillian McCain, whose artistic medium is the prose poem, sprinkles her work with references to Florenceville and Moosehead beer. She also hints at the huge burden and gift of family legacy in her poem "Time": "I was reared on simple storytelling, franchised legends that created puppets of patented blarney. I only became a black sheep after a disagreement over succession, you fill in the gaps."

CHAPTER 2

K.C. AND THE SUNSHINE BAND

SAINT JOHN CITY COUNCILLOR Glen Tait is one angry man. The retired city fire chief is dismayed at his council's cave-in to pressure tactics used by Irving Oil to extract a long-term municipal tax break for its latest mega-project. In his view, it's a form of blackmail. "They're big enough to come down with a hammer," says Tait, describing the ultimatum that forced city council to ram through a 25-year tax deal for Irving's $750-million liquefied natural gas (LNG) terminal— or risk losing the project for the city of Saint John.

In March 2005 Tait had become one of the central figures in the debate over the role of the Irving family in the economy of Saint John, of New Brunswick, indeed of all the Maritimes. It is another episode in the love-hate relationship between this wealthy family and the part of Canada it dominates so totally. But Tait makes it clear that while aghast at the pressure tactics, he is not anti-Irving. He respects the family, which has been very good to Saint John, and accepts that the Irvings have every right to look after their own interests. Much of his anger is directed at the Saint John mayor who negotiated with the Irvings on his own and, he says, thrust the deal on the council with a lack of proper process. Besides, his opposition to the tax break has been fairly covered by the Irving family-owned Saint John *Telegraph Journal*, whose new publisher, 27-year-old Jamie Irving, is the first member of his generation to enter the family empire.

For the minority of councillors who oppose the Irving tax break—it passed by a seven-to-four vote—it smacks of the old days in Saint John when K.C. Irving would lock up generous 15- to 30-year tax and water deals for his mills and refinery from grateful municipalities. Now, his grandson Kenneth, who runs Irving Oil, has won a 25-year tax bill of $500,000 annually, with no inflation indexing, on a terminal project whose value would otherwise yield $3 million to $5 million a year for the city.

In poverty-afflicted Saint John, that amounts to a potential $60 million to $100 million in lost revenue over 25 years. "The bottom line is we have 69,000 people living in the city, and one-third of them are seniors on fixed incomes," dissident councillor Ivan Court says. "They have no room at all to pay additional taxation. On the other side, you have a billionaire family who is getting tax avoidance."

That billionaire family is, of course, Atlantic Canada's toughest, most powerful, and most reclusive business clan. The tax controversy highlights what is both old and new about the Irvings. The grandchildren of empire-builder K.C. Irving carry on the family tradition of getting what it wants, but also delivering jobs and investment to this economically pressed region. They remain the most secretive members of the Maritime Mafia, the only major Atlantic family that refused to be interviewed for this book. They are a kind of mafia of their own, in that they value family, loyalty, and privacy above all. Unlike their New Brunswick alter egos, the McCains, they consort very little with the wider circle of successful Maritimers, let alone the elites of the rest of Canada.

Generally, they are not joiners or club-goers. In Brahmin Boston, it was once said, the Cabots spoke only to the Lodges and the Lodges only to God. In Saint John, the Irvings speak only to the Irvings. They would not trust God with any of their business secrets.

But this time, there are new elements in the family story that make the LNG terminal particularly fascinating. For one thing, the Irvings have a powerful partner, Repsol, a Spanish firm that, observers say, is pushing the low-tax agenda. The Irvings do not usually take partners, or take their direction from partners, but this is a crucial project. Also, the public relations fiasco over the LNG terminal is being zealously covered by one of their own, Jamie Irving, the oldest child of the fifth generation, who claims to love newsprint and balanced reporting ahead of pulp mills and oil refineries. His stewardship of the *Telegraph Journal* will be closely watched, both by media critics and corporate-power junkies, for he is a potential titan-in-the-making.

The empire he may command, or help command, some day is a sprawling privately owned conglomerate that can be traced to 1881. That's when founder J.D. Irving purchased a small sawmill in Bouctouche, New Brunswick. J.D.'s hard-driving son, K.C. Irving, built an integrated industrial powerhouse, taking it into pulp and paper mills, shipbuilding, oil and gas, retail, and food processing. While most family firms lose their drive and ambition by the third generation, the Irvings sustained their aggressiveness and vitality under K.C.'s three sons, James (J.K.), Arthur, and Jack, now all in their 70s. *Forbes* magazine in early 2005 estimated the family's wealth at $4.4 billion (U.S.), making it the world's 117th-largest fortune.

The liquefied natural gas terminal represents a big move by a key member of the fourth generation, Arthur's son

Kenneth, president of Irving Oil, to stamp his own legacy on Saint John. It signals Kenneth's bid to emerge as the fourth generation's most important leader, in none-too-subtle competition with Jim Jr., his first cousin, boss of the huge Irving forestry operations and Jamie Irving's father. The family sees the terminal, to sit beside Irving Oil's existing deep-water tanker port, as a key building block in a hub of petroleum, power-generation, and plastics production that would feed the U.S. market from Saint John.

The project will provide about 700 jobs at peak construction, but only about 20 when it begins scheduled operation in 2008. That, of course, is a drop in the bucket compared with more than 5,100 employed in the Saint John area by forest products giant J.D. Irving Ltd. and its sister firm, Irving Oil. The two organizations, on their own, make up close to 10 per cent of the local workforce, and through suppliers and spin-off businesses probably account for more than a quarter of the Saint John economy. "The bottom line is that Irving is a good employer," concedes Ivan Court, the councillor who opposes the terminal tax break. "This is not about the Irvings, this is about taxation."

THE IRVINGS ARE ALSO THE benefactors of perhaps the most beautiful university complex in Canada, a monument to environmental research and philanthropy with a cost that observers estimate at more than $75 million. The K.C. Irving Environmental Science Centre rises out of a hillside on the red-brick campus of Acadia University in Wolfville, Nova Scotia, a neo-classical amalgam of dark wood, pale yellow walls, and lush greenhouse gardens. The building, along with the adjoining Harriet Irving Botanical Gardens, named for K.C.'s first wife, speaks volumes about how the Irving family sees itself as it moves into the fifth generation. For the three sons of the late K.C. Irving, this building represents a new self-image: more philanthropic, more public, more eager to please. The most private billionaires in Canada, they are feared and respected, but they are not loved. This magnificent building is the Irvings' cry for love.

It also furthers the image of the Irvings as environmental pioneers and benevolent capitalists. Even the Irving involvement with Acadia is the subject of myth-making. Although K.C. Irving and his three sons all attended Acadia, none graduated. Arthur Irving, known more for his rugby playing than hitting the books, writes on a plaque that "I have a good many memories of my time at Acadia as a student." Wallace McCain, who went to school with Arthur, smiles at the reference. The Irving boys, he says, weren't in love with university life and stayed for only two years. When Arthur became Acadia's chancellor a decade ago, Wallace was startled: "No disrespect, but it surprised me—he didn't strike me as the type." But, in fact, it is Arthur who has driven the Acadia building project.

To dig into the reality of the Irvings, leave pristine Wolfville and travel 100 kilometres to the west, out into the Minas Basin and across the Bay of Fundy, to the old Loyalist city of Saint John, the grimy, downtrodden base camp of the Irving empire. This is where K.C. Irving came as a 26-year-old from rural New Brunswick to make a fortune and where the Irving empire still stands tall.

While Wolfville is a pastoral gem of stately homes and inns, Saint John is a hard city to love, a place of grinding poverty, urban decay, dense fogs, and the lingering whiff of sulphur from the giant Irving pulp and paper mill in the west of the city. It is a town of shocking contradiction, where you turn a corner and find a perfect 19th-century white frame home, and a moment later confront a ragged kid in the middle of the street giving you the finger. There are other major businesses, including the executive base of phone giant Aliant and the Moosehead brewery, but the Irvings stand by themselves, with the country's largest oil refinery, a major pulp and paper mill complex, a once-thriving shipyard that is now closed, a couple of head office buildings, and plans for the new liquefied natural gas terminal. As befits the masters of the mills, the Irvings pour their largesse into the town, creating a splendid nature park, planting trees along the highway, and undertaking various other public works. But they also rule with a tough-love paternalism, squeezing out suspected adversaries, battling unions, and quietly dispensing noblesse oblige to those they like. "Ah, Saint John," a union leader once told the *Globe and Mail*, "this is Irvingville in Irvingland."

The contrast tells you what you need to know about the Irvings: They are environmental benefactors in a pristine college town and tough birds who tower over Saint John's old-economy stew of oil refinery, pulp and paper mill, newspapers, and abandoned shipyards. These two sides make the Irvings the most closely watched and least understood wealthy family in the Maritimes. No Irvings sat down for interviews in the preparation of this book, but every conversation ended up speculating on what they are doing and who is up and who is down in the pecking order. Through their reticence, they have become notorious.

The three brothers, all in their 70s, are very much in charge, particularly James and Arthur, but day-to-day operations have shifted into the hands of a group of their children in their 40s and 50s. The uneasy aspirants to the throne are Jim Irving Jr., the 54-year-old son of James, who runs the forestry, pulp and paper, and forest products side; and Kenneth, Arthur's son in his mid 40s. There are others to consider, such as Robert, Jim Jr.'s ambitious brother, and Mary Jean, his sister who runs her own food and packaging businesses, but Jim Jr. and Kenneth are the ones to watch. At times, there have been real fights between the two, says one Maritime business leader who insists on anonymity. "That tension has been there." Unlike the McCains, they have never allowed these rifts to come to the surface. But as the generations move out and become more splintered and diverse, it will be harder to keep the iron discipline that the patriarch K.C. Irving imposed and his three sons have maintained. The simmering tension suggests that when it all blows, the Irving eruption could make the McCain feud look like a garden party.

There is so much at stake in this next generational transfer. The other Maritime plutocrats, even the mighty McCains and Sobeys, are small stuff beside the Irvings. Frank McKenna used to joke that when he was premier, the Irvings controlled a third of the province, the McCains a third, and he was allowed as premier to control a third. He no doubt underestimated the Irvings, who in land alone own 3.5 million acres of forest in the Maritimes and Maine, and manage another 2.5 million acres of Crown land. The family runs an estimated 300 companies, involved not only in primary industries such as petroleum and pulp and paper, but also in real estate, media, and transportation. They own tissue plants, potato-processing plants, a diaper plant, a trucking firm, and a Junior A hockey team.

It is estimated that the Irvings have about 2,000 gas stations in eastern North America, and their strict ethic of spotless efficiency is reflected even here. According to a *Toronto Star* piece describing the Irving empire, "Even the company's fiercest foes stop there, for any regular traveller in the Maritimes knows that at an Irving station, the bathroom is always clean, the coffee is always hot and there is always a fresh green apple in the cooler, an apple that isn't bruised and doesn't look as if it was picked three years ago."

On the energy side, they own the largest refinery in Canada, a huge factor in Canada–U.S. trade, accounting for 50 per cent of Canada's exports of finished petroleum products to the United States. The refinery, upgraded and expanded since its opening in 1960, handles 270,000 barrels a day in crude oil. It receives the crude from the Middle East, the North Sea, and other parts of Canada, and produces refined gasoline, largely for the U.S. market. The tankers travel to and fro from the huge Canaport terminal at the entrance to Saint John Harbour. According to Hart Energy Publishing—which in 2004 named Irving "North American Refiner of the Year"—each day Irving Oil exports more than 200,000 barrels of petroleum products to the northeastern United States, including 100,000 barrels of gasoline, approximately 20 per cent of all U.S. finished gasoline imports.

The LNG terminal, which will be completed in 2008, will only augment the Irvings' economic ties to the United States. Called the Canaport LNG terminal, it will receive liquid gas transported by tankers from offshore suppliers, convert it back into a gas form, and pipe one billion cubic feet per day to a market largely in the U.S. Northeast. Repsol will be responsible for providing all the LNG and, most significantly, will be marketing the gas in the United States and areas of Canada outside the Atlantic region, where Irving Oil will handle the marketing.

The Irvings own an empire dedicated to the antiquated joys of vertical integration, which means controlling the entire supply chain from raw materials down to retail. For example, J.D. Irving controls the forestry process from seedlings, to trees, to pulp and paper mills, to its Majesta and Royale tissue plants, and the Kent Building Supplies stores. Meanwhile, the Irving Oil side handles petroleum products from the refinery to the gas stations. The idea is to impose rigid control and to capture the margins at every stage of the supply chain. The Irvings disdain giving up this control to any outsourcer, except for Repsol, perhaps, which has vital supply sources of natural gas in Latin America that will feed the tankers hauling the liquefied gas to Saint John.

This integration also means that no matter who challenges them for power, it is very hard to dislodge the Irvings. The most vulnerable business they own now is Kent Building Supplies, which faces deep-pocketed rivals such as Montreal-based Rona and Home Depot, the big-box giant from Atlanta. But Home Depot Canada boss Annette Verschuren contends that, while she and the Irvings duke it out, the Irvings cannot entirely lose this fight. After all, their forestry division supplies Home Depot with a lot of its wood products.

As in so many things, this vertical integration represents the legacy of K.C. Irving, whose heavy hand still stretches from the grave, through trust agreements, through wills, and through the force of the man's personality. Various likenesses of the old man are scattered throughout Acadia's environmental centre, including a large oil painting of an older K.C., sitting at his desk in dark pants and a blazer. From the window of his office, there is the profile of the Irving refinery and the signature six oil tanks that spell out, letter by letter, I-R-V-I-N-G. On the desk of this calculating man lie, significantly, a calculator and a pen.

Elsewhere, there is a photo of a teenaged K.C., looking natty in a three-piece suit, posing in front of Willett House, which today stands across the street from the K.C. Irving Environmental Sceince Center. His three sons comment in an inscription that "father lived here in Willett House. He left early to serve overseas in the Royal Flying Corp." Another photo of K.C. shows him as a 19-year-old training pilot, sitting in the open cockpit of a World War I aircraft, looking both proud and nervous. It is perhaps the only public picture of K.C. Irving that portrays him in anything but a supremely confident gaze. But the war ended before young K.C. could see any action.

To understand K.C. and his legacy, you must travel northeast of Moncton, up the coast of Acadian New Brunswick, to Bouctouche. It too is sacred ground for the Irvings, and they have poured money into a monument, a chapel, and to the preservation and enjoyment of the vast white sand dunes, where the family has supported a boardwalk and the Irving Eco-Centre. In this town, also known as a vital Acadian cultural centre, the grandson of Scots immigrants, J.D. Irving, bought a sawmill at age 21 in 1881 and it is where his son, Kenneth Colin (K.C.), was born in 1899. He was reared in a house of devout Presbyterianism, with all the thrift and enterprise that went with it. At 10 years old, young Kenneth, unknown to his family, bought a used Model M Ford car for $8. According to John DeMont's book, *Citizens Irving*, the boy's father found out about it and ordered it sold. So the vehicle was unloaded to a neighbour for $11, a tidy 38 per cent profit. "He wanted me to go lower, but I wouldn't drop my price," K.C. later recounted.

After a young K.C. went into the service station trade as an agent for Imperial Oil, the big oil company made the now legendary decision to revoke his licence, or as author John DeMont says, he may have just felt too restricted by a territorial licence. Whatever the facts, Imperial Oil unleashed a tiger. He quit doing business with Imperial and started buying his own gasoline from as far away as Oklahoma.

In 1925, he came to Saint John to play on a bigger scale, making his home in that proud city buffeted by trade and war, an amalgam of Loyalists, transplanted Yankees, and Irish and English immigrants. He took over a Ford dealership at 300 Union Street, which is still one of the head office addresses for the Irving operations. As the business grew, he moved into a nearby office building called the Golden Ball Building, after the odd-looking ball that dangles along one of its corners.

The empire spread to a bus business, sawmills, the pulp and paper mills, and a big refinery in partnership with Standard Oil of California, which he later bought out. As other businesses left or closed, the Irvings' weight on the Saint John economy became magnified. He bought all the province's English-language newspapers, a small business in the context of the empire, but symbolically important as a primary source of information and comment.

Never a lover of the Canadian tax system, he left Canada in 1974 for the Bahamas and later Bermuda. He set up an iron-clad trust based in Bermuda, with the condition that any of his sons would have to leave Canada if they wanted to administer control of the fortune. When he died in 1992, he was on a return visit to Saint John but his body was flown to Bermuda. Twelve years later, K.C.'s and Harriet's remains were repatriated to a Bouctouche churchyard. The boys, Arthur (known locally as Greasy), James (nicknamed Oily), and Jack (Gassy), took over the job of running the Irving empire in Canada. James and Arthur, near-clones of their father, got the core pieces of the business, while the more congenial Jack got bits and pieces, making him part of the inner circle but not a significant player.

These men have merged into a single entity called "the Irvings." People can't remember who said what, it was just one of "the Irvings." They all demonstrate the same top-down control, the economy with words and spending, combined with quiet acts of personal kindness. "There is no family business like the Irvings," says seafood titan John Risley, who is the K.C. Irving of his age, a demanding, unflinching entrepreneur. Risley says if you meet Paul, Donald, or David Sobey, you are aware of separate personalities. "But if you talk to the Irvings, it's all the same, they speak as one, they're magical at it."

They are totally consistent in tone and message, and the overwhelming message is a thirst for business knowledge and intelligence. "When you talk to them, you never get to ask them a question," Risley marvels. "They answer a question with a question. They pump, pump, pump, pump all the time and it doesn't matter which Irving you are talking to, they're looking right at you, they're asking a question and it's one question after another, bang, bang, bang," says Risley, now pounding the desk in syncopated harmony with the Irvings' conversation style.

A man who grew up with the Irvings is astonished by the same 24/7 attention to business. Now relocated to another Canadian city, he remembers running into Arthur Irving at an airport and exchanging the usual pleasant inquiries about family, health, and the weather. Then, as quickly as the conversation started, it was over. "Time is money, gotta run, goodbye," Arthur snapped and in a flash he was gone.

Their obsession with loyalty has become mythical. There is a story that has circulated for decades around one family from the tough south end of Saint John. One of the uncles, let's call him Gerry, was a great salesman who had one major flaw—he was a heavy drinker who would disappear for days on end. As a result, he was regularly fired and rehired by the Irvings. At one point, he was sent afield to open a bunch of service stations and, in his new capacity, hired a manager who would take over the business from him at some point. He warned the new recruit that if the Irvings ever called from Saint John when he was on a bender, "You don't know where I am."

So Gerry went off on a toot for a couple of days, and when "the Irvings" did call and asked this new guy, "Where is Gerry?" the manager replied that "he told me not to tell you." "Well, we want to know," the Irvings said, and so he told them about Gerry's little drinking holiday. The next Monday, the Irvings summoned Gerry to Saint John, sat him down, and said, "Gerry, now look, you told this guy that you didn't want us to know where you were, and yet he told us." Finally, they got to the point: "Gerry, I don't think he's the kind of guy you want around."

This story speaks volumes about how Saint Johners view the Irvings—that brew of fear, pride, and astonishment that a family can be so single-minded in its demands for hard work and loyalty and is so willing to give loyalty in return. For decades, they have been viewed as a family of public toughness and private kindness, made up of people who almost defy you to like them.

One prominent Saint John family tells of the death of their patriarch, and how the Irvings diverted their private jet in order to whisk the deceased's family members back to Saint John from Toronto. When young Wallace McCain was a hardware manager for the Irvings in 1957, he was stricken with a serious bout of ulcerative colitis that landed him in a Fredericton hospital. He had been there for two months, and doctors felt there was nothing more they could do for him. Then K.C. Irving, his employer and family friend, stepped in and provided his plane to fly McCain to the elite Lahey Clinic in Boston, where K.C. had been a patient for years. Wallace got the care he needed at the Lahey, which conducted a number of operations to help him live with the condition. Wallace and his brother Harrison, as they built their fortune, also became patients of the Lahey.

But this demand for loyalty and hard work placed almost unbearable pressure on executives, who could expect to be called at any hour of the day or night. It is a favourite ploy of the family to drop in without warning to inspect operations. Lino Celeste, a retired Saint John business executive, had a first-hand view. A son of Minto, New Brunswick, and an engineering graduate of University of New Brunswick, he joined New Brunswick Telephone and did well in the telecom company. But in his early 30s, while seconded to a government agency, he met the Irvings and they offered him a job. For three years, he worked for James Irving, labouring on such projects as the development of one of the family's modular-house manufacturing plants. It was a great business finishing school, he recalls, but it was a tough way of life, particularly for a young man with two small children. "It is a demanding organization," he says with a shrug in explaining his decision to quit the Irving group. Soon Celeste was back working at the telephone company. The story sounds like another tale of a guy who couldn't hack it, but Celeste is no stiff—he rose to become CEO of NB Tel, which was at the time the country's most innovative telecommunications player.

The Irvings often seem like classic Calvinists, tough and unbending in business, pious and charitable as friends and neighbours. Every New Brunswicker I know has a story about someone they know who had switched a small contract from the Irvings to a competitor, and then got a call suggesting they might reconsider, since they earned a lot of their revenue from some other part of the Irving empire. People marvel at the family's intelligence-gathering system.

Nothing stands in the way of their commercial reach. Robert Zildjian, an Armenian-American businessman who came to New Brunswick 30 years ago, was first drawn by the rich salmon fishing. He built a highly successful musical cymbal factory in Meductic, west of Fredericton, and bought one fishing lodge and a half-interest in another, both on the Miramichi. But he leased the fishing rights each year from the Irvings, whose timberland surrounded the lodges. After an investment of more than $35,000 in the camps, Zildjian suddenly got a letter from the Irvings saying they needed the forest and were cancelling the rights.

In New Brunswick, fishing lodges are sacred ground, and the Irvings themselves own one of the grandest ones, at Downs Gulch on the Restigouche. Understandably, Zildjian was hopping mad. He threw out everything Irving-related from his plant—the propane, gasoline, and printing contracts. "You know there are always alternatives," he says. He figures the Irvings lost more than $1.5 million in annual revenue from the fishing lodge fracas, but they did not bend. "One of the Irvings wrote me a letter saying 'I'm sorry we upset you. Would a couple of weeks at one of our fishing lodges repair the damage?'" Zildjian says with contempt. "I said I want to frame this, it is so ridiculous."

It reminded him that there are two families that run New Brunswick, the Irvings and the McCains, and he was determined to stay out of their way. He was in the music business, after all, not in trees or building supply stores. He co-exists nicely with the McCains who live close by, but the Irvings remain a sore spot. And he has remained an alien to the tight club of Maritime business people.

Irvings are also total traditionalists in that they are still hands-on family managers in a multi-billion-dollar business. There is not the wrenching debate you see in the Sobey family about how to step back from management or the value of independent boards. The only Irving board that still matters consists of the three brothers. One family member jokes that all the big decisions used to be made by the brothers over lunch at an Irving Big Stop service station, although Jim Jr. and Kenneth have brought in more modern management methods.

Still, family members are expected to master both grand strategies and picayune details. That is illustrated in a story that has gone around Aliant and its predecessor company in

Nova Scotia, Maritime Telegraph & Telephone. A number of years ago, Maritime Tel was having trouble negotiating its pay phone contract with the Irving Oil service stations in Nova Scotia. Negotiations became so difficult that Colin Latham, the utility's president, was invited to Saint John to meet with the Irvings themselves.

He remembers sitting down with an Irving family member, whom he refuses to identify but was very likely Kenneth Irving. The phone company would pay a percentage of revenue from the pay phones to the service stations, but Irving Oil wanted a higher percentage. "I might consider that," Latham argued, "but we need to have better location of the pay phones so we both can win." At that point, the presiding Irving agreed—in fact, he said, the situation was really bad at the Canso Causeway truck stop where the pay phone was too low for the truckers. "He knew exactly how many inches it was off the ground," marvels Latham. "And I was just stunned that this guy would know so much detail when running a multi-billion corporation. We came to an agreement, needless to say."

Latham was also astonished that this particular Irving had to rush from that meeting and take the corporate jet to New York so he could purchase the next round of crude oil supplies for supertankers at his port. "The juxtaposition of his dealing with this minutiae of pay phones, and going straight from there to New York to negotiate the crude oil for supertankers was even more amazing."

Latham was greatly amused, and unnerved, by another aspect of the Irving negotiating style. At the time, Maritime Tel managers were using Irving credit cards to buy their gas at Irving service stations. The Irving family member had walked into the meeting and was able to tell Latham the last time he had used the card and where he had bought the gas. It was clearly meant to knock Latham off balance before the talks.

But one aspect of the Irvings is a constant source of debate: Have they been bad or good for Saint John and New Brunswick? The prevailing feeling is that if they had not invested so heavily in the province, no one else would have stepped forward as industrial benefactors. Against this is arrayed the view that they stifle creativity. Whenever anything of value is created, the Irvings snap it up. The overbearing presence of the refinery and the pulp mill discourages new industry. The city of Saint John is often contrasted with Moncton, which has enjoyed an entrepreneurial awakening from an injection of new blood, including the arrival of Robert Irving on the scene. There are observers who say the city of Saint John badly needs a leading family that is more outward looking and engaged with the rest of Canada and the world. In 1998, Saint John lost its sugar refinery, when Lantic Sugar chose its Montreal refinery to stay open while the Saint John site would close. The closing was a blow to the hard-pressed south end, which had already lost some important industries. Some speculate if the Irvings were less inward-looking and had a wider network, they might have called the right people with connections at the sugar company, and it might have turned out differently. One critic admits the family is far more engaged now, but it is still very self-contained.

The Irvings are perhaps classic Maritimers—they are very good managers and operators in a strictly technical sense but they are not gifted in new product development, new technology, or new ideas. Their combination of strengths works well in the Old Economy industries they inhabit—forest products, oil refining, dry docks, gas stations, and basic processing. It has allowed them to dominate their province and their region. But if they were to venture into New York, London, and Toronto, and into industries that require marketing or financial innovation, they would have to employ new kinds of people, and they would have to cede some control. Says one New Brunswick businessman, "One reason they are more insular is once you get out into Montreal or Toronto or New York or London, you get into people who do creative things either in marketing or finance. The Irvings would have problems dealing with people like that, whom they would see as wide-tied high fliers or a lot of flash. They wouldn't realize there was this ability and they would need them."

So how does a company that is so insular, so top-down, get new ideas? The Irvings hire good people who often stay for life, but Saint John is a tough sell for the brightest young managers, especially partners in two-income families. The spouse cannot always find a job he or she wants in the community. Besides, you know you are never going to run the company —the Irvings run the company, and that is not going to change.

It's an issue that perplexes other members of the Maritime network. John Risley shakes his head over the Irvings' sublime timing in investing more than a billion dollars in an oil refinery expansion, a process that began in the early 90s, just in time to capitalize on a global tightness in refinery capacity in 2004–2005. "Their timing could not have been absolutely better. Did they know that this tightness in refinery capacity was going to happen? Did they do the studies? We'll never know but you just have to take your hat off to them."

"I felt 10 to 15 years ago that they were so inward-looking that they might not make it," concedes John Bragg, the Nova Scotia blueberry and cable TV entrepreneur. "You know, they wouldn't consider an outside board or anything like that." But the new generation seems to have shifted the company to a new openness. "They've become much more outward-looking and invested a lot in technology, a lot in management training and bringing good people to the table. They've made a real breakthrough. I thought they were so inward looking that they would struggle but I think Robert and Jim [Jr.], and Arthur's family, they're all very aggressive. And they run their businesses well. They're very efficient, and you won't hear of any sloppiness."

Also, the tendency to talk about "the Irvings" as a monolith ignores the variety of personalities inside the family group. Among the three brothers, James is tough but humanized by a strong family life and a wife, Jean, who has a genuine social conscience. "Morally, Jean Irving has a lot of sway," one friend says. A nurse raised on a New Brunswick farm, she is prominent in the non-profit area and has influenced her husband in taking a more front-and-centre role in anti-poverty initiatives in Saint John. "She really drives a lot of that—not just to write the cheque, but in the idea that you've got to be there," the family friend says.

The Jean Irving influence is best captured in a self-published cookbook that showed up a couple of years ago in Kent building stores. *Old Farm Favourites Cookbook* revealed a different side to the austere Irvings. There are pictures of Robert wearing a baseball cap, barbecuing in the backyard; the vivacious Mary Jean and Judith with their mother; a picture of all the grandchildren; and Jim Jr., often seen as a harsh and unbending figure, shown amiably cutting the Thanksgiving turkey.

Of the three brothers, Arthur is seen as the most volatile with a hair-trigger temper. Although troubled by health problems, he seems more relaxed in his second marriage to a devoutly Baptist wife, which may explain the renewed attachment to Acadia, a traditionally Baptist school. But his stormy divorce from his first wife caused strains in the family, which have run deep. Meanwhile, the youngest brother, Jack, plays a more background role, clearly second fiddle to his older siblings despite his command of a collection of construction and steel assets. The victim of a foiled kidnap attempt in 1982, his relative lack of clout makes him a sad figure to some observers, but to others he is the most balanced of the Irvings in interests and lifestyle.

Of the next generation, James's older son, Jim Jr., is raw-boned and all-business, every inch an Irving. He is the one who incites the most debate: Some see him as a compulsive cost-controller who is bereft of vision; others defend him as an injector of new management ideas. Those who know the family say he was once a wild kid who was brought to heel in a meeting with his father and uncles. Others can't remember when he was any other way than he is now. He has exhibited all the necessary Irving workaholic tendencies, sometimes seen leaving his wife, Lynn, alone at neighbourhood parties so that he could tend to the woodlands properties.

The core forestry business has been a slow-growth, mature enterprise in recent years, while the more dynamic side of the J.D. Irving forest products group has been run by younger brother, Robert, an amiable fireplug who is the most out-going of the Irving children, described by a family friend as a real "rock 'n' roller." The wonderful thing about the Irvings is that there are enough businesses to go around. Robert has built a power base in Moncton, a couple of hours away from his brother, where he tends to the tissue operations, the Cavendish Farms food business, Midland Transport, and his hockey team. People who know the family say there is an undercurrent of rivalry between the two brothers, although in the final analysis, Jim Jr. is clearly the one in charge. The Irvings are unshakable in their dedication to primogeni-ture—the oldest guys get the prize.

Yet James Irving's family is also one of the most female-friendly among the Maritime Mafia. One of the daughters, Mary Jean, is a business force unto herself, with a packaging plant in Moncton and sizeable potato farms in Prince Edward Island that are separate from the Irving family trust. "Mary Jean is an important business woman," says a family friend. "Her father meets with her all the time and coaches her like he coached Rob on new businesses." Not to be denied is younger sister Judy, who runs Hawk Communications, a marketing business based in Moncton, which claims many of the Maritime Mafia as its clients. She is married to Paul Zed, Liberal member of Parliament for Saint John and the son of a prominent Lebanese-Canadian dentist, but as of mid-2005, the marriage was in trouble.

The energy side of the family is now managed by Arthur's son, Kenneth, a bit of a mystery man, who observers say appears very smart because the energy moves have recently seemed so right. His brother, Arthur Leigh Irving, is a marketing man who is respected but his impact on the company is not well known. The lack of profile of these two men may reflect the fact that Arthur is still such a powerful presence on the refining side. But the massive LNG project will be their opportunity to make their mark.

Kenneth, who dotes on his four daughters, is considered athletic and disciplined—he has been an avid rower to keep in shape—and progressive as a manager. Says one family friend, "Ken has a dramatically different style, a much more empowering personality, while the traditionalist Irving regime is to manage things tightly and almost to not trust employees. Ken has come up in that but is not of the same mindset. Ken is a very nice guy."

Even more of a mystery is John Irving, Jack's eldest son, and the best educated of the fourth generation with an MBA from Harvard Business School. But formal education doesn't give you any inside track in the Irving group. There is greater emphasis on street smarts and savvy than pretty degrees. He has bounced around the organization and now operates largely in real estate. Says one observer, "John never seemed to click. He is probably on the other side of the spectrum from most of the Irvings, who would have no hesitation to reach for the terrible swift sword to take off someone's head. He is not tough enough by their standards."

John, however, makes his mark in other areas. He is, for example, very active among the Canadian alumni of the Harvard Business School and is part of a concerted effort to attract and financially support young Maritimers for enrolment in the prestigious school. John should not be dismissed in any final reckoning of the fourth generation. It is assumed that the empire is run by a trust, and day-to-day operations are governed by an operating agreement. While his father, Jack, may lack operating clout, John shouldn't be discounted because he could in time inherit significant ownership weight in the family complex. This would create fascinating dynamics, because John and Jim Jr. do not get along.

Still, among the 14 grandchildren of K.C. Irving, Kenneth and Jim Jr. are clearly the operational heirs, and the battle is between them. There have been arguments between the oil and forest organizations over such things as the price of gas that the energy Irvings charge the forestry side or the trucking operations. "It is James's and Arthur's presence that has contained the fighting between Jim Jr. and Kenneth," one family friend says. "When they are not around, it will be interesting to see whether Kenneth and Jim Jr. have matured enough in terms of their relationship, and understand that they can't do this any more. I think they do it now because they know they can get away with it, because it doesn't matter in the final analysis." But what happens when the three brothers pass from the scene? And then there is the fifth generation, whose members are beginning to enter the companies. Will they continue to sublimate their own goals to the greater good of the Irvings?

Clearly some cracks are already forming in the Irving façade. Jim Jr. wanted his own older son, Jamie, to follow his steps into the forestry business, but the young man resisted and chose the family newspapers instead. The newspapers are a backwater compared with forestry or energy, but Jamie was following his heart. He simply loves newspapers and wants to make the Irving media properties much better. There is evidence the family is listening. In early 2005, the family gave $2 million to endow chairs of journalism at Université de Moncton and St. Thomas University in Fredericton, as well as money to fund media internships. Cynics might wonder if the gift is timed to coincide with a Senate committee investigating media concentration, but it does indicate the Irvings may be willing to put their considerable money behind better journalism.

The fact that Jim Irving Jr. bowed to his son's journalistic ambitions is good news for the Irvings, suggesting that new ideas and out-of-the-box thinking may be tolerated if it is seen to benefit the empire. Jamie is the first of more than two dozen of the fifth generation of Irvings to be old enough to join the companies. Judging by Jamie's independent streak, it will be fascinating to watch how this emerging generation challenges and changes the Irving ethos. Despite the familiar sound of the raging battle over an LNG terminal, there are signs of a new openness, in philanthropy and managing, which is both un-Irving and unnerving. You can almost feel the tremors as K.C. Irving rolls over in his grave.

CHAPTER 3

DOUGHNUTS TO DOLLARS

WHILE DAVID SOBEY WAS growing up as the son of the business-man mayor of Stellarton, Nova Scotia, Ron Joyce was down and out in nearby Tatamagouche, as one of three children raised by a working-class widow. When David Sobey was getting started in his father's grocery stores, Ron Joyce was shipping out to Korea for a stint in the Canadian navy. While David Sobey was a rising young executive in his father's super-market chain, Ron Joyce was scraping enough dollars together to buy a doughnut shop in Hamilton, Ontario, desperate to escape the job he despised as a cop in the Steel City.

Now these two lives, so dramatically different yet geograph-ically linked, have come together in their old age. Joyce and Sobey, both retired, immensely wealthy, and in their mid-70s, have become warm friends. They are both unpretentious men's men, hunting and fishing buddies, who like heading off to Alaska on one of Ron's planes, swapping stories and golf games at Ron's fabulous Fox Harb'r Golf Course, or sitting around the boardroom at David Sobey's supermarket company, where until recently Ron was a director. It's entirely possible that Ron Joyce is wealthier than David Sobey, having sold his monstrously successful Tim Hortons doughnut chain to

Wendy's in 1995 for almost $600 million. But David Sobey's friendship is more valuable to him than dollars. Beyond the male bonding, which is an important thing in Ron Joyce's macho world, the friendship represents affirmation that Joyce has made it; he is part of the inner circle of the Atlantic establishment. He is the kid from Tatamagouche who went on to become a near-billionaire doughnut vendor in Ontario. Ron Joyce's story is where *Goin' Down the Road* meets the Maritime Mafia.

The other affirmation of this arrival is Fox Harb'r itself, a jewel of golf courses, estimated by local people to have cost $75 million to build and still counting. It is just 20 minutes away from Tatamagouche, across the causeway and up the road from the small fishing village of Wallace on the Northumberland Strait. Since Ron first put a shovel in the ground in 1997, it has become the gathering place for the Maritime elite, less than two hours from the region's economic nerve centre in Halifax and an hour down the highway from booming Moncton. It has its own landing strip to accommodate come-from-away types, as well as serving the peripatetic lifestyle of Ron Joyce, who operates an air charter business out of Hamilton, Ontario, and has homes in Calgary and Burlington, Ontario, as well as a luxurious abode in Fox Harb'r.

Indeed, this 1,000-acre property is much more than the stunning 18-hole golf course with its $75,000 membership fees—there is the spa with its generous pool and the clubhouse with its sumptuous restaurant, where Joyce likes to play the gracious host, circulating among the tables, joshing with the golfers and their guests. There are the ponds teaming with fish, the $660,000 condo units and the luxury guest suites, stocked with Tim Hortons coffee—but alas, no Timbits. The full-court press of features and activities is all part of the effort to boost the all-season appeal of Fox Harb'r, whose real estate sales are not going as well as the owner would like. "My plan was, 'I will build it and they will come,' " Joyce says ruefully. "You spend a lot of money and try to sell an idea, which is difficult."

But on a bright sunny day in late fall, the financial clouds are swept away for a moment. Joyce is tooling around Fox Harb'r in his black Mercedes, eager to show off his Xanadu to a journalist from Toronto. He has a couple of free hours before he boards one of his six aircraft and heads back to Hamilton for a fundraising dinner for the Tim Horton Children's Foundation, which helps disadvantaged kids. He stops for lunch in the club restaurant and lingers with guests in the dining room, which is dominated by a huge fireplace on whose mantle sits a bronze fox sculpture, a gift of David Sobey and his brother Donald.

Dressed in a dark suit for the evening event, the stocky, silver-haired Joyce adjusts the monogrammed RJ cuffs on his white shirt and explains that "I want to change the demographics of the north shore of Nova Scotia." What he means, of course, is he wants to change the region's economics, which he is doing by providing 150 seasonal and permanent jobs in an area with few prospects. And that's just the beginning, for Fox Harb'r is a gold mine for tradespeople and contractors, who can use the work. This is a beautiful region with rugged shores and beaches, but it contains economically challenged communities like Tatamagouche and Pugwash, whose claim to fame is a pewter factory and an annual peace conference founded by late American industrialist Cyrus Eaton. Joyce continues to invest, recently building a hunting lodge with live pheasants and grouse for the hunting crowd. He promises that his estate has provided for Fox Harb'r, ensuring that the golf course will go on long after he has left this earth.

But for now, Ron Joyce is collecting earthly toys like some men collect stamps. There is his 134-foot sloop, *Destination Fox Harb'r*, with its 17-storey-high mast, which he has dry-docked in Newport, Rhode Island but keeps moored at Fox Harb'r during the summer. There is the house that juts out into the strait, with 13,000 square feet and 10 bedrooms, a vast wine cellar, and a movie theatre for 15 people. Down the shore, there sits a faux lighthouse in whose shadow Ron holds concerts for his friends, featuring the likes of the Tragically Hip and East Coast troubadour Bruce Guthro. Inside the house, the vast living room contains wooden sculptures from gnarled driftwood collected in the Galapagos. The room is dominated by a spectacular painting of a nude woman that once hung in the restaurant dining room until some patrons objected to its distracting presence. The house is a who's who gallery for Maritime art with the usual Colvilles and Pratts and Blackwoods. But tucked away in one of the house's many nooks is a picture of the little cabin where Ron and his two siblings were raised by their mother, Grace, after their trades-man father was killed in a work accident. The painting is Ron's Rosebud, the symbol of the insecurity that drives his wandering existence.

Back in the late 1940s, there wasn't much happening in Tatamagouche for a 16-year-old with a grade 10 education, so like so many young Maritimers, he headed off to Ontario to work in a factory. After three years at American Can and Firestone, at 19 he joined the navy and ended up in Korea as a Morse Code operator just as the fighting was easing up. After the navy stint in Korea and Japan, he returned to Hamilton and joined the police force at 26. It was a good living but not what Ron Joyce wanted out of life. An outgoing, positive guy, he couldn't stand the cop's natural suspicion about human nature. "You become a cynic; you just don't trust anybody. People would tell you something, and you'd say, 'What's the real story?' It becomes hard to differentiate between the two, what is truth and what is fiction." Besides, he adds, "I was bored and I had a high energy level."

As a police officer, he would drive the streets of Hamilton at night, past the shops, garages, and the new wave of take-out places that were the product of the new post-war affluence, and he kept thinking, "How do I get into business?" To supplement his income—he had a wife and four kids by then—he took odd jobs, driving a banana delivery truck for a while. One night, he and his wife went for a walk to one of the new Dairy Queen ice-cream and burger outlets. When he walked in, he noticed the guy at the counter was another ex-Maritimer who had served with him in Korea. "Jesus, it was old home week," he recalls. His old pal finally shut the lights off in the store and brought out a bottle of whisky, and gestured around: "Ron, get yourself one of these, it's a licence to print money." A few drinks later, Joyce wandered home, picked up the *Hamilton Spectator*, and spotted an ad for a new Dairy Queen for sale. "So I called the guy the next day, put $200 down and paid $3,000 in all for the store."

Ron Joyce had found his calling and a life more positive than being a cop. It was entertainment, it was fun, it was about being a good guy; nothing like doling out speeding tickets or locking up booze artists. Besides, it was good money. While he was making less than $5,000 a year as a cop, in his first year with his own Dairy Queen, he cleared $17,000. Joyce was hooked on fast food and tried to buy another Dairy Queen but got shut out of that deal because of his lack of financing.

At that time, doughnuts and crullers were a new twist in the rising fast food business. Tim Horton, a star defenceman for the Toronto Maple Leafs who had come from a hard-scrabble life in northern Ontario, was another young guy lusting for the good life in southern Ontario. After some hard knocks, he had started up a franchise business based on the lowly doughnut and coffee. When Ron Joyce was working as a motorcycle cop, he had often stopped at the first Tim Hortons restaurant on Ontario Street in Hamilton, and he liked what he saw. So for $10,000 in borrowed money, he bought the place and became the first Tim Hortons franchisee.

He got to know Tim Horton, a basically sweet guy who had been burned so many times by get-rich-quick ventures and whose new doughnut business was suffering from misman-agement. "Guys would rip him off. He was hurt so many times when we got together, he didn't trust partners," Joyce says. But Joyce was honest and smart and eventually beat down Horton's defences, buying his way into the parent fran-chisor business as a 50-50 partner. Horton insisted that they keep their desks face to face in a big office so that he could look Joyce straight in the eye.

They shared everything, including the wild party life of young guys on the make, and by the early 1970s, they were splitting equally both the doughnut profits and Horton's hockey salary. The rationale was that Horton was an absent owner most of the year, and Joyce carried the weight with the fast-rising doughnut trade. Therefore, all proceeds should be split equally.

The company began to expand quickly, and some of the new franchisees were success-hungry Maritimers like Ron. *Tales from the Rim*, a book by Tim Hortons' former marketing whiz Ron Buist, tells the story of Eddie Mattatall, who grew up in Tatamagouche as a friend of Ron's, and on his sugges-tion, moved to Hamilton at 17 to work in the plants. He spent 18 years at American Can and in 1967 took a flier to become the third franchisee in the Tim Hortons system by buying Store No. 1 in Hamilton from Joyce. Then he quickly bought two more, based on the enthusiasm of his old friend. Buist says Joyce "made his blue-collar franchisees feel like million-aires, going from $7,000 jobs to $30,000" by working for the company known as Tim Donuts Ltd.

Word of this success reached the offices of Sobeys Stores, a growing supermarket chain in Stellarton, Nova Scotia. Bill Sobey, the eyes and ears of the family, called up his brother David who was on a business trip to Toronto and suggested he head down the road to meet these Tim Hortons guys at their head office in Oakville. The Sobeys figured there might be a way to get one of these outlets into the ailing Scotia Square office and retail complex in Halifax.

So David and a colleague motored to Oakville, a suburb on the Queen Elizabeth Way between Toronto and Hamilton, entered an old stucco building, ascended a flight of stairs, and found themselves in a big room with two desks in the middle facing each other. At one desk sat Ron Joyce, and at the other, Tim Horton, face to face, the way Tim wanted it.

Sobey and Joyce immediately hit it off; they were the same age and both from northern Nova Scotia. Ron was anxious to get into the Maritimes because he saw its potential as a low-cost development region; Horton was much cooler on the Sobeys because he was keen on western expansion, which might be more expensive but lucrative. An excited David Sobey headed back to Stellarton to tell brother Bill and father Frank about his great find—to be on the front end of the Next Big Thing. But the other Sobeys were not as enthu-siastic, and the idea died on the vine. They were mainly interested in filling retail vacancy in Halifax, not ending up in the doughnut business.

The chance to lead Tim Hortons into Atlantic Canada was a lost opportunity that the Sobeys would later regret as the doughnut chain became Canada's leading fast food vendor. But David Sobey doesn't lose a lot of sleep over what might have been. There were plenty of lost opportunities over the years—the Sobeys also passed up on McDonald's—but "you can't do everything, you lose your focus." Besides, he says, the tensions of being in business together might have cost him and Ron Joyce their friendship. It could be an easy rationalization but it's also a classic Maritime approach, where friendship is considered more important than an extra buck or two.

Joyce recalls that David Sobey "went back to his family and they made a decision that they didn't think there was money in doughnuts and coffee." As the chain grew, he was constantly trying to get people involved in the system, but he heard a constant refrain: "Are you nuts? Coffee and doughnuts?" Joyce didn't miss a beat though. His first Maritimes store, and the 43rd in Canada, opened on July 5, 1974 in Moncton—he can recite the date instantly from memory. He was so excited he called up Horton in the middle of the night. "I said, 'Timmy, I got the first deal and I just signed the paper, $35,000 for a piece of land on Mountain Road,' and I was so pumped I got him out of bed. Then I drove to Halifax and did my second deal."

Joyce's enthusiasm about Atlantic Canada turned out to be entirely justified. Along with his adopted hometown of Hamilton, the East Coast has proved to be the prime property for Tim Hortons. Nova Scotia, with 180 stores in early 2005, boasts a Tim Hortons outlet for every 5,000 people, just slightly better than New Brunswick's average of one store per 6,000 people. Contrast this to Ontario, which has a store for every 8,000 people. While Hamilton boasts 63 outlets and Toronto 85, Moncton is still considered the doughnut-tiest of Canadian cities. Although it is a small city by Toronto standards, it boasts a Tim Hortons for every 2,900 people, according to Ron Buist's calculations in 2003.

Late in 1974, tragedy struck the Horton and Joyce duo. As they were building the chain together, the hockey world was also changing. The original six NHL teams expanded, the World Hockey Association came along, and Tim Horton got older. In late 1974, he was a savvy but banged-up veteran of 44, playing for the Buffalo Sabres. After a game at Maple Leaf Gardens against his old team, the Leafs, Horton, juiced on painkillers, tore down the Queen Elizabeth Way toward Buffalo in his sports car and spun out of control at St. Catharines. The car ended up in a tangled wreckage, and Horton was declared dead at the scene.

When Ron Joyce talks about Tim Horton, it sounds like something close to love. "He was a great, great guy. We all have weaknesses, but he was kind, honest, straight." And the ultimate tribute: "He loved to party." His partner's death left Joyce alone at the top of Tim Hortons, sharing ownership with Tim's widow, Lori. Then in 1975 the widow sold him the other 50 per cent for $1 million. That deal would lead to more heartache, ultimately sparking a lawsuit by Lori Horton, who insisted she was incompetent when she sold out, the victim of a serious drug dependency. The judge threw out the suit, Lori lost on appeal and, in 2000, she died of a massive coronary. At the time, there were more than 1,700 Tim Hortons outlets, and there are more than 2,700 today. But Lori was living on a $3,000-a-month pension. Joyce told the media that he harboured no animosity toward Lori, who had been highly critical of him in a book and TV biography. What makes it even more poignant is that one of Lori's daughters is married to Ron's son. Relations with his seven children have always been complex, friends say, although one son, Stephen, is the Fox Harb'r CEO.

The Horton family could not appreciate Joyce's contention that however much he loved Tim, it was not the hockey player's name that sold the doughnuts. In his view, the chain's success was built on himself, on Ron Joyce, whom he saw as the Canadian version of Ray Kroc, the operational and marketing genius who built McDonald's into a fast food colossus. Nobody remembers much about the McDonald brothers, the original owners whom Kroc bought out, but they sure remember Ray Kroc. "I used to say, 'Timmy, I don't care what you call it—to me, your name is two bits and cup of coffee.' I never believed the name Tim Horton had any intrinsic value to it. It never did."

He points out that the first store featured pictures of Big No. 7 in a characteristic pose, skates flashing as he was rushing up the ice. But Joyce couldn't see the business appeal of the Horton name and image, and after they had built two or three stores, he ordered the removal of the pictures. "I said to Tim that 'your name is meaningless; the key is operations, operations, operations.' The success of Tim Hortons had nothing to do with a hockey player—it had to do with trying to be the best of anyone else in that [fast food] segment."

The deification of Horton irritated Joyce long after his friend's fatal crash. "For a long time even after Tim died, a lot of people believed that I was riding on his coattails, that Tim Horton gave me a big break in life. He was broke when I got involved with him; he was losing the goddamn equipment; he had nothing to do with the success of this, except that he was a beloved guy that I fell in love with, and I worked my ass off to make it work."

After 10 years of working with a mostly absent hockey-playing Tim Horton, Joyce now had sole control over Tim Hortons, its 40-odd stores, and the dream of expansion. "I was the sole owner, and my board meeting was in front of a mirror." But as with many Canadian entrepreneurs, the stratospheric interest rates of the early 1980s almost did him in. He had some problem stores and he was ponying up 22 per cent interest payments. "The shit hit the fan—I was lucky I survived 1981–1982." He laid off people, cut back his construction activity, and actually was able to expand through the toughest times, while other fast food chains were floundering. But with that came a certain wisdom. Banks are always ready to lend you money in the good times, he learned, but are equally prepared to close you down in the bad times. He was determined never to get in that deep again.

The company recovered, and the Tim Hortons phenomenon continued to roll, fuelled by Joyce's creativity, street smarts, and an unusual talent for marketing an image. It diversified from doughnuts into lunches with soups and sandwiches. More than just a fast food chain, it became a Canadian institution stoked by clever ads that made Tim Hortons, the doughnut chain, as much a Canadian icon as hockey and medicare. Through the chain's "True Stories" of Canadian students abroad or elderly ladies walking to the local Tim's, it tapped latent Canadian nationalism and a fuzzy feeling of community that touched a nerve, particularly in the Maritimes.

But Joyce faced the reality: Where do you take it from here? The United States beckoned, but it takes bucks and expertise to succeed in what has been the graveyard of many Canadian retailers. Companies as diverse as Peoples Jewelers, Canadian Tire, and Mark's Work Wearhouse had foundered on U.S. expansion, and restaurant concepts are the most perilous and ephemeral of any retail approach. Canadians often forget that the United States is a foreign country where the people are truly different. But Joyce had an ace up his sleeve: He had got to know Dave Thomas, the aw-shucks builder of Wendy's who had a similar bootstrap background. The two started developing combo stores, Wendy's and Tim Hortons, on the same sites. Finally, the two firms decided to get together, and in 1995 Wendy's bought Tim Hortons for $600 million in shares, making Ron Joyce the largest shareholder of the U.S. fast food giant. At first he thought he would be a major player in the Dublin, Ohio, firm, but he soon discovered he was a fifth wheel whose role was continually circumscribed. He eventually sold the last of his Wendy's shares in 2001 for what he describes as estate-planning purposes.

Joyce is tormented still by his decision to sell Tim Hortons, both endorsing and regretting his move in a single breath. "I should have taken it public rather than sell it. I'll regret it as long as I live," he grumbles. "If I had kept it, it would still be owned by Canadians." But he believed in what he was doing at the time. "The ultimate move would have been south of the border, and for that you had to have a strong partner. Look at the history of chains down there, they are not all successful. To do the United States, I needed a partner."

The irony is that in summer 2005, 10 years after the sale, his former partner Wendy's was announcing plans to spin off a piece of Tim Hortons as a publicly traded company, just as Joyce had once contemplated. Some analysts were estimating the Canadian doughnut chain's total value at an eye-popping $4 billion (U.S.), which was at least twice the estimated valuation of the Wendy's burger chain.

The sale also left the former doughnut king with a huge hole in the centre of his life, which he tried to fill with his boat, his cars (a red Viper RT10 sports car sits in his garage), his planes, his houses, and his rootless lifestyle. Twice divorced, he is single again and insists he loves the life. "It's freedom," he says. "I get up in the morning and I don't have to ask anyone to go someplace." He is legendary in the business world for being seen with an endless variety of women, many much younger than he. Apparently it is hard to resist an engaging 74-year-old man who is worth close to a billion dollars.

After the sale, he also started going back to Tatamagouche, partly to see his mother but also to forge new relationships. Since their lapsed doughnut deal in the early 1970s, he had maintained close ties with David Sobey and was buying buckets of blueberries from John Bragg. In 1987, he put up a Tim Hortons Camp for underprivileged children just outside of his hometown, and his local profile started to grow. One morning, a friend who was manager of the kids' camp took Joyce out to the northern coast of Fox Harb'r and showed him a windswept expanse of swamp and sandstone that had been on the market for three years. He fell in love with the rugged location. At 10:00 a.m. on a Saturday he first saw it and at 3:00 that afternoon he owned it. It cost him $200,000 in cash. But the land stood there for 10 years, used for outings by the children from the Tim Hortons camp. Then Ron Joyce, bored by the loss of his doughnut and coffee empire, came up with the dream of Fox Harb'r, a golf course where he and his friends could play. After all, he had the time and the money. But was he really just showing up the Nova Scotia bigwigs who were once better than he?

"I don't think I'm that way," he says now, although he adds, "At one time I thought I would gloat about certain things. After all, my father was a tradesman, a bricklayer, and plasterer. I was glad I did very well, but after a while, it became meaningless."

He wanted a nice place to play golf, but the idea took off from there—to build a world-class destination course, designed by the Canadian course architect Graham Cooke, whose work includes the Glen Arbour and Highland Links courses in Nova Scotia and Royal Montreal and Grey Rocks in Quebec. The economic payback would be the real estate—the selling of condos and building lots to people from around the world. It has not been easy, and Ron has gone through a number of sales and development people—but of course, it's not as if he is running out of money.

Most of all, he wants to transform this depressed part of Nova Scotia with its secondary roads and lack of entertainment and shopping. Cape Breton, he says, gets lots of financial grease from government, but in this area, people have learned to live with low expectations. Most of the infrastructure has been built, with the hunting lodge as one of the final touches, and plans for skeet shooting and the release of live birds that are being raised across the road. A nine-hole golf course is also in the cards to complement the 18-hole mother course.

Of course, whenever a local boy makes good and comes home, there is the inevitable envy and accompanying tensions. He is now Ron Joyce, centimillionaire, instead of Ron Joyce, a regular guy. Down at Chester, Nova Scotia, one day, he overheard a pair of fishermen debate the scale of his wealth. Lapsing into an exaggerated East Coast accent, he quotes one of the men: "Jaysus, boy, did you see that sailboat? God, that mast is high." The other guy said, "That's that doughnut guy, that Tim Hortons guy. The boat costs $400 million." Joyce won't say how much the boat costs, but he clearly revels in the speculation. A friend, however, says he was told by Joyce that the boat cost "only" $50 million Canadian.

Still, there are some sour moments. He feels betrayed after being fined $180,000 in 2004 for offshore blasting at Fox Harb'r, which federal officials said harmed the fish in Northumberland Strait. He finds it sad, when he is creating so many jobs and not requesting any government assistance. "We spent a lot more money than it makes any sense. I'll never get my money back, but I'm not concerned about that." His hope is that the golf course and its real estate development will soon become self-sustaining. He says one of the questions he often gets from prospective members is what will happen when he departs the scene. "Well, it would be awful dumb to spend all the money I've spent here if I didn't have some kind of estate planning. And I have very strong estate planning. It will be sustained and I have the capital to do that.

"I'm not an empire builder in the sense that I want to be the richest guy in the graveyard. But I have a lot more money than I could ever spend, and I might as well use it on what is the right thing to do."

He was honoured that Frank McKenna chose Fox Harb'r in 2003 as the site of his third annual Maritime networking event. (McKenna first proposed the course for his 2002 clambake but it could not be arranged in time.) The guest speaker in 2003 was John Major, the former British prime minister. But the real thrill was attracting the star power of Bill Clinton in 2004. The former president wasn't able to play golf that day, but later wrote Joyce to thank him and say that he hoped to come back just to play some rounds. The boy from Tatamagouche clearly loves that proximity to power. The combination of vast wealth and ownership of an elite golf course have enrolled him in a club of wealthy and powerful people. He met George Bush Sr. at the first McKenna conference and has gone fishing with him two or three times, including a high-security excursion at Hilton Head, North Carolina, right after the terrorist attacks of September 11, 2001. He goes off on fishing expeditions with Alberta millionaire Peter Pocklington, former Ontario premier Mike Harris, one-time Liberal cabinet minister Ed Lumley, and of course, David Sobey. So Ron Joyce is living the perfect life? He doesn't argue with that appraisal. His major regrets are that he waited until his mid-30s before he got into business, and that he is now as old as he is.

There are occasional health concerns, such as the accident he had recently in his boat off Grenada. A kid working on the boat opened the anchor well and left it open. Ron went out for a walk and fell down the well, ending up with a painful compression fracture of the vertebrae. He didn't realize the extent of his injury for a few months, until he couldn't stand the pain. "I can hardly walk now. The left side of my butt is in constant pain, worse than my back, sounds like the sciatic nerve. So I'm sitting here with this pain in the ass."

Besides Fox Harb'r, Joyce, a licensed pilot, runs his air charter business with the fleet of six planes at the airport in Hamilton, Ontario. He is also very active as an equity investor, particularly in U.S. stocks. The rise in the Canadian dollar cost him a fortune. He also owns a stake in a number of oil-fields in Argentina which, he says, "is like Alberta was 30 to 40 years ago." In his investing, as in most facets of his life, he values personal relationships, and particularly with former and present Maritimers. Among his co-investors in the Argentina venture are David Sobey and Grant Bartlett, another wealthy former Nova Scotian who lives in Calgary.

Bartlett, born to a family of ordinary means, is also a rags-to-riches story, the highly successful product of the strong education given in the small rural schools of Nova Scotia in the 1950s and 1960s. His father was a jack-of-all-trades, a carpenter and fisherman, with a passion for learning. No one in Bartlett's family had gone to university but young Grant got scholarships to attend Mount Allison, and then to pursue graduate degrees in marine geology and ended up teaching at Queen's University in Kingston, Ontario, in the 1970s. But, itching for more hands-on action, Bartlett went west in 1980 to make money in the oil patch, and did very well. He met Ron Joyce and for a while, the two men were part of the nine-person syndicate that owned the Calgary Flames of the National Hockey League. Joyce and Bartlett sold their interests but they are still an item in the investment game. "I've invested with him over the last 10 years, and every deal we did turned out very good," Joyce says. Bartlett, meanwhile, goes back to Fox Harb'r to participate in Joyce's charity events and see family members. "He's such an unbelievably generous person," Bartlett says of his old friend.

Joyce has other friends, however, who find this rootless lifestyle to be rather sad. He has every toy imaginable and consorts with powerful and rich people, one friend says, but "he is the loneliest person I know." All the baubles buy him companionship among powerful men and attractive women, but, except for his mother, whom he adores, there is no one he can really love, the friend says. He fills this void with short-term relationships, the camaraderie of his buddies, and a generous sociability that is both charming and touching. "He needs to be needed," the friend says, adding that he is easily bored and flits from one obsession to another.

Others say his hard-scrabble background and lack of formal education make him a bit of an outsider in the Maritime Mafia.

Yet this is not a group that judges people by their university degrees. If you talk to David Sobey, you get the impression that his relationship with Joyce is a strong, enduring one, buttressed by Joyce's role as a Sobeys director for about a decade, until he stepped off the board last year. The Sobeys credit Joyce, along with John Bragg, for giving the family a lot of support to pull off the massive merger with Oshawa Group and to integrate the plethora of retail banners under the core Sobeys umbrella.

It is hard to summon a lot of sympathy for a man who, at least outwardly, seems to be enjoying himself so much. Joyce himself says he has no personal regrets: "I've been divorced a couple of times; marriage didn't work for me, which is why I'm single, I guess. I loved my wives, I love my children.

They're all grown up, have their own families, and I'm a great-grandfather."

As for his mother, he is clearly devoted to her and feels he owes her a lot. He has set aside a suite for her at his home in Fox Harb'r, but he admits sadly that she is rarely there. Grace prefers to live in a nursing home in Middleton, Nova Scotia, in the Annapolis Valley. On this late fall day at Fox Harb'r, as Ron Joyce ponders the financial future of his golf course, he is trying to get through by telephone to the nursing home. "Mum's 94, she's as healthy as hell, and I can't find her right now," he mutters. For a near-billionaire, he sounds just like any exasperated son.

CHAPTER 4
....

THE AMBASSADOR FROM APOHAQUI

ANNETTE VERSCHUREN WAS facing the toughest decision of her life—whether to give the final order to evict 110 destitute people from their makeshift homes in the Tent City on Toronto's waterfront. The rise of this community of homeless people had become a *cause célèbre* in Toronto's media and political circles, creating an aura of solidarity and sanctity around the band of squatters. It also put intense pressure on the owner of the Tent City property, Home Depot Canada, of which Annette Verschuren, a 48-year-old Cape Breton Island native, is the chief executive officer.

In September 2002, Verschuren organized a surprise eviction raid, a decision backed by Home Depot head office in Atlanta. But before she issued the final command, she made a call, as she often does in tough situations, to her friend Frank McKenna, the former premier of New Brunswick. "Frank, here's the story," she said, taking him through the issues: the health dangers, the threat of drug dealing, and the large potential liability to Home Depot, which is the world's major home renovation retailer.

McKenna's response was quick and supportive: Verschuren had to stand up to this challenge, she had to deal with it, and she had the guts to do it. Within 10 minutes of the conversation with McKenna, she gave the order and security guards swept into the Tent City. "It was really tense. It was so orchestrated," she recalled later. Before long, the area was cleared of people, tents, and debris, and the debate between the defenders and critics of Verschuren's preemptive strike dominated the radio and TV airwaves.

A year later, almost all the Tent City occupants were successfully relocated to city-funded housing. The debate had cooled down quickly in the media, and Home Depot suffered no reputation backlash. In early 2005, reformist mayor David Miller announced a no-tolerance policy toward homeless squatting in Toronto's city hall square, which many saw as a public affirmation of Verschuren's bull-by-the-horns policy.

"These are defining moments in a person's character," said Verschuren, a sunny blond woman who blends a self-revelatory candour with the tough core of a seasoned corporate executive. "When you've got a guy like Frank saying, 'Look, it's right, let's go'—that means a lot. I use Frank for that."

Indeed, a lot of current and former Maritimers lean on Frank McKenna for that kind of moral support. After leaving his premier's role in New Brunswick, where he created an economic and business revolution, he had channelled his impressive energies into being a professional director, corporate lawyer, and non-stop salesman for the benefits of living, working, and doing business in Atlantic Canada. With that came the role of unofficial sounding board for Maritimers living in Atlantic Canada and around the world. The list of McKenna contacts is probably rivalled in size and prestige by only two other members Maritime Mafia, Toronto corporate lawyer Purdy Crawford and Sir Graham Day, the charming lawyer and corporate director.

Verschuren, the daughter of Dutch immigrants who became dairy farmers in Cape Breton Island, is the ultimate product of the Maritime network because of the way her career intersects with two of its central figures, McKenna and Crawford. Each has mentored her at different stages in her life. Purdy Crawford first noticed her as a 28-year-old executive vice-president at the coal-mining giant, Cape Breton Development Investment Corp., where he served as a board member in the early 1980s. He hired her as an executive at the Montreal holding company Imasco Inc., where he was CEO and later chairman. That was the big step in her career transition to retailing executive, which finally landed her the top job at Home Depot Canada. Some see her now as a potential future CEO of Home Depot worldwide.

McKenna is a more recent friend, but for Verschuren the relationship is just as important. A decade ago, when he was still New Brunswick premier and she was the Canadian boss of Michaels, the big crafts retailer, they met on a CBC radio program discussing the economic prospects of eastern Canada. Some time later, she got a call from McKenna, who asked if she would be interested in opening a Michaels store in New Brunswick. It was classic McKenna all the way—it's always about selling the region and using the network to make connections. Ten years later, both Verschuren and McKenna have moved on to bigger leagues, but he is making the same pitch, only now in the role of Canadian ambassador to the United States.

FRANK McKENNA, SITTING IN his car in Washington on a June day in 2005, is missing the fresh sea air of Cap-Pelé, the small village on the New Brunswick shore of the Northumberland Strait that he calls home. But there is no time to relax for the hyperactive McKenna, who is just settling into his role as Canada's emissary to the most powerful nation on earth. One day, he is lecturing Americans on the distinct Canadian society; another, he is defending Canada's decision to opt out of the U.S. Star Wars program. "I love this new job," he says. If only he could bottle the fresh ocean breeze of the Maritimes and carry it with him.

In fact, McKenna is already bringing a fair bit of the Maritimes to Washington. He's introduced New Brunswick wood carvings to the embassy, and he's put Atlantic paintings on the wall of his residence. The ambassador is giving away gifts of New Brunswick chocolate. He has told his chef to order New Brunswick salmon for state occasions. His first Canada Day celebration at the embassy featured strawberries and ice cream from Atlantic Canada. "I've got an opportunity to use the embassy as a bit of a selling platform for the region and we're doing it," he told me over his car phone from Washington. "I've got a little bit of home around me everywhere I look."

Frank McKenna was still selling New Brunswick, just as he had been doing for the past 20 years of his life; his salesmanship was the hallmark of his years as premier from 1987 to 1997 and was the focus of his incessant networking after he retired from the premier's job. Even though he had assembled an impressive array of international contacts, his continuing obsession was introducing these powerful players to his Maritime friends and business associates. He was always connecting people. So it was inevitable that the Atlantic provinces would capture a big part of his splintered attention as ambassador in Washington. He remained an indefatigable booster of the region's business people: "When you look at the entrepreneurial skills of the Sobeys, Irvings, McCains, and Braggs, these are superbly managed businesses."

Prime Minister Paul Martin's choice of McKenna as ambassador to Washington made sense in a lot of ways. McKenna is a centrist, pragmatic politician who is unlikely to make ideological waves at a time when the minority Liberal government was trying to get on the right side of the conservative Bush administration. Also, the former New Brunswick premier had spent his time and energies building an impressive personal network of business connections that would be useful operating inside the Beltway. In Canada, he had become legendary, almost notorious, for the 10 public company boards he sat on at the same time, which he had to give up when he became ambassador. He was consorting with present and former world leaders, and was an adviser to the Carlyle Group, a controversial U.S. private equity firm that has served as a retirement home for former government heavyweights. And, of course, for five years, he has hosted a summer networking event that brought Atlantic Canadian and national business and public policy figures together for good conversation and good golf.

McKenna, a fireplug-shaped former hockey player, also has a facility for delivering tough talk, like many of the Atlantic business people he consorts with. On becoming ambassador, he immediately took the Americans to task for not understanding Canada. It's the kind of thing he could get away with, as a sports-playing, non-intellectual jock in a country that boasted a sports-playing, non-intellectual jock president. He could deliver a hard message to an American audience and then play a jocular round of golf with the group afterwards. "I've found during my time in New Brunswick that just being straight saves a lot of work and effort," he said from his car phone. "It's just much easier to just talk straight and expect the same thing in return. I'm kind of in an enviable position in that I'm not from the career diplomatic world and I don't need to retain the job. So I can probably afford to be more direct than someone who is trained in this job and has a career in it." McKenna also found that this direct approach played well in the United States, where people are very straight-talking and take offence at any sign of smugness or hypocrisy. "If they push and you push back, I find they respect you. I don't gratuitously look for fights but I don't walk away from them either."

If McKenna seemed like the right guy for the job, the job was also just right for him. He had walked away from the premier's job as a relatively young man at 48. After his retirement from politics, he had kept busy with a break-neck schedule of directorships and public speaking engagements, and he spent quality time with his family, but he admitted that the absence from politics had left a huge void in his life. McKenna gave the impression of a caged tiger who was restlessly prowling around his enclosure. "There is a hole in my life but I am resigned to not having it filled," he told me at one point. "I mean, I don't have to have it filled. I got such intense satisfaction out of my time as premier that I can't replace that, but I can replace the workload and I do that with a lot of activities."

But now, as ambassador, that vacuum of public life had been filled again. Frank was back, and there was talk again of his taking a run at the leadership of the federal Liberal Party. McKenna refused to comment on his political future but the new job "gives me back a lot of the public life." What's more, East Coasters were coming through Washington all the time, and he was on the phone with someone every day. If anything, his new role made him a more valuable link from the Maritimes to the wider world.

Like many success stories in the Maritimes, this one has a Horatio Alger element. Frank McKenna was born in 1948, in Apohaqui, a small town between Moncton and Saint John, one of eight children of a hog and dairy farming family. Ambitious and smart, he was immersed in hockey, baseball, reading, and school studies in the confines of a close but not affluent family.

Frank won a scholarship to go on to St. Francis Xavier, where he entered the network of ambitious young kids from small-town Maritimes. Even for someone in St. FX's hothouse climate, he was a rather large man on campus, becoming the first student appointed to the university's board of governors. He also got to know Kevin Francis, another young upward striver, the son of a trucking entrepreneur in Sydney on Cape Breton. Frank also met his future wife, Julie Friel, and Kevin met Sharon, his wife, and the two couples got married right out of university. Frank was bound for political glory; Kevin was heading for teacher training, but got sidetracked and ended up as a Xerox salesman and, ultimately, CEO of Xerox Canada and a Silicon Valley technology executive. Through the years, the two men remained good friends.

Gaining a Beaverbrook scholarship, Frank went on to law school at University of New Brunswick in Fredericton. After graduation, he set up practice in the small city of Chatham in New Brunswick's Miramichi region, the home of Julie's mother's family, whose members were retailers in the area. There he achieved some reputation as a lawyer, notably by representing the battered old Miramichi boxer Yvon Durelle in a murder case, and Durelle was freed. "A murder trial before a jury is probably the most stressful experience you can encounter," Frank McKenna told a reporter later. "It's good preparation for politics."

Meanwhile he was a rising star in Liberal politics in New Brunswick of the mid-1980s, which was going through the last scandal-plagued years of the Richard Hatfield Conservative regime. The premier, the son of a great lumbering family, had been a meteor in New Brunswick politics and held the government since 1970. But he was now making headlines for wild parties with university students and being busted for pot possession. The province was poised for another of its massive swings between the Liberals and the Conservatives. After a short stint as an MPP, McKenna won the Liberal leadership in 1985 and swept to power in 1987, with the Liberals winning all 58 seats. He was eager but also very green. A reporter at the time asked about his feelings that day and McKenna replied that he had the sense of being "like a dog with a whole bunch of new puppies." It was bound to get a rise from opponents, but also from his own members. "I walked into caucus and they all started barking," he recalled in an interview with John Lownsborough in *Report on Business* magazine. "I was very naive."

He faced a formidable task in New Brunswick: a heavy deficit, and a burdensome debt in a have-not province that lacked the taxation base to attack the fiscal challenges. Wealth creation seemed an impossible task when so many of the best and brightest were leaving the province. But McKenna, a centrist Liberal sometimes called the best leader the Conservatives never had, was the man for the times. He realized that other have-not constituencies had turned around their prospects, such as Ireland, or Arkansas under another boy wonder named Bill Clinton. "He was a governor in a very poor state, and yet he did not give up on opportunity," McKenna recalls.

McKenna was also the beneficiary of a timely shift in business thinking. The modern corporation, particularly in the United States, had fastened on the concept of the call centre, a growing tool to boost their productivity by farming out customer service functions to low-cost jurisdictions. Using modern telecommunications technology, large companies could locate their customer service and telemarketing anywhere in the world—in India, in Houston, or in the rural Maritimes. New Brunswick had the right formula to attract these new offices, whether company-owned or outsourced to independent companies. The province had well-educated people, many of them bilingual; a loyal but underemployed workforce with no place to go and few other income alternatives; a favourable low-value Canadian dollar; and now a can-do government with an indefatigable premier.

Once it woke up to the promise of call centres, the McKenna government had to enter a partnership with a key technological support player—NB Tel, the province's telephone company. There was the need for seamless and immediate interaction. When a customer in Dubuque, Iowa, called Xerox because the photocopier wasn't working, he or she had to think that the call was being fielded next door, or in Rochester, New York. The challenge was compounded by having massive amounts of communications with diverse customers around the world. Fortunately, NB Tel had emerged as one of the most dynamic telecommunications enterprises in North America in its dedication to the latest technology and customer service.

NB Tel had a run of great leadership, including a crack engineering team recruited by long-time president Ken Cox and his team. Cox, as president in the 1980s, groomed an outstanding succession of leaders, such as Lino Celeste, Ed Graham, and Gerry Pond. The reason was simple: The telephone companies offered good jobs, and the chance to remain in New Brunswick for a cadre of engineers and professionals who came out of University of New Brunswick, Technical University of Nova Scotia (TUNS), and other schools. The best and brightest flocked to the local phone companies and particularly to NB Tel, which developed a reputation as a technology hothouse with the intimate scale of a small company.

The exemplar of this generation of NB Tel stars was John MacDonald, who came from Cape Breton Island and picked up his engineering training at Dalhousie University and TUNS. MacDonald joined NB Tel and quickly made his name as a brilliant engineer with a strong grasp of the future of technology. Lino Celeste, who succeeded Cox as CEO in 1986, remembers the day he asked his chief engineer to send up his brightest prodigy to explain a difficult technology to Celeste. It turned out to be John MacDonald, who blew Celeste away with his insight. Celeste told the chief engineer from that day forward, he would be in charge of John MacDonald's career development. "I saw all the potential," Celeste says, but "I had to fight with him on every promotion, including taking my job." Celeste admits now that was probably a mistake. "He wanted to be a top technical guy and we wanted to put him into the business jobs. His love was the technology."

Indeed, as chief engineer, chief information officer, and then CEO, MacDonald helped propel NB Tel into the Internet age before it was fashionable. But MacDonald was attracting attention from NB Tel's much larger sister company, Bell Canada, the telephone giant of Central Canada. He was approached by fellow Cape Bretoner John McLennan, now president of Bell Canada, to move to Montreal as his chief operating and technology officer. The road from NB Tel's base in Saint John to Montreal and Toronto was already well worn. The Maritime phone company was continually being raided by Bell Canada.

MacDonald did well, helping push Bell into the Internet age as the developer of its Sympatico on-line product, and he ultimately rose to the president's job at Bell Canada. But, Celeste says, "It was hard for John because he came from a small organization where he was the best of breed and when he went to Bell he didn't have the same authority to move."

MacDonald learned that Bell Canada was big and bureaucratic, while NB Tel was smaller and much closer to its customers. "With NB Tel, you looked someone in the eye, you shook hands, and you did it," recalls MacDonald. As NB Tel president, he would invite people in from Bell to learn about the New Brunswick company's dedication to customer service. It was like the New Brunswickers were speaking in code—the Bell types from Upper Canada just didn't get it. They were used to thinking in spreadsheets, not about being present and responsive in their communities.

MacDonald had a good run at Bell Canada, but both he and McLennan got chewed up and spit out in the politics of the telephone utility and its parent company, BCE Inc. But soon the two were teaming up again, both of them running AT&T Canada, a telecom company that provided services to big companies. AT&T Canada was renamed Allstream, and in 2004 it was taken over by an expanding Manitoba Telecom Services, which was headed by St. FX grad Bill Fraser. MacDonald became the president of Manitoba Telecom's Allstream division, which became the major instrument in the company's national assault on Bell Canada. It proved that Canadian telecom industry is a very small world.

But during his 18 years at NB Tel, MacDonald had helped create the kind of corporate culture that was just right for Frank McKenna. In the late 1980s, the new premier came knocking and said, "I need a technology partner," and NB Tel was ready. Under Cox, Celeste, and MacDonald, it had already built customer service into its DNA. The key was that the new premier was not an outsider; he was a player, a business guy, he was one of them. Lino Celeste, who was president of NB Tel when McKenna started to woo call centres to the province, said, "That was when McKenna became my vice-president sales, because he could get a crowd together and sell what we were trying to do." He saw it right away when he was invited by McKenna to attend a call centre convention in Toronto, where the premier hosted a luncheon of key industry executives. The NB Tel crowd soon learned that McKenna knew how to work a crowd of corporate bosses.

"We had a [New Brunswick] workforce that was over-trained for the jobs that were here," Celeste says. "When a call centre came in and had to hire 50 people, I tell you, they got some top-notch people. And Maritimers are very loyal to the employer; they don't jump around so much. People found retraining costs went way down, there was little churn, and they got skilled people."

"The provincial government was looking for a job creation strategy and we were looking for a growth strategy, and the two blended perfectly," remembers Gerry Pond, NB Tel's customer service whiz who became president in the later years of the McKenna revolution. "A guy like McKenna driving the entrepreneurial flair around that, a businessman who was a lawyer by training but he was really a good businessman, he thought business, he understood business people, and they understood him."

And he was always using that global network of alliances formed in high school, university, law practice, and now as a globe-trotting salesman for New Brunswick. If a phone call didn't work, it might be clinched by a fishing trip to the Miramichi or the Restigouche. He played the network relentlessly, often flashing that St. FX ring at prospective customers. "I've been to a lot of meetings where we've been talking away and then someone says, 'Look, we're with you on this.' And he just puts out his ring like that. The X is very distinctive and it's got a strong network. The networks here are quite extraordinary; a lot of the business we did is based on this mafia."

When he was luring a Royal Bank centre for Moncton, he talked it over with then chairman Allan Taylor while fishing on the Restigouche. Then vice-chairman Gordon Feeney came on board, because after all, he was a native New Brunswicker. When Air Canada needed a reservation centre, Frank got a call from chocolate tycoon David Ganong, who is on the airline's board, and "I immediately landed the centre for 500 big jobs in Saint John." Every business he went after, he would check the board, find out who was on it, and work the Maritime relationship.

Sometimes he didn't have to look very far. By the time Frank was lining up call centre customers for New Brunswick, his old friend Kevin Francis had risen through the Xerox ranks and had become the copier company's Canadian president in Toronto. Out of the blue, Frank called him one day and said, "Why don't you put some Xerox call centre jobs in New Brunswick?" McKenna explained that he needed some brand names to get the call centre thing off the ground. Francis was receptive to at least talking to his old friend about it. "He was up to Toronto in a flash with a couple of officials," Francis says. "He sold his little heart out. He is probably one of Canada's great salesmen."

Xerox was beginning to understand the power of selling its technology over the telephone and through the Internet. Francis travelled down to its Connecticut headquarters to make a presentation to the then chair of Xerox, Paul Allaire. The business case was that Xerox could save millions by consolidating its customer service centres, moving them north to Saint John in Canada, and eliminating duplicate centres south of the border. The Canadian team made the case, and a team of finance boffins went through the numbers. "I would say there was a high degree of skepticism that we could staff it and on time. Not only did we open on time and on budget, to this day it is one of the most efficient Xerox operations in the world."

In Francis's view there were several things McKenna did brilliantly. If he was going to take New Brunswick out of a traditional resource economy into a high-tech economy, he needed a good communications infrastructure, and NB Tel came through.

There is no point selling opportunities if you can't staff the call centres, so he invested heavily in community college education. Then he came up with financial incentives, including provincial seed money in the form of forgivable loans to help cover the call centres' start-up costs. Companies had to guarantee the job would be maintained for a minimum of three years; after that, the loan would be forgiven.

"Over and above that, it is the quality of Maritimers that makes it work," Francis said. "Maritimers are enormously loyal, we are not easily transferable—we give loyalty and so there is a very low turnover." In his time, Xerox's annual turnover rate in New Brunswick was in the single digits, compared with 40 per cent in some areas of United States.

But at 50, Francis felt he had gone as far as he wanted at Xerox. After 28 years, he exercised his right to an early retirement and looked for a new opportunity. He ended up in Ottawa running a high-tech company called Jetform and helped guide it through a hostile takeover bid and a merger. Then he was invited to move to San Jose, the heart of California's Silicon Valley, to run CenterBeam, a rising new company specializing in customer-service outsourcing, the very kind of business that the Maritimes had specialized in.

At his very first interview with CenterBeam's board, Francis made a daring proposal. The company's core research and corporate marketing should be retained in pricey San Jose, but all the growth areas of customer service should be immediately shifted to the Maritimes. "The board wanted to know, where are the Maritimes?" Francis chuckles, as he recalls that first reaction to the name of his home region. He has heard that kind of question many times in Silicon Valley, which is why he advocates a permanent Atlantic Canada office in the technology capital of the United States.

CenterBeam soon had 50 people in downtown Saint John providing customer support for 40 companies operating around the world. If CenterBeam holds to its growth trajectory, Francis figures to have 500 people working there by 2010. No Californians have had to be moved to Saint John. The employees are all Canadians, including many transplanted Maritimers who have come home. "We have a technical manager from Newfoundland who worked in Singapore and came back to Atlantic Canada; she's now running a technical team in Saint John. We continue to get applications from across the country, and they all have Maritime roots." For Francis, it provides an opportunity to repatriate top technical talent, pay them well above average salaries, and start growing the critical mass of companies and talent that allows people to build careers.

To find a home for CenterBeam in Saint John, Francis went to see John Irving, the family member who handles a lot of the real estate business for the powerful clan. The Irvings had been looking for an anchor tenant for a splendid century-old office block in the centre of Saint John, at the corner of Prince William and Canterbury streets—56,000 square feet of original brick and wood beams. A large section has been customized to CenterBeam's high-tech needs. But the building holds particular meaning for Kevin Francis: In 1972, when he was a sales trainee at Xerox, he made his very first sale to a company located in this building—"15 dollars a month and five cents a copy."

But isn't there the danger that Francis, an old Cape Bretoner whose heart still lies in the Maritimes, is putting sentiment ahead of business? He is indignant at the suggestion: "I'm not doing this out of social democracy, I'm doing it because it's good business sense." He concedes that in any case where the economic returns are equal, his bias would always go to Atlantic Canada. At CenterBeam, the company considered a number of possible locations, including India. "We evaluated that and determined that the cultural fit would not work well for the North American business focus we were going after. Whereas the NAFTA alignment sells very well down here in California."

The McKenna years were a golden age, and the question is how to sustain it. The province is still attracting good jobs, but the McKenna formula needs to be adapted to the times. In 1999, NB Tel merged with the three other Atlantic telephone companies, largely at the instigation of their major shareholder, BCE. The product of that merger, Aliant, has been plagued with integration issues. It has been run by a bright accountant, Jay Forbes, who is the son of a Canadian Tire dealer in Woodstock, New Brunswick, but it is now considered more a component of BCE's national machine than a separate Maritime institution. Some of the best technical people at NB Tel have left Aliant, but a number have stayed in the Saint John area, starting up new companies. Gerry Pond, who was displaced at Aliant by a manager brought in from Bell Canada, quit the telecom utility to go into the consulting and venture capital business with some ex-NB Tel colleagues. They have developed a network of information technology companies that hold considerable promise. The game isn't over in New Brunswick, Pond insists, even though the players have traded uniforms.

But in the global call centre business, strong rivals have emerged, including Nova Scotia, as well as the new outsourcing powers in India, Pakistan, and South Africa. In addition, New Brunswick has a finite supply of skilled people coming out of its universities and community colleges, and immigration numbers are notoriously low to the Maritimes. Not to mention the higher Canadian dollar, which has hurt New Brunswick's ability to attract new businesses into the province.

Still the momentum has been rolling on. Kevin Francis, who estimates that he has created 1,000 jobs in New Brunswick, says his numbers look good for a number of currency scenarios. A business proposition like this cannot be based on currency shifts; it has to offer a sustainable competitive advantage. "Once a Maritimer, always a Maritimer, but I could never in good conscience be a responsible steward for shareholders if it did not meet the test of time. I've been doing this for 10 years, and it has stood the test of time."

The biggest change was that McKenna left politics in 1997, ceding the political limelight and now the premiership to a new young premier, Bernard Lord, who has a different style. Lord has many gifts—he is a smart and careful consensus builder—and he may yet be the federal Conservative leader, but he is not a high-energy salesman in the McKenna mould. That has taken some adjustment for one business leader who is a member of a dyed-in-the-wool Conservative family. The businessman, who requested anonymity, said he used to get a call from Premier McKenna at least every year, just to shoot the breeze: "It was always: How's business? How's this? How's that? What are you hearing? It was his personal inventory of what was taking place." But in December 2004, five years after Bernard Lord took office, this high-profile Conservative businessman said, "I have never ever talked to Premier Lord."

As a private lawyer working with McInnes Cooper in Moncton, McKenna had been defiant that New Brunswick's "nearshoring" would not lose jobs to the "farshoring" alternative of India or South Africa. Sure those countries were getting the low-level assignments but New Brunswick was moving up the value scale, offering technical assistance and other more advanced chores. "We wanted to be at the very high end of this business and we continue to grow our job base at the high end, as much as our labour force can handle: sophisticated applications, computer diagnostics, sophisticated customer support."

He sounded like a man who still saw himself as premier, even though he was technically out of the office and practising law. He admitted that being a former premier is a difficult role. You see a lot of opportunities but you have to tread very carefully. "When you are a former premier, it is not clear what your role is. What I didn't want to be was kind of an interfering busybody with those who were duly elected to run Atlantic Canada or my own party, which has its own leader. I didn't want to be critical of other premiers, didn't want to interfere on the national stage." But he felt that he could speak occasionally on issues that affect Atlantic Canada and use his network to support the Atlantic economy and bring business in.

In mid-2004, there was a flurry of speculation that McKenna would throw his hat in the ring as a federal candidate, positioning himself as a future leadership candidate when Paul Martin retires. But he turned down the Liberals' offer on the grounds that all the Moncton-area Liberal MPs were running again in their constituencies, and he didn't want to become a commuter MP, trundling off to remote ridings, far from his home and family.

McKenna was spending about a third of his time in Toronto, where he tended to his second legal career as a rainmaker and consulting lawyer to the giant Bay Street firm Osler Hoskin & Harcourt and to his various board roles. "I used to say as premier I go to Toronto for the same reason

Willie Sutton robbed banks, because that's where the money is," he joked.

When I met McKenna in fall 2004, in the wood-panelled Moncton offices of McInnes Cooper, he was dressed in jeans and a red T-shirt with "Glenwood Kitchens" emblazoned on the front. "It's our kitchen cabinet company," he explained, pointing proudly at the T-shirt message displayed above the cherubic swell of his belly. "My wife and I and my son bought it two years ago. It's like the Victor Kiam story: We liked the cabinets so much we bought the company."

For the past few years, Frank McKenna had been building a different kind of cabinet than he did as premier. He has been twinning sales meetings in Toronto and Boston with speaking engagements and board meetings. Frank and Julie were putting their personal faces on a public policy issue in New Brunswick—how to keep children at home in a province with limited employment prospects. The McKennas' youngest son, James, had been working in Toronto for a gas brokerage but wanted to come home. As the family looked around, they decided the best bet was buying a kitchen-cabinet company with 130 employees, one of the largest employers in Shediac, the coastal town not far from Cap-Pelé. James, working with the former owners, the Belliveau family, helped run the company, Julie did the books, and Frank did sales calls from Boston to Toronto.

In early 2005, however, the prime minister announced that McKenna's hiatus from public life was over and he would be the new ambassador to Washington. For his friends, it was a signal that Frank was back in the action again. But it also meant that McKenna's short career as cabinet salesman, and Julie's as bookkeeper, would have to be put on the shelf. With their departure to Washington, James took an expanded role in the company, working with general manager Robert Belliveau, a member of the founding family.

But McKenna, the irrepressible, constant salesman, was keeping informed. Sales, he said, were going great in New England, the Caribbean, and Canada. "My son has really stepped up," he said. "It shows how quickly you can become redundant when you move out of the picture." The nice thing, he said, was that his ownership of Glenwood Kitchens presented no conflict of interest because it did no business with the government.

That would be a useful detail if McKenna assumed what many of his Maritime friends believe is his natural calling—to become prime minister of Canada. With his new role, the Maritime Mafia could once again entertain the hope that, after striking out with Conservative Robert Stanfield in the 1960s and 1970s, they might soon have one of their own in the prime minister's residence at 24 Sussex Drive.

CHAPTER 5

THE KING OF ECONOMY

IT IS A LONG WAY FROM northern Nova Scotia's Colchester
County, where Purdy Crawford grew up, to the towering
First Canadian Place office complex on Toronto's Bay Street.
But travel up the 63 floors and you will find a piece of the
Maritimes housed in the quietly hectic offices of the giant law
firm Osler Hoskin & Harcourt. This is one of Canada's
premier corporate law firms, and it is where both Purdy
Crawford and Frank McKenna kept offices for several years.
Frank was a consulting counsel who came from Moncton
and spent a few months every year as a rainmaker, corporate
director, and adviser. But all that ended when he took his
show to Washington as the new ambassador. Crawford
remains part of Osler's very lifeblood, a retired counsel with
46 years' experience who maintains a small office and a
secretary, but continues in his role as the avuncular conscience of Canadian business.

Purdy Crawford, at 74, is the grey eminence of the Maritime
Mafia, the *consigliere* to a half-dozen of the families who sit
at the core of the Atlantic network, and mentor to many others. Besides fathering six of his own children, he is teaching a
generation of young Maritimers how to prosper in the high-

pressure hot spots of world business. He is a close confidant of Wallace McCain, whom he met at Mount Allison University in Sackville more than 50 years ago, and a mentor to Michael McCain, Wallace's son and the CEO of Maple Leaf Foods. He is also a close adviser of blueberry king John Bragg and chocolate chief David Ganong, and sits on the board of fish tycoon John Risley's Clearwater income trust. He is a friend and a business partner to the Sobey family and has been known to join Donald Sobey for the annual pilgrimage to Warren Buffett's media circus, the annual meeting of Buffett's Berkshire Hathaway in Omaha, Nebraska. But the six degrees of Purdy Crawford extend beyond his fellow Atlantic Canadians. To dozens of managers and directors across Canada, he is Mr. Corporate Governance, a sane and sound voice in a corporate world gone mad.

Yet to people who don't know him well, the power of Purdy Crawford is a bit mystifying. He lacks the athletic dynamism of Paul Tellier, the former chief of Bombardier and Canadian National, or the ambitious brio of Manulife Financial's Dominic D'Alessandro. He is an unprepossessing public speaker who tends to mouth the usual platitudes about good governance and fair free markets. Once a skilled athlete, Crawford now looks like a portly favourite uncle.

Crawford's strength is in small groups and one-to-one counselling and mentoring. He can be tough and decisive, whether firing a senior manager at Imasco Inc., where he was once CEO, or developing succession policies on one of his boards. In explaining what he brings to the party, he says, "I have a lot of know-how and experience with things that happened in the past and may happen again." He brings particular expertise in two areas: He has deep business savvy and understanding, and a great interest in human resources and leadership development, which he pursues on his various boards.

While Frank McKenna is the Maritime Mafia's salesman, Crawford is its intellectual ballast, bringing a depth of learning and reading that is rare in a business class that favours action ahead of book-learning. No one is better briefed or better prepared than Crawford, and that is his continuing power: He reads widely and distributes his views through Purdy's Picks, a guide to articles and ideas that is sent to about 200 of Osler's young lawyers, other friends and colleagues, and a huge slice of the Maritime business mafia. Essentially, he tells Canada's business elite—busy people distracted by their awesome responsibilities—what they need to read to be effective managers. His Purdy's Picks of February 2005 contained, among other things, a *Barron's* piece on Indian economic prospects; a couple of pieces on corporate governance from a publication called *Board Alert*; and a *New York Times* story on the complex quirks of high-tech cars. Thus, Crawford serves as the ideas filter for the Canadian ruling class. That is why he is possibly the most influential figure in Canadian business today. When the Ontario Securities Commission needs someone to undertake its five-year review, it is Purdy. When someone needs a speech on corporate governance, it is Purdy. And when the Maritime Mafia needs a leader, it is still, undeniably, Purdy.

His career is a model of how the Mafia works. On the surface, this is a classic story of the son of a coal miner who through luck and pluck becomes a powerhouse attorney. But it is also a classic Maritimes success story, built on two of its defining institutions, Mount Allison and Dalhousie Law School, and his membership in that large, quiet, and influential club of male Maritimers who make things happen all over Canada. The only Maritimers who even approximate him in influence are his old Osler office neighbour, Frank McKenna, and Sir Graham Day, the former small-town lawyer and corporate fix-it guy for Margaret Thatcher, who has retired to Hantsport, Nova Scotia, as a director and elder statesman. Crawford likes to kibitz with both men and gently chides McKenna for trying to put him out to pasture as a networker. Day and Crawford are cut from a similar cloth: relaxed charm blended with iron discipline and intense loyalty to the families they serve. When they confide to a journalist that a certain family consists of "good people," that's code for "they are my friends and I will be very unhappy if you slag them in print."

To understand Purdy Crawford, head back to Five Islands, Nova Scotia, a pretty village between Truro and Parrsboro, looking out on the gorgeous Minas Basin and the cluster of flowerpot islands that gives the community its name. He went to school in a shingled white building high on a hill, still standing, with a plaque commemorating 125 years of schooling, from 1877 to 2003. Now it sits empty across the road from the KC Jay Diner, which closes on a Sunday in November but serves good clams in the summertime, Crawford says—and just down the road from the United Church and the ball field he once owned and recently gave away to his niece.

Purdy was a much-loved only child of second marriages for both his mother and father. His father was a coal miner in Springhill who went to work underground as a 14-year-old and rose to the job of shift boss. He lost his first wife and two children to the global influenza epidemic just as World War I was ending. A 50-ish widower with a family, in about 1930 he married Purdy's mother, a young divorcee with a family of her own. His body broken down by disease and accidents in the Springhill mines, he retired at age 55 to nearby Five Islands, the hometown of his wife, where they raised young Purdy, the gift of their later years.

Crawford grew up with a great thirst for schooling. After elementary school in the shingled white schoolhouse, he travelled to nearby Bass River for high school. Those were the days before school busing, and students often had to board near their high schools on weekdays because it was hard to traverse the 24 kilometres. To get to Bass River each week, he had to travel through the little communities of Lower, Central, and Upper Economy.

From those roots in Central Economy, Purdy would eventually play a central role in the Canadian economy. He became a trailblazer among the young people of rural Nova Scotia who would head off for fame and fortune in Britain, Upper Canada, and the United States. They were products of the fine education available from teachers in the small schools of rural Nova Scotia. A number of people interviewed for this book, from economist Judith Maxwell to oilman Grant Bartlett, attribute their success to that superb small-town schooling. In this way, Nova Scotia has played a role similar to Scotland itself, whose stellar education system produced the superb lawyers, engineers, and doctors who built and extended the British Empire in the 19th and early 20th centuries. "Nova Scotia is very Scottish and it exports learned people," says Graham Day.

As a product of that background, Crawford headed off to Mount Allison University, 60 kilometres up the road in Sackville, New Brunswick. He already knew a classmate, Margaret Norrie, whose family, like Purdy's, was much involved in Liberal politics in the Truro area. He also met Margaret's future husband, Wallace McCain, but they weren't close friends like they are now. Wallace, a year ahead of Crawford, was a hellraiser who was attending his third university in three years, and Crawford, even then, was clearly a student. "To say he was a better student would be an understatement," Wallace says. "Purdy was a real student; he was there to work."

Today, Crawford remains a bit puzzled about why his career took the turn it did. The family wanted him to be a schoolteacher, but Purdy, the first of his family to go to university, loved the idea of the law. He figures that he might have ended up in Nova Scotia practising law and eventually going into politics, but he just kept upping the ante. He did well at Mount Allison and headed off to Dalhousie University Law School in Halifax, where he did very well. At Dalhousie Law School, Crawford stood first in his first year, second in his second, and third in his third. "It's a good thing it didn't last longer," he once told a classmate, "or I would have been at the bottom."

That academic standing is a tribute to Purdy's intelligence and competitiveness, for the mid- to late-1950s was a golden era at Dalhousie Law School, a period that produced a constellation of legal, business, and political stars. Graham Day was just behind Purdy; John Crosbie and future New Brunswick premier Dick Hatfield were there at the same time. James Palmer, who became one of Calgary's legal titans, was another near-contemporary. For most of these young men, it was one of those experiences that laid down lasting connections. "When you go to law school, you got a congregation of people who maybe didn't know each other, but maybe knew of each other. You congregate for three years and those contacts last a lifetime," says Sir Graham Day. "I don't know of any of whom you would say, what a miserable shit he was."

In those days, legal and business careers did not gravitate to Toronto but to London, England, or to Boston and New York. Graham Day was the son of a British immigrant father in what was, in the 1950s, a very anglophile province. Pictures of the British king and queen hung in classrooms, and there were role models of earlier Maritimers, such as Max Aitken, later Lord Beaverbrook, who had made it big across the seas in England.

One of the most influential Dalhousie law teachers for both Purdy Crawford and Graham Day was Roland Ritchie, son of a prominent Halifax family, brother of diplomat and diarist Charles Ritchie, and later a justice of the Supreme Court of Canada. "We got taught culture by people who were like the Ritchies, who viewed the world and the law in a very British way," Sir Graham says.

Day had one of the most unconventional careers of them all. After graduation and joining the bar, he acquired a law practice in Windsor, Nova Scotia, where he worked for eight years. One day he got a call from a law professor friend, a Newfoundlander, who had contacts at Canadian Pacific, the big railway company. Asked how long he intended to keep practising law in Windsor, Day replied that he was getting stale from doing the same thing over and over again. So he was hired by the railway company and did a lot of international work, which led him to assignments in Britain. There, he made a deep impression on the British government and was recruited by the Conservative government of Ted Heath in the 1970s to deal with a shipyard that was going bankrupt.

Day became a fixer, the kind of guy that British prime ministers could rely on to take a company private, turn it around, or downsize a workforce. He remembers that at 38 years old, after a number of challenging jobs, he finally asked a British minister why he kept getting these tough assignments. The minister said it was easy: "If you make a hash of it, you are not one of us. It's always easier to shoot the colonials than it is to shoot the natives." Grateful for the candour, Day said, "My God, you are an absolutely honest man."

As British prime minister through most of the 1980s, Margaret Thatcher got to depend on the can-do attitude of

Day, who combined a steel will with a charming, witty demeanour. He went from challenge to challenge, in the ship-building, automobile, and aerospace industries. He always had a page-and-a-half letter from Thatcher, outlining her expectations and what he was pledged to do—in other words, the terms of his assignment. "Periodically, some civil servant would phone up and say, 'Graham, it would really be helpful if....' But I would have my piece of paper and I would say, 'Would you like to speak to the lady or shall I?' And there were never any takers."

The key, he says, was that "once she said, 'We are agreed, are we not?' then that was the line in the sand." It was an exhilarating period when he was present at the making of history in Britain. His role in a number of touchy privatizations and rationalizations made him the scourge of Britain's left, but his charm softened the edges. *The Times* of London once described him as "the nicest man who ever axed an entire workforce."

After the Thatcher years, he sat on several British boards, such as Cadbury and British Aerospace, but suddenly gave it all up in the early 90s to return to Canada. He was in demand as a director in Canada and took on more boards, including the chairmanship of the Ontario power distributor, Hydro One, which had been spun out of the former Ontario Hydro with an eye to privatization. He now wishes he had obtained a Thatcher-like letter from then premier Mike Harris when he got involved in the energy industry of Ontario. Harris retired, and the premier's job was inherited by his former finance minister, Ernie Eves. That precipitated a rare blot on Day's career, as he found himself in the middle of a botched privatization. It led to his resignation, amid allegations of an excessively rich compensation deal for the utility's chief executive, Eleanor Clitheroe. Day argued that the compensation packages reflected market rates, the advice of consultants, and the pattern of other privatizations he had participated in. Faced with a collapse of political will at Queen's Park, he grew nostalgic for a prime minister such as Thatcher, a lady who was not for turning. But Day through it all remained the epitome of grace under fire.

While Day was building his career in Britain, his former schoolmate Purdy Crawford was gravitating in other directions. Like many Dal law grads, past and present, he won a scholarship for a master's degree at Harvard University Law School, where he did very well indeed. Harvard was an eye-opener for the kid from Five Islands and Economy. He developed his knack for being better informed than anyone else. He audited courses, becoming a master of legal thought across a range of disciplines. He became enamoured with labour law and took a course on the subject with Archibald Cox, who later became special Watergate prosecutor in the Nixon White House and quit dramatically in the Saturday Night Massacre, which is widely viewed as the beginning of the end of the Nixon presidency.

He decided that he wanted to practise law in a major centre. The choices were New York, Boston, and Toronto, because Montreal, while exciting, would have meant a mastery of French civil law and language, which he did not have. Boston was particularly beguiling because he loved the city, the Red Sox, and the Bruins. There was also the traditional Maritimers' ties to what they called "the Boston states" of Massachusetts and environs. "A lot of my relatives lived and worked in the fishing business and the ice business, delivering ice to tenement buildings," he recalled. Near Five Islands, there was a community up in the hills called New Boston, which was once populated by people who had come back from the Boston states. But practising law in the United States in those days would have required him to become a U.S. citizen.

So he returned to Halifax to article under Roland Ritchie, who was well connected in Central Canada and helped line up job appointments in Toronto. Crawford got offers from a pile of firms, but chose Osler's, then a firm of 23 lawyers—there are now more than 400.

Crawford started as a labour lawyer, helping to negotiate union contracts on behalf of management. One of his great learning experiences was helping to convert Bethlehem Steel's contracts with the United Mineworkers into pacts that would apply to the company's workers at an iron mine in Marmora in east-central Ontario. Those sessions in Pittsburgh gave the young lawyer exposure to employee benefits and pension plans, which would serve him well later. The son of the coal miner from Springhill found himself on the other side of the table, but he felt he hadn't really switched sides. In negotiating contracts, particularly with small companies, "the biggest challenge was getting your own client to be reasonable. You could take off your necktie and relate to the guys across the table."

Meanwhile, his career was taking him into different directions. He became a member of a committee of lawyers, headed by securities lawyer Jack Kimber, who prepared a report in the mid-1960s about what securities laws should be. Then he and another lawyer, Howard Beck, were retained by Kimber, the head of the Ontario Securities Commission, to draft a new securities act that became the foundation of the law today.

It was the kind of back-breaking intellectual life that the over-achieving Crawford revelled in, involving hours of reading and preparation. After working most of the day at the law office, he would leave in the late afternoon for Kimber's office, where he worked into the night. With the tabling of legislation, he became an authority on securities law and mergers and acquisitions. It was a splendid learning opportunity and a certified career-builder, which he was able to exploit with stunning success.

As one of Canada's top young corporate lawyers, he quickly accumulated board memberships, including in the late 1970s a directorship with Imasco, the holding company for a big slice of the Canadian economy, including Imperial Tobacco. It now seems odd that Purdy Crawford, the Mr. Clean of the Canadian corporate world, would have thrown his lot in with a company that has taken such a heavy toll on Canadians' health and public finance. But his association was a long one, back to when cigarette smoking was not a big issue. Indeed, he joined the company's board just as it faced a crisis: The U.S. Surgeon General's report linked smoking with cancer, which led CEO Paul Paré to embark on a major diversification program to lessen Imasco's dependency on tobacco.

As an Imasco board member in the early 1980s, Crawford got involved in the search to find a successor to the company's builder, Paré. But one of the candidates left the company and the other was clearly not ready for prime time. The board turned to Crawford and asked whether he would take on the job as president and COO, with an eye to succeeding Paré as CEO.

Despite all the health warnings, in the 1970s and 1980s the number of cigarettes sold in Canada kept increasing, and Imasco had been able to use its strong cash flow to fuel its diversification. As a director, he had seen the company acquire the Shoppers Drug Mart and Pharmaprix drugstore chains and Hardee's Food Systems in the United States. When he joined Imasco, Crawford became immediately caught up in Imasco's biggest diversification bid to take over the giant holding company Genstar, whose holdings ranged from real estate and construction companies to its prize asset, Canada Trust, the country's best-run trust company. The pressure mounted because Paré was suffering from heart problems and underwent surgery shortly after Purdy joined in 1985.

Paré returned to action but he couldn't deal with negotiating the financing of the Genstar takeover. "Paré was part of that but the pressure was so great he walked away from it. He would break out in a big sweat, but I had to go head to head with Genstar in New York," Crawford recalls. Of course, he loved the job. "It was a fascinating deal, I ran it, no damn investment dealer did. I called the strategy." For advisers, he enlisted the investment bank McLeod Young Weir in Canada and First Boston in the United States, a hard-driving firm run by Bruce Wasserstein, then the wunderkind of Wall Street. Purdy negotiated fees that were absurdly low by the standards of today. It was particularly thrilling on the final weekend when the team worked to make the Sunday advertising deadline to get the offer published in the Monday *New York Times*.

Once he had won Genstar, Crawford had to make the hard transition from lawyer and deal-maker to the operator of a company. Imasco faced some immense challenges, including the purchase of the Peoples Drug Store chain in the United States. Peoples was a collection of small drugstore chains assembled by a brilliant entrepreneur and industry visionary named Bud Fantle. But once the chains were put together, they became a sleepy group that failed to perform according to expectations. When Imasco took over, Purdy's team concluded in 1986 that the problem lay with Fantle, who was now Peoples' CEO. "He was a great entrepreneur who knew how to put the pieces together; he wasn't a great operator, and I had to sack him," Crawford says. The plan was that Purdy would give Fantle the boot and replace him with an Imasco manager named David Bloom, who was later to head Shoppers Drug Mart. It was Purdy's darkest moment.

He decided he was not going to do it before Christmas because it would ruin Fantle's vacation. "So I worried about it all over the holiday. It spoiled my Christmas and not his—although his being Jewish, it probably didn't matter that much."

On January 10, 1987, the *Wall Street Journal* reported Imasco's release that "Sheldon W. Fantle retired as chairman and chief executive officer of its Peoples Drug Stores Inc. unit, which has been posting poor earnings." An Imasco spokesman told the *Journal* that "Mr. Fantle's retirement followed discussions with Imasco's president and chief executive, Purdy Crawford, but the spokesman declined to say whether Mr. Fantle was asked to leave."

Crawford's other operating challenge was Hardee's, a burger restaurant chain whose decline was a big blow to Purdy because he was deeply involved in its acquisition as a director. Purdy and the Imasco team realized the fast food industry was moving to a more mature stage from a period of indiscriminate expansion. "We didn't have the leadership or the understanding of what was happening in the marketplace," and Imasco exited that business, selling out to CKE Restaurants for about $500 million (U.S.).

It was at Imasco that Purdy began to hone his ability to find and mentor future business leaders, particularly in his native Atlantic region. He found one of his most successful projects when he joined the board of Devco, the hard-pressed Cape Breton coal company kept alive through massive federal government subsidies. At one board meeting in the early 1980s, a young vice-president named Annette Verschuren was giving a report on the strategic options facing the coal-mining industry. Verschuren recalls that Purdy grilled her on her presentation, then took her aside after the meeting and said if she ever wanted to leave Devco, she should contact him. "She was a breath of fresh air around the place," Purdy recalls.

Verschuren had come from a dairy-farm family in North Sydney and had developed a take-charge personality. Her confidence came out of helping keep the dairy farm going, along with her mother and siblings, after her father suffered a heart attack at 42, an event that dramatically reduced his role in the operations. After helping milk the cows in the morning, she would come to school with the aroma of manure on her clothes, which earned her the charming nickname of Poopie. She had also overcome a damaged kidney that landed her in hospital for long dark days as a teenager. As a young manager, she was ambitious and left Devco to take a job in Ottawa selling off Crown assets for the federal government. She renewed her relationship with Purdy and, after some negotiation, he hired her at Imasco as a vice-president, corporate development.

In time, she was eager to run a business, and he put her in charge of Den for Men, a chain of gift stores that needed a turnaround. Once she had served some time there, she came to Purdy with yet another career plan: She wanted to own something. "So I quit Imasco and there was a little bit of friction with Purdy, but he understood subsequently what I did." The relationship survived, and Verschuren became a retail powerhouse. She took a year off to check out retailing investment possibilities, then joined Michaels as it was expanding into Canada. One day, she got a call from a headhunter who had an intriguing proposal for her. Verschuren, who had personally invested in the Michaels venture, kept putting off the headhunter, until the woman said, you'd better look at this, this is big. The company was Home Depot, and Verschuren went to the interview. After extricating herself from the

Michaels contract, she joined the big retailing company and she never looked back.

BY THE MID-1990s, Crawford, now Imasco's chairman, had bigger fish to fry. Britain's BAT, which owned 40 per cent of Imasco, decided to consolidate its tobacco business, bring it inside, and cut loose its non-tobacco affiliates. The UK company had been under increased pressure from British institutional investors to clean up its corporate portfolio and gain a more focused business outlook. So BAT came to Imasco and said it wanted the Imperial Tobacco business for itself, and it wanted out of Imasco's diversification assets.

"We could have said no and had a serious disagreement," Crawford says, but instead he and CEO Brian Levitt launched the long, complex breakup of Imasco. These turned out to be devilishly intricate negotiations, involving BAT, an Imasco shareholder committee, and Imasco management. One of the primary considerations was getting the deal done without a crushing tax blow for Imasco's shareholders, which Levitt and Crawford were able to accomplish.

There are some who feel it was Purdy's greatest moment, but he sees it as a mixed highlight, a bit of sadness and joy. The Imasco team found buyers for the non-tobacco assets, including Canada Trust, which the Toronto Dominion Bank bought in an $8-billion deal that changed the structure of the banking industry in Canada. The one remaining unsold asset was the land subsidiary that had come as a fragment of the big Genstar takeover. The property company had great assets, particularly in western Canada, but undervalued by potential buyers. Crawford was able to use his Maritime connections, and the Sobeys came in as a major investor, along with Toronto developer Rudy Bratty and Genstar management.

The idea was that Purdy Crawford, Wallace McCain, and John Bragg would join in another ownership group, but McCain didn't like the risk and Bragg got caught up in a major cable investment. "So I took a deep breath and leveraged myself in debt," says Crawford, who prides himself on making his own investment decisions. It was a big gamble but it paid off in spades. "Look what's happened, housing went on a boom, and we have all this low-cost land in Calgary and we have gone back into the U.S. with some pretty good deals. So it is a good story."

The unbundling of Imasco was Crawford's last big deal, and in the past eight years he has reduced his role to that of a counsel and superstar director. Asked what his talents are, he says it is his wide-ranging reading—at the time we were talking, he was poring over Ron Chernow's biography of Alexander Hamilton. "I bring a broad perspective, an ability in a relaxed sort of way to make decisions and move on and an ability to delegate, see the big picture."

As he got older, he would go back to his old alma mater, Mount Allison, as a member of the board of governors. He had picked up his acquaintance with Wallace McCain and his wife, Margaret. Ultimately, Purdy and Wallace became one of the most effective tag-team fundraising duos in corporate Canada. "Purdy has got first-class people skills, and he's obviously a man of high integrity," McCain says. "I think he gets enjoyment out of the success and building other people. He enjoys people. If he likes you and thinks you're a good guy and can help you do better, and lets you do that, it gives him great satisfaction. He likes smart people, likes people who are going to do something, and he wants to help them if he can, and he does."

Crawford has in late career cut back to "only" six corporate boards, plus a number of non-profit boards. By mid-

2006, he hopes to have dropped a couple more. It gives him time to linger at his winter place in Naples, Florida, and play a little golf. But he remains very plugged in, tied closely to almost all the power bases in the Maritimes. There are only two major family lines of the Maritime Mafia that he doesn't connect with. While he knows the Irvings, he does not advise them. Indeed, who does, for they keep their own counsel. The other one is the Jodrey family, the powerful family of investors who have their roots in the Annapolis Valley. They are friends but not confidants. As far as everyone else, they are connections in Crawford's amazing network.

He uses his immense credibility to challenge the accepted wisdom in Atlantic Canada that governments need to pour their money into job-creation schemes. He can attack that orthodoxy because he is a Maritimer, not some Stephen Harper outsider who gets his jollies by dumping on the Atlantic Canadian work ethic. He is very harsh on the political leadership, which has been obsessed with being elected rather than making the hard choices. He wants to see the four Atlantic provinces working together on economic development. To get it going, he wants a full study on the competitive advantages of Nova Scotia—not some pricey consultant's report but a committee of government, public service, and business.

Meanwhile, after 46 years in Toronto, he continues to go back to Five Islands. He and his wife, Bea, have taken over an 1890 farmhouse once owned by her family just down at the bottom of Economy Mountain, the area he used to travel through as a young boy heading to school in Bass River. He spends the summers there, and the kids and grandkids come home and stay for a while.

But he is never far away from the Mafia and looking out for the future careers of some of his protégés. He is particularly pleased to see his Osler colleague, Frank McKenna, head off for Washington. Crawford feels that as long as McKenna was immersed in corporate boards, he did not have time to chart his future role in the public policy scene. But going back into politics is a much easier step when you are a high-profile ambassador to the United States. "He's definitely back in the picture," Crawford says. "He had too many boards and advisories; he was handling them well but busy. This gives him a chance to dump them all and start over if he wants to."

CHAPTER 6

ON BLUEBERRY HILLS

THE GLITTERATI OF CANADA'S business class were out in force for the induction ceremonies at the Canadian Business Hall of Fame on May 1, 2003. It was the first event to be held in the recently re-opened Carlu Theatre, the art deco masterpiece that had been closed for almost 30 years in downtown Toronto—on the seventh floor of what used to be Eaton's College Street store. After taking in the splendour of the refurbished Carlu, the audience settled in for the lavish tributes to Hall of Fame inductees and the gracious acceptance speeches from the still-living inductees.

But then something fascinating broke out, which could make sense only to insiders of the Maritime Mafia. Inductee Richard Currie, the brilliant Saint John boy who built a formidable career at the Loblaws-Weston food empire, launched into a lengthy promotion for the company he now serves as chairman—BCE Inc., parent of Bell Canada and dominant player in the telephone system in much of Canada. He described the Bell system as the best in the world with the lowest rates, based on the superior Canadian regulatory model.

It was classic Currie, a heady blend of self-importance and self-parody, capped off by a quote from the Eagles, one of his favourite rock bands: "Take it to the limit, One more time." It's a hard act to follow, but John Bragg, the balding, unprepossessing Nova Scotia blueberry king, is more than up to it. While blueberries are his core business, Bragg, now in his early 60s, also owns EastLink, the pioneering cable company that has emerged as a fierce competitor to Bell's affiliate Aliant in providing local telephone service in Nova Scotia and Prince Edward Island.

As he wrapped up his own acceptance speech, Bragg paid tribute to his "great little blueberry company," but also to "my great little telephone company, which offers service in Atlantic Canada at discounted rates from the great company that has the best rates in the world." The hall erupted in laughter, and Bragg acknowledged that he would get in trouble for that remark. This wasn't what the glitterati had expected; they heard not the usual platitudes but an edgy exchange by two of the Maritime Mafia. In various parts of the hall, the Bragg fans and the Currie groupies were jabbing each other in the ribs: "Take that, eh!" Later, as the evening wound down, an enraged Currie confronted Bragg, complaining bitterly that the EastLink owner had shown disrespect to BCE.

For people who know John Bragg, the verbal comeback wasn't all that surprising. Over the past 50 years, much lesser people than Dick Currie had been upstaged by the soft-spoken, tough-as-nails son of a lumberman in Nova Scotia's Cumberland County, who built a frozen food empire out of a diverse stew of wild blueberries, carrots, cranberries, and onion rings. He took the great leap into cable television by building EastLink, a company that other cable tycoons could only dream of emulating. There is no low tech or high tech for John Bragg, there is just business: hold a line on costs, hire good people, be a smart operator, take chances but always watch your ass. He is the typical Maritime managerial package—a firm man with a practical touch. Worth more than $360 million according to *Canadian Business* magazine, he remains humble, helpful, decisive, the kind of guy that the other Maritime Mafia want on their side—and many of them do, because John Bragg's quiet influence graces a plethora of boards, including the Sobey family's two public companies.

But the base of John Bragg's success lies about two hours north of Halifax, around Truro, Oxford, and Springhill, where in the autumn the wild blueberry plants form a crimson mantle over the smoky hills and faded farmland of the lightly populated back roads. In the middle of this riot of blueberries, there sits an industrial mega-complex—the sprawling frozen food factory in Oxford, the little town (population 1,300) that forms the hub of the Bragg blueberry industry, complete with museum and a shop that sells blueberry ice cream and chocolate-covered blueberries. On a Sunday afternoon, somebody has dumped a load of carrots on the pad in front of the factory, waiting for just-in-time processing and freezing. A few kilometres to the south, a twisty road takes you to tiny Collingwood Corner, with its complex of Bragg homes and businesses—a lumber yard, a blueberry harvesting equipment maker, and the white frame house that was the home of John Bragg's parents and which is kept ship-shape for visiting family members from away. Across the road is the grey Cape Cod house that John and Judy Bragg built as newlyweds and where they raised their four kids, all in the business now. It is where, in the wry observation of John's son Lee, the couple keep adding rooms as the number of people living at home keeps shrinking—and even though John and Judy also maintain a vacation home in Hawaii. Collingwood Corner presents an idyllic picture: In River Philip behind the old Bragg homestead, a man is fly-fishing in the soft fall rain. But it is also deceptive in its calm—this is the home of one tough businessman.

This is where John Bragg was born 65 years ago to a hard-working Baptist family in the lumber business. In Nova Scotia, lumber producers tend to own their own land on a freehold basis rather than lease it from the Crown. And there was a lot of land available as people moved off the farms in large numbers, often searching for a better life in town, or down the road in Ontario or Alberta. In a strange way, the Braggs benefited from the Maritime diaspora by accumulating large land holdings from exiting small farmers for the value of the woodlots alone. But young John saw not only the woodlots but other possibilities in the old farm fields, horse pastures, and back lots fading to bush—he saw the wild blueberries that grew in great profusion.

A teenaged John Bragg seized the opportunity by growing and harvesting berries on those old marginal farms. "I kinda fell into the blueberry business," he says now. When he was 15, he hired a team of students to help him pick 4,700 pounds of blueberries, and then sold them to a jobber and "I just went on from there." In his final year of high school, he made $4,000 picking blueberries, which tidily covered the $1,200 it would cost him to go that year to Mount Allison University in nearby Sackville, New Brunswick. During the summers, the blueberry business took off, and by his last year in teacher training at Mount A, he was grossing $25,000 a year from the berries. Meanwhile, he was being offered $3,900 to teach school at nearby Pugwash, as well as coach basketball at recess.

With that kind of choice, it was an easy decision to come home to help run the lumber business and build his tasty little sideline of blueberries. He had plenty of role models in his own family with a five-generation history of entrepreneurial endeavour, including his older brother Doug, who had joined his father, Elmer, in the lumber business. But soon the sideline was taking over from the core lumber trade, which was going through tougher times. When he was 28, John Bragg borrowed a wad of cash to build a frozen food plant in Oxford, which became the foundation of his Oxford Frozen Foods. He is shocked today by his innocent faith in the future. "Although it was part of a family business, it was my initiative. I had great support from my father and older brother but it was mine to run—live it, sleep it, and work it night and day."

John Bragg borrowed heavily from the province to fuel his expansion, putting up the family's landholdings as collateral. He bristles at any suggestion that he was subsidized by the province in the manner of the classic job-creation fiascos that, in the minds of many Canadians, have characterized the Maritimes. "We have never received a penny of subsidy from the province," he says. Sure, the Braggs borrowed money from Nova Scotia at a decent rate, but they paid it back. In John's view, the province was simply filling a void in rural Nova Scotia, where lending institutions failed to provide adequate financing for budding entrepreneurs. The province never lost a penny lending to John Bragg. It helped form his view about the need for government to stimulate rural development. "I don't think there is anything wrong with the province lending money to an entrepreneur," he says.

Bragg also developed a life-long relationship with the Bank of Nova Scotia, as did many of the Maritime Mafia. Scotiabank emerged as the lead lender to the rising business class, including the Sobeys, McCains, and Irvings. Bank leaders over the years, such as Horace Enman, Arthur Crockett, Cedric Ritchie, and Peter Godsoe, had Maritime roots themselves. But in the early 21st century, Bragg severed his relationship with the bank in a split that closely approximates the painful divorce of a long-married couple. "They've got a new guard and a new philosophy. They were great supporters but we just couldn't agree," Bragg says sadly. Like the rebounding partner in a failed marriage, Bragg quickly joined the board of Scotiabank's bitter rival Toronto Dominion Bank, now his cable TV banker. His food business lenders are led by Rabobank, a Dutch institution with deep experience in agribusiness.

In the 1970s and 1980s, rural Nova Scotians kept moving away, and John Bragg continued to buy up farms. Starting with 100 acres at Collingwood Corner, he accumulated 20,000 acres across Nova Scotia, New Brunswick, and the state of Maine. He assembled what his managers consider to be the largest fruit farm in North America, a 10,000-acre blueberry plantation in Cherryfield, Maine, near the Canadian border. The Braggs bought the farm in blocks, first 3,400 acres and then adjoining lots. This Ponderosa of blueberries is like a vast Texas ranch, except it lies amid the faded farmland of eastern Maine. "You can drive 75 miles on this one farm; you can't see it all in a day," Bragg marvels. "I fly down to visit it and spend a day and a half to see it all. I walk it." In its efficiency, it is the Toyota or Wal-Mart of blueberry farms, with 8,000 acres under irrigation. The crop goes primarily into the United States, but Oxford Frozen Foods sells its produce everywhere around the world. It pioneered the export of Canadian blueberries to Japan, and Bragg tirelessly promotes the fruit for its health properties—reduced memory loss and slower aging, he claims. Like many Maritimers who operate on both sides of the border, John Bragg sees the boundary as an artificial barrier for commerce and views Canada and the United States alike as the domestic market.

John Bragg also developed a legend as a very wise man, and along with his close friend, Purdy Crawford, he is the most quoted business leader by his Atlantic peers. There is a sense that if John says it, it must be true. The Bragg business principles are like the man himself, down to earth and practical. For one thing he is not big on five-year strategic plans. "We've had all kinds of people, including our banks, say what are you going to do in the next five years? And we always say we don't know. If we look back five years, we've done a lot more than we anticipated and that's been true in every five years." The business has an expansionary spirit, combined with a lack of timidity concerning debt; but in every expansion, there is also a carefully considered exit strategy. John Bragg likes to quote Frank Sobey, a man he never knew but whose sons he counts among his close friends. "Frank said, 'Always leave the back door open,' and we believe in that."

The Bragg story contains parallels to that of the McCains, another family close to John. Oxford is a business that grew out of the father's smaller operation—just as the McCain brothers extended beyond their father's seed potatoes, Bragg burst out of his father's woodlots and into food processing. What's more, the sons created an entirely new global business and ran it from the small rural community. Today, John points out, the family still owns a lot of trees, which is part of the family heritage. "It is still a great satisfaction for me to walk a nice woodlot." But blueberries, carrots, and other frozen food are a much bigger part of his life. "We took that industry from a cottage industry to a professional business, with all the bells and whistles that go with that. When it started, we had a small factory and small farm; now we market all over the world. We grew it dramatically, grew the entire industry with us."

He has been a tremendous mentor to other Maritimers, including Steve Parker, a Halifax communications consultant. "John Bragg is a driven entrepreneur," Parker says. "A lot of people think he's crazy but there is no evidence that John Bragg is crazy." Although Bragg has branched out into cable television and owns a chain of Pierceys lumber stores, it is his success in frozen fruit and vegetables that is truly remarkable. "He created a category in wild frozen blueberries by selling them around the world. That is hard, getting people to buy something they never bought before."

Bragg sits on one of Parker's boards, a role he fills in countless companies and organizations. One day, when Parker was trying to articulate his business model, Bragg told him, "Steve, if you can't write the key elements of your business on the back of a cigarette pack, you don't understand your business." Thanks to Bragg, Parker and his team have become obsessive about knowing the essence of their business and its key operating ratios.

Being somewhat isolated in rural Nova Scotia also taught Bragg a sense of initiative and can-do improvising that has served him in all the businesses. That too is a McCain and Irving characteristic: If you are isolated in the Maritimes, you have to create your own supporting technology and your own service industries. If you process potatoes, you build harvesting and processing equipment, as the McCains have. You buy trucking companies, as the Irvings and McCains have done. The Irvings have taken this all the way to a rigid vertical integration in which they control the entire supply chain, from refinery to gas pumps, forests to tissue paper. The Braggs are not that extreme, but they are unusually self-sufficient.

To hear it from John's older son Lee, a lot of the extemporaneous thinking comes during the evenings in the Bragg household, when John and one of his children fasten on a problem and thrash it over.

Consider, for example, the Braggs' appetite for many thousands of bees to pollinate the blueberry plants that tumble across the Cumberland County rough land. Oxford used to rent bees from Nova Scotia and New Brunswick beekeepers, but they were always running a little short. Then Nova Scotia, in a protectionist move, closed the border to out-of-province bees, and Braggs had to improvise. Lee and John figured out one evening that they should go even further, starting up their own apiary operations with 100 or so hives. They launched a head-hunting search for a beekeeper, and faced with a choice of two top-flight people from western Canada, they hired both of them. Now they run about 15,000 hives of bees, a regular pollination machine, as well as continuing to rent 25,000 hives for their Maine operation. Less successful have been plans for honey production from these hives—they have yielded hardly a drop of honey. That will be tackled at some point in the future.

John Bragg feels this flair for improvisation is part of the Maritime management tradition. Atlantic Canadians, he says, are often terrific operators, but with some exceptions, "we are not the greatest marketers, salesmen, and pizzazz people in the world. We start with the rubber boots on; we are all operators. Raising the money is secondary—you have to run the business right first. That's where companies like GM lost their way: They became marketers, and they started turning out crap for a few years."

The Braggs' operating juices got squeezed hard when John took a big leap across the technological divide. In the early 1970s, the Canadian Radio-Television and Telecommunications Commission was looking for local entrepreneurs to take up licences in the growing area of cable television. John Bragg was fascinated and applied for a licence in nearby Amherst, Nova Scotia. Having got the Amherst cable business up and running, he acquired licences in Springhill and Sackville, New Brunswick. But the real breakthrough came with the great consolidation of the cable industry in Canada, combined with the launch of new and costly Internet technologies. The Braggs had to make the choice of whether to get out or get big.

At one point, in 1997, the family forged a joint venture agreement with Maritime Telegraph & Telephone to link their networks and invest jointly in new broadband technology, including high-speed Internet. The deal sparked an angry response from Charles Keating, a Halifax entrepreneur and a minority shareholder in the Bragg-controlled Halifax Cablevision. The Keating family claimed its interests were being disregarded by Bragg. They went to court asking, among other things, for full disclosure and protection of their role on the Halifax Cablevision board. The judge tossed out the action, and the decision was supported on appeal.

It was a fascinating glimpse into Bragg's business style and his willingness to make tough decisions when he had to, even if it meant alienating another charter member of the Maritime elite. The legal dispute at times got very personal, with Bragg and Keating trading allegations about their respective business ethics. Judge Goodfellow of the Nova Scotia Court of Appeal observed in his judgment that Bragg had excluded Keating from knowledge of negotiations because of his concerns about the confidentiality of the talks. The judge noted that the two men did business with each other and shared a certain degree of mutual respect, but there was no mutual fondness. That relationship "has probably been irreparably damaged," he concluded.

The ironic outcome was that Maritime Tel decided it didn't want to do the Internet deal after all, which was the best thing that ever happened to John Bragg. It meant that he would march into the Internet and broadband future by himself, with no major partner. That outcome coincided with a dramatic change in the Braggs' passive approach to the cable business. Lee Bragg remembers he was running the family's woodland operations when he was summoned to a family meeting. The family's advisory board was pushing the family to come to a decision: sell the cable business, stay static, or make it bigger. Lee, then in his late 20s, made the argument for selling. After all, there was no direct family involvement on the cable side; the business was a relatively passive undertaking: "Put the picture on the television and collect the money." The Braggs thrashed it around, and then John came up with the answer: The Braggs were staying in, and, by the way, Lee, you're now in the cable business. Lee started working in the Truro system, then in New Glasgow, and has helped forge the integration of the Braggs' cable systems into a single company called East-Link Communications.

In the nine years since that decision, the family has made its mark in cable. The Braggs bought the cable systems that had been consolidated by Calgary's Shaw Communications in the Halifax area, an investment of $250 million that signalled their clear intentions to be a serious player. Then life got more interesting when they took the leap into the new technology, including fibre-optic networks and high-speed Internet. The next step was something very revolutionary— offering local telephone service over cable TV lines. Other cable tycoons such as Toronto's irrepressible Ted Rogers had talked for decades about taking on the Bell system in telephone, but the blueberry guy from Oxford actually did it. The technology was based on digital telephone switching, rather than the new wave of voice-over Internet protocol (VoIP), which in time will revolutionize the industry. A few U.S. cable systems were offering local phone options, but they usually would cherry-pick big apartment buildings for customers. "We went down the street and into the homes," says Bragg. For a while, no one else in North America was doing it except Cox Broadcasting, a giant U.S. company with annual revenues of $6 billlion. People from all over North America were paying attention to the little company from Oxford.

The way John tells it, it was simply his response to the highly competitive Halifax communications market that was taking shape in the 1990s. There was Aliant, the Bell affiliate formed out of the merger of the four major Maritime telephone companies, and a rising interloper named Fundy Cable. The Braggs, meanwhile, had bought the Shaw Cable systems, and there were a ton of service resellers. Bragg's approach to telephone was simple: The residential customer was his core market, and he was already selling Internet and video services to that market. Surely, there are ways to bundle those two with a cost-effective telephone service. In the great Frank Sobey tradition, he asked, "What would it cost us to try this? What could we afford to lose?" So EastLink set up its initial trial with a $10-million maximum cost. "We actually got in business for $10 million. We decided we could afford to do that."

Since then, much more has been invested—far in excess of $100 million, Bragg says. As of early 2003, it was estimated that 30 per cent of EastLink's 240,000 cable subscribers in Nova Scotia and Prince Edward Island were taking the telephone option, often selecting the bundled package of full-tier cable TV, high-speed Internet, and local telephone for about $100 a month. Since then, the numbers have grown, but EastLink does not disclose the exact amount.

But what was a blueberry king doing getting into the business where a blackberry is a portable e-mail device, not a type of fruit? Lee says, "[My father] really has no idea behind the technology in this business or, in fact, the technology in the food business." What he does know is the bottom line, and he has the ability to hire good people (in this case, émigrés from Maritime Telephone) and an unflinching honesty. "He can't run a hammer," laughs Lee, who is co-CEO of the family's cable business and with his closely shaven head qualifies as a younger version of his father. "His skill is knowing the right questions to ask. For him, technology is just a tool. He finds four to five things to measure—right away."

John doesn't argue with that. "I get the basics of technology, but I'm not a techie." He can tell whether the cable company is doing well by the key financial numbers, its revenue growth, and percentage operating profit. "All the key ratios which bankers measure are very good," he pronounces.

Understandably, the telephone service lost money in the early years, but as 2005 began it was on the right side of the ledger, according to Bragg.

Bragg has depended heavily on his technical team, led by David Caldwell, a talented manager who joined EastLink from Maritime Tel. EastLink faced a major challenge: To provide long-distance service, it needed to connect with the network of its major competitor, the telephone company. "The CRTC was telling them they had to interface, but they were dragging their feet. David worked his way through that, working with Maritime Tel."

Meanwhile, Bragg kept bringing his common sense to the table, including his experience as a low-cost, top-quality producer of blueberries. Still, the cultures of commodity food production and high-flying telecom innovation have clashed at times, such as when EastLink's managers, led by Lee Bragg, approached the parent company for $5 million to spend on a software package for automated provisioning, which involves sorting out the source of communications in Internet and telephone messages. It is a very complicated process, which EastLink wrestled with, going as far as sending Lee down to Cox Communications to have a look at what they were doing.

When the request came in for $5 million, John's response was "Whoa, what about a scribbler and a lead pencil?" At a time when the Internet service was making hardly any revenues, he figured there must be a low-cost, manual way to do it—not ideal perhaps, but affordable at that stage in East-Link's development. So the EastLink techies had to make do with a manual solution, until, as the service took off, they were able to justify the purchase of their software package.

Lee smiles at the story because it underlines his father's philosophy: Technology is a means to an end, not an end in itself. Although the manual way was not perfect, his father's words still ring in his ears: "Lee, remember your roots." John would remind his telecom managers that in his experience, a lot of innovation occurs on the farm, not in a lab. "In our blueberry business, we built all our specialized equipment; nobody else could build it. So there is a tremendous amount of innovation at the operating level if you create the climate for it."

John Bragg believes this is a Maritime facility—to develop technology on the fly. Oh, you have to have labs and PhDs, but consider what NB Tel did, he says. Frank McKenna had a plan to develop the province's wealth base through call centres and he needed the technology to do it. So NB Tel wired the province and figured out solutions as it went along.

In fact, this skill at improvisation suggests the Atlantic region has a stronger technology base, particularly in telecommunications, than people give it credit for. After all, Alexander Graham Bell's telephone is a product of his work in Cape Breton Island, as well as in Brantford or Boston, the two other places that claim the birthplace of telephony. Engineers who came out of the Maritimes went off to join the local phone companies and often graduated to the mother company, BCE and its subsidiaries, Bell Canada and Northern Telecom, now Nortel Networks. Indeed, the ranks of BCE, Telus, and Manitoba Tel are stuffed today with ex-Maritimers, and, of course, some have stayed home to work with Aliant and EastLink.

Meanwhile John Bragg figures EastLink is in good shape when it moves up to the next frontier of VoIP, which promises to be the most efficient way to provide telephone service over fibre-optic networks. "We have a customer base, and we can switch it over to VoIP anytime, when the technology works," Bragg says. "Is that the right strategy? We've spent a lot of money doing it; we are very happy with it." He suspects that EastLink will offer VoIP and standard switching at the same time. The capital costs will be less with VoIP than with switching, but still a major investment for a small independent stacked up against Aliant and its giant shareholder BCE.

Dean MacDonald, a Newfoundland cable executive who has become close to John Bragg through the Canadian Cable Television Association, says the EastLink venture shows that Bragg is cut from the same cloth as the McCains and the Irvings. "They all run real, real strong businesses and are very hands on and disciplined. John never gets knocked off the puck. During blueberry harvest, you're not going to get John to come to a cable meeting. It's too important, he doesn't allow himself to get diluted in effort or cost. I admire him and am impressed like hell by him."

All this success in food processing and telecommunications has made Bragg a core member of the Maritime Mafia. As he took on more advisory and fundraising work at Mount Allison, where he is now chancellor, he came into contact with two men who have become his mentors, Wallace McCain and Purdy Crawford. He became very close to Donald and David Sobey, and now sits on their boards. The Sobeys say Bragg was a tower of strength when the family had to decide whether to take a run at Oshawa Group, the takeover that vaulted the Maritime family into the front ranks of Canada's grocery titans. Paul Sobey, in recalling the 1998 boardroom discussions, says, "I remember John turning around and saying, 'You should let management have an opportunity to go after this thing. You are really setting your course for the next 20 years, and if you make mistakes you know how to fix them and you *will* make mistakes.'" Sobey adds that they did make mistakes but Bragg's predictions are turning out. Sobeys is also a direct competitor of Dick Currie's former employer, Loblaws, which explains some of the electricity in the air at the Carlu. John Bragg is where many of the lines of the Mafia intersect, making him a key figure along with his good friends Purdy Crawford and Frank McKenna.

More than many Maritime business people, John Bragg has also become a passionate and vocal Maritimes advocate, who regularly locks horns with his friend Purdy Crawford about the future of the region that spawned them. Bragg is a zealot about rural development, pushing the argument that governments have to be activist pump-primers for rural communities in Nova Scotia and other provinces. What good does it do the country, he asks, if all the development takes place in a tiny band of territory along the St. Lawrence River, with the money concentrated in the Greater Toronto Area?

This is a troubling issue in Atlantic Canada, where people have been slower to move from rural to urban centres than in other parts of the country. For many economists, this heavy rural concentration accounts for much of the Atlantic region's income gap versus the wealthier regions.

It angers Bragg to hear outsiders say the long history of government handouts to Atlantic Canada has created a "culture of dependency," which has corrupted not just the underprivileged or the marginally employed, such as Newfoundland's fish workers, but the region's entrepreneurs. Bragg points out that governments across Canada support all kinds of economic development projects, from auto industry grants in Ontario to low stumpage fees in the West Coast forestry area. But is anyone calling those giveaways "a culture of dependency?" And what about the requests for federal subsidies for urban roads and mass transit? In Central Canada, that is considered essential investment, not welfare. He agrees that not everything in Atlantic Canada is perfect, and some money gets squandered, but there has to be a positive role for government in supporting rural development.

What got Bragg hopping mad was a comment by Conservative leader Stephen Harper—speaking in 2002 when he led the Canadian Alliance—that Atlantic Canada's problems could be linked to a "can't do" attitude and a culture of defeat. That set off a firestorm in Atlantic Canada, which may have doomed the Conservatives' political chances in the region for elections to come. The funny thing was that many Maritimers, or ex-Maritimers, were saying many of the same things. But Harper, as an outsider, lacked credibility; he was simply taking gratuitous shots at Maritimers without living the life.

Certainly, Harper's comments are not much different from those emanating from Bragg's friend Purdy Crawford, a Nova Scotia native who has worked for five decades as a corporate lawyer in Toronto. Crawford argues that the top-down grants, from agencies such as the Atlantic Canada Opportunities Agency, have created a "look after us attitude" in eastern Canada. Crawford keeps coming back home to Atlantic Canada and hearing about families where the mother or father is working just long enough to qualify for employment insurance. He has been much influenced by some of the research coming from the Atlantic Institute for Market Studies, a free-market think-tank of which he and John Bragg are both members. "People are great and hard-working," Purdy says, choosing his words carefully, "but well-meaning governments have created a sense of dependency. The reality is that so many parts of Atlantic Canada turn on getting enough time in to get your unemployment insurance. That's the best thing they have going for them. And the other thing is going to Ottawa to get money for this and that. They are entrepreneurs, and that's the easiest source and least-accountable source of money—all those agencies." Crawford's solution is to pull back on the top-down grants and subsidies and develop Atlantic Canada as a low-cost, business-friendly place, taking advantage of easy access to the immense U.S. market.

Of course, this is an argument over nuances among old friends, who want to know how their own success can be somehow broadened to encompass the region that spawned them. Bragg would have no argument with most of Crawford's prescriptions, except that he sees a stronger positive role for government. The underlying reality is "we don't want to have everyone living in Toronto," he says, and to avoid that necessitates a proactive role by governments. He would contemplate the revival of Industrial Estates Ltd., the Nova Scotia Crown corporation of the 1960s that used government financing to lure companies to the province. IEL, the brainchild of then premier Robert Stanfield, had some well-publicized failures, but it also left some real winners. Bragg would not throw away the much criticized Atlantic Canada Opportunities Agency—he would just make it more effective.

He sees his own company as a model of what can be done with progressive government support, in providing investment capital when private institutions fail to step forward. It happens in other provinces, he says, pointing to the role of the *caisse de dépôt* pension fund in Quebec and the Heritage Fund in Alberta. "They are creating jobs that create wealth," which is no different than governments providing good highways to factories in Nova Scotia. "We've got ACOA money to build infrastructure, and most of the money has created a great benefit. Was it a handout? I wouldn't apologize, and neither would Wallace or Harrison McCain, for creating a couple of thousand jobs in the Saint John River valley."

He is proud that all four of his children remain in the Maritimes; in fact, all work in the family businesses. Lee, 38, and Carolyn, 33, are at EastLink and Mathew, 36, and Patricia, 31, are in the frozen food business. They have all bounced around in their father's companies, building experience and allowing a bit of space for each to develop on his or her own. The Braggs have done a classic estate freeze, a tax-saving and estate-planning device, in which each child has ended up with 20 per cent of the business's equity, and therefore will reap the bulk of any future growth. Meanwhile their father, who has retained 20 per cent of the shares, still has voting control.

While none of the children has emerged as their generation's leader, the early betting is on the eldest child, Lee Bragg, an open-faced likeable guy, who as co-CEO of East-Link works out of the cable company's Halifax headquarters. His office attire tends to the informal, khaki pants and olive-green sweatshirt—fitting for a former college athlete. He played basketball at his father's alma mater, Mount Allison University, before he blew out his anterior cruciate ligament. He then finished his university degree at the University of New Brunswick, where among other things he helped coach women's basketball. He had always worked as a kid in the blueberry business, and after university, it was a natural transition for him to move into the family companies.

He shares the EastLink CEO role with another young manager, Dan McKeen. Bragg focuses on operational aspects such as information technology and human resources. McKeen is the sales and marketing expert. Lee says the split works well because he doesn't need to let his ego get in the way; it is enough that the company does well, because that enhances the value of his own ownership stake.

As it goes head to head with Aliant, EastLink has to offer comparable product offerings if, as John Bragg says, it intends to supply all the needs of the residential consumer. Early in 2005, it did a deal with Toronto's Rogers Communications Inc. to sell the Rogers wireless product at a 15 per cent discount to EastLink's residential customers. It was seen as a breakthrough because it signalled the cable companies' intention to present themselves as a full-service alternative to the telecom giants. The deal was not a big financial benefit, Lee admits, but it does fill a key product gap.

EastLink is now the fifth-largest Canadian cable company and the largest that is entirely privately held. Lee says the private status gives it a leg up. "We're so efficiency-sensitive, we'll spend money to get it right. That's the advantage of being a private company, to build assets rather than cash or quarterly results. We're a little more aggressive on innovation."

But will the Braggs want to own EastLink, as the industry continues to consolidate? It is an appreciating asset that would command a great price on the market. Lee admits that at times he worries that the company is running out of "$30 products to sell to our residential customers." But he sounds more like a man who would rather buy than sell. If, for example, Rogers wanted to sell its remaining Atlantic Canada cable systems some day, "we'll be interested." Meanwhile, "there doesn't seem to be a big killer application we can't handle for the next three to five years."

His father, at 65, continues to back away from day-to-day involvement in EastLink, although blueberries still command a lot of his time. After all, when you grow half the blueberries in the world, what you do has significant effect on the global market, Lee says. Also, you have to be continually plotting crop strategies, based on the outlook for other commodities, such as apples and cherries, which are competing ingredients for pies. The Braggs have brought in a new chief operating officer for their food group, who comes from ConAgra in the United States. The new manager has injected further professional management—although, as Lee says, "Dad wants his say."

He says his father calls him regularly, questions what he does, and gives advice. At the end of the day, John Bragg's down-to-earth business savvy is the link that still connects the family's far-flung and diverse assets. "The strong management practices are the synergies we get from one business to another," Lee says. "Our rivals are big, stodgy, and bureaucratic."

CHAPTER 7

FOOD FIGHTS

FRANK SOBEY WANTS TO go to lunch, so he wheels his black Audi sedan out of the snow-packed parking lot beside the modest office building in Stellarton, Nova Scotia. His destination is the Swiss Chalet restaurant over on the Westville Road, less than a mile away. Short-haired, slight, bespectacled Frank Sobey is the likeable fourth-generation standard-bearer of an $11-billion supermarket powerhouse, the namesake of his late grandfather, the empire-builder who lent his name to the Sobey chain itself. Frank Jr., who looks after the family's real estate holdings, lunches at Swiss Chalet, where he likes the $6.95 quarter chicken dinner with fries. It is classic Sobey—modest, down-home, no flash or pretension.

But before hitting Swiss Chalet, an errand forces him to wheel past the Atlantic Superstore, a grocery outlet owned by rival supermarket titan Loblaws. Frank chuckles as he points out the store, finding some irony in the presence of the enemy just a stone's throw from his own office. They're expanding the store, he notes with a studied interest. The Sobeys pay a lot of attention to that store, and to Loblaws, the supermarket arm of multi-billionaire Galen Weston's corporate empire, a company with more than twice the annual sales of Sobeys.

The store symbolizes the one blemish on Sobeys' great advance to become a major national company: While it was making huge gains in the rest of Canada, mainly by buying Oshawa Group in 1998 in a $1.5-billion deal, arch rival Loblaws was moving ahead in Atlantic Canada. Frank Sobey says it used to bother the family a lot more, but they are satisfied that they are neck-and-neck in a two-horse race in the region. Still, it sticks in the Sobeys' craw, intensified by the personal nature of this battle.

The architect of Loblaws' 30-year advance to become the dominant Canadian supermarket owner is another Maritimer, Richard Currie, a product of the hard-scrabble south end of Saint John, New Brunswick. Now retired from Loblaws and chairman of telecom giant BCE Inc., he is still regarded as the key builder of Loblaws into the $25-billion juggernaut it is today. Unlike most of the Maritime Mafia's self-effacing plutocrats, Currie stands out as a real character, as brash and opinionated as the Sobeys are reserved and low-key. He wears his hair long and leonine, in the manner of some superannuated pop star. It is his way of saying to his pompous critics that you can't judge a person by such surface things as hair length. "I like it long," he once told me. "If you like it long, God love you. If you don't like it long, God love you. You wear yours any way you want. It's not how you wear your hair." But he and the button-down Sobeys have something in common: They are intense competitors, whose rivalry is saturated with elements of class and history.

Currie and the Sobeys are wealthy beyond imagination. *Canadian Business* magazine, in its "Rich 100" rankings of 2005, put the Sobey family wealth at about a billion dollars and Currie at a cool $341 million. But the Sobeys are fourth-generation owners. Along with the McCains and the Irvings, they are one of the great business families of the Atlantic region. In his heart, Dick Currie is still the son of a machinist in the Saint John iron works. He has been an employee all his life, albeit a gifted, fiercely competitive, and lavishly paid employee. People who know him say his ambition has been partly fired by a chip-on-his-shoulder disdain for the silver-spooned squires of Pictou County. Yet the irony is that Currie has spent almost all his life in blue-chip organizations— Harvard Business School, the prestigious management consulting firm McKinsey & Co., the Weston organization, and now BCE, the ultimate corporate monolith. Until the 1990s, the Sobeys were pretty much a regional business clan, more just-folks than plutocrats. But the image of Sobey status and entitlement, at least in the Maritime context, has driven Currie and made him that much tougher a competitor.

Both Richard Currie and the Sobeys come from regions of the Maritimes that blend grim industrial pockets with achingly beautiful natural landscape. Currie is from Saint John, a smoke-spewing town on the splendid Bay of Fundy; the Sobeys from Pictou County, which is pockmarked by coal mines and aging steelworks amid the fine Northumberland shore and beaches. Currie, born poor, went off to make his fortune and reputation in Toronto; the Sobeys have stayed planted in the soil of Pictou County, determined to make it a better place. It has made for a creative and restless tension between their roles as stay-at-home benefactors and ambitious players on the national scene.

PICTOU COUNTY IS BOTH THE cradle of Scottish immigration to Canada and the birthplace of industrial Nova Scotia. Pictou Harbour is where *The Hector* dropped anchor in 1773, bringing 189 Highland Scottish refugees to a New Scotland and unleashing the waves of Gaelic immigration that have defined this part of North America. The Highland Clearances and the battle of Culloden still burn brightly as grievances in the soul of this region. Even today, one-quarter of the local phonebook consists of names that start with Mc or Mac—Macdonald, McNeil, MacDonnell, McIntosh et al., and that's not even counting the Campbells, Frasers, Rankins, and so on.

To understand the Sobeys you have to understand their Scottishness, their thrift, their lack of flash and pomp, and their ties to tradition. Sobey is not a Scottish name—family legend has it that a Polish noble ancestor named Sobieski made his way to the West Country of England. But the family ethos derives from the Scottish forebears, including Janet McIntosh, who married William Sobey in 1862, the union that spawned the Sobey supermarket line in Pictou Country.

From the harbour of Pictou, the early Scots moved inland and up the East River, founding new settlements, creating a string of towns, Trenton, New Glasgow, Westville, and Stellarton, which is the home of the Sobeys. These mill towns spawned entrepreneurs and industries in the 19th century, creating what is called the birthplace of the steel industry in Canada. Above all, Pictou is Coal Country, and coal has exacted a huge toll on the community in lost lives and grieving families. Underground coal mine deaths have been a fact of life since the 19th century, all the way up to the infamy of Westray, the methane gas explosion that killed 26 miners in 1992. The Sobeys grew up in that world: The site of the Westray mine lies just beyond the tracks in Stellarton, within sight of the Sobeys' head office building. The Sobeys' new regional head office is located smack dab on top of the dreaded Allan Shaft, which killed legions of men in a series of underground accidents. "We'd be at school, and we would hear the sirens go," Donald Sobey says, "and we knew someone had died or was in trouble." The Industrial Museum of Nova Scotia, a project the Sobeys have backed with money and enthusiasm, details with spellbinding horror the culture of fear and death surrounding the coal mines.

There is still a coal mine in Stellarton, and it is still touching lives. The community is moving a secondary road so that the narrow coal seams underneath can be mined. But the industrial superpower these days is the Sobeys Stores, which have created 1,000 clean, safe, good-paying jobs in the region. The family is looked on both as benefactors and local heroes. You walk into the Heather Hotel in Stellarton, and you come face to face with posters celebrating Donald and David Sobey, who have been inducted into the Stellarton Chamber of Commerce Hall of Fame. Their pictures flank a tribute to a local insurance agent, who is photographed wearing a kilt.

Around the turn of the 20th century, the Sobeys' business founder, J.W. Sobey, son of William and Janet, came off a nearby farm to move to Stellarton as a carpenter helping to build the Allan Shaft. When the shaft was constructed, he stayed in town, and in 1912, he opened a butcher shop on the village's main street. In Sobey parlance, that shop was No. 1 in a retail empire that has grown to more than 1,300 stores across Canada. But while J.W. Sobey led the family into retailing, it was his son, Frank Hoyse Sobey, who built it into a regional retail and investment powerhouse.

Frank was a man of huge ambition, a tough son of a bitch, a risk-taker and dreamer, with a careful sense of hedging his bets. I never met him, but the photos tell all you need to know—no-nonsense, determined, with sharp, cool flinty eyes in the nature of that other Atlantic tycoon, K.C. Irving. Although he lived humbly for a millionaire, he was a public figure, mayor of Stellarton for 22 years, and a restless investor who seeded the family fortune in supermarkets, movie theatres, real estate, and myriad other ventures. He regularly wrestled with the classic Maritime lack of growth capital. His sons remember how he would stuff bonds in his pockets and take the train to Montreal, selling to the institutions and investors in the canyons of St. James Street, then Canada's financial capital.

Frank Sobey was prominent in one of the grandiose but ultimately futile efforts to foster industrial development in the Maritimes. He was chairman of Industrial Estates Ltd., the provincial venture launched by then-premier Robert Stanfield in the early 1960s to stimulate industrial investment. There were some real wins, such as new Volvo plants, but some spectacular losses, such as the much ballyhooed Clairtone stereo venture co-founded by Peter Munk, who later emerged as Canada's gold baron. About all that remains of Clairtone today in Pictou Country is a lovely old wooden stereo cabinet, complete with black-ball speakers, which sits in Frank's former home. The building, "Crombie," on Pictou Harbour, is a kind of museum that also houses his Krieghoffs, Tom Thomsons, Emily Carrs, and Riopelles.

Frank built a great regional supermarket business and started to venture into Central Canada and Newfoundland. He was unstoppable—when he ran into a local supermarket owner, he would simply buy him out. In the 1960s, he swung into Grand Falls, Newfoundland, only to discover that the town already had a modern supermarket, owned by a local entrepreneur named Ches Penney. Sobey went to Penney, a young man, and disclosed his plans to put a store in Grand Falls that would rival Penney's and probably drive him out of business. So Sobey made an offer to buy the young man's store, not for cash, but for shares in the Sobey company. Penney took the offer and went into the construction business, ran into trouble, and had to sell his shares for approximately $300,000. Penney, now one of Newfoundland's wealthiest men, recently asked one of the Sobey brothers how much the shares would be worth today. "You don't want to know," was the reply. Penney just shakes his head, thinking of his foregone wealth, although he has done very well even without the Sobeys shares. Frank Sobey created an empire—in fact, his holding company was named Empire, but not because Sobey was a flamboyantly conceited man. In order to buy a store site in New Glasgow, he had to buy the whole company, which was called Empire, and he just kept the name.

He had three sons, who would each play an important role in the future of the company. The family likes to say that if you took the old man and split him three ways, you would end up with the relative talents of the three. Bill was a great networker, real estate chief, and idea generator. The garrulous David was the innate merchant, a guy who got his jollies visiting supermarkets. "When you cut his arm, it is retail that he bleeds," says his nephew, Frank Sobey. Tall, angular Donald was younger and quieter, a commerce graduate of Queen's University in Ontario, an aesthete and art collector. He was a highly cerebral investor, whose idea of a good time was taking off with buddies Purdy Crawford and John Bragg to attend the Warren Buffett annual meeting in Omaha, Nebraska, a sort of Woodstock for the value investor set.

But it was not an easy upbringing for the boys, because the old man was as hard as nails, more monster than mentor at times. Asked if his grandfather gave him advice, his grandson Paul laughs. "He wasn't exactly the cuddly type." David Sobey, who worked closely with his father, says it was hard being Frank Sobey's kid. "He could cut you down pretty fast, and it didn't matter if you were with your peers or who you were with. I guess we survived it, suppose it made us better but at the time I didn't think so. He could switch pretty quickly and be the bad guy and the good guy pretty fast."

Indeed, John Risley says the Sobey sons accomplished something that is extremely rare: to continue to build what the old man started, but in their own way. "The real true entrepreneur was Frank, and he was very hard on the three sons," Risley says. As far as verbal abuse goes, "he beat the shit out of those guys," Risley says. "In meetings he would be really tough on them, almost to the extent that he risked snuffing out any entrepreneurial spirit. I've got respect for them because they persevered and learned, and they didn't take huge risks, didn't need to and were smart enough to put good operating people around them."

Frank Sobey built a reputation for quiet and sometimes ruthless efficiency. In many of his deals, he partnered with Roy Jodrey, an eccentric entrepreneur from Hantsport in the Annapolis Valley. They did real estate deals and bought companies together, often playing the role of Nova Scotia loyalists who would keep the industry from falling into Upper Canadian hands. For many years, Nova Scotia seemed to be a neat little compact between these two Anglo-Scottish multimillionaires. Alexander Bruce, in a 1987 article in the *Report on Business*, quotes one Halifax lawyer: "Frank was like a terrier. He would sit there and watch for mistakes or openings. He wouldn't say much at board meetings. But once he saw a weakness in an opponent, he'd go away and figure out ways to turn it to his advantage. Roy was more like a bulldog. He'd sit there like a country bumpkin and disarm the people around him who didn't know what he was like. Once he had an idea in his head, he just wouldn't let go of it."

After Roy Jodrey died in 1973, his successors continued to build the investment portfolio and do deals with the Sobeys, including the notorious takeover of Nova Scotia Savings and Loan Co., where the two families tried to play the roles of white knights in turning back the bid of Moncton financiers Reuben Cohen and Leonard Ellen. This triumph was undercut by allegations that the Nova Scotia Savings board had bent the rules to allow the Sobey-Jodrey bid to succeed, thus blunting the ambitions of Cohen and Ellen, sons of Russian Jewish immigrants who had often tweaked the Nova Scotia Anglo-Scottish establishment. Today, the Jodreys continue to play powerful investing roles, with interests in golf courses, real estate, and nursing home operator Extendicare, but they have never developed a brand, a single company, that carried their name. The Sobeys were different—they put the name on their stores and took the chain westward into Quebec and Ontario. But this expansion was almost reluctant, as they were forced to grow or face extinction in the supermarket wars.

In the mid-1980s an aging Frank Sobey was dying from cancer, just as the company was making its big forays into Ontario. David went to tell him that the company was going to push far beyond its then-level of $800 million in annual sales and that $3 billion was within its reach, an unheard-of level for the little guy from Stellarton. "I never would have thought we would have what we have," the old man marvelled. David can only guess he would be thunderstruck if he were alive today. "Now we're at $11 billion." The patriarch died in 1985, and to the end he was tough on his sons. Asked near his death if he was proud of his progeny, he is reported to have said, "Absolutely. And I'll be even prouder when they learn how to make money."

The combination of three sons worked well until 1988, when Bill died after a long battle with cancer, a terrible blow to the family. But the two surviving brothers simply took up his duties, and new family members emerged—John Robert, who is the son of Frank's brother Harold; Bill's sons, Frank Jr. and Karl; and David's son Paul, an accountant who had worked in public practice and spent time in Harvard Business School's advanced management program. Young Frank Sobey gravitated to the real estate side, while Paul was groomed to take over Empire, the holding company where his uncle Donald held sway.

They came to rely heavily for advice on an army of financial and legal professionals, led by the powerful Halifax law firm, Stewart McKelvey Stirling Scales, which has served the

Sobey family for four generations. Just as the first Frank Sobey was advised by superstar lawyer Frank Covert in the 1950s, his children and grandchildren have developed close relationships with current Stewart McKelvey attorneys, including Rob Dexter and Sir Graham Day, who also serve as directors of Sobey company boards. Just as Stewart McKelvey helped make the Sobeys' fortune, the Sobeys were instrumental in making Stewart McKelvey into the legal titan of the Maritimes. Every new crop of lawyers is pressed into serving this valuable client, and as these people mature, they often become personal confidants of the retail family from Stellarton. "If any young lawyer goes into Stewart McKelvey, the thing he or she learns from Day One is you're going to be doing a little bit of Sobey work, maybe tax, property or a joint venture in theatres," one attorney says. "Let me tell you, you absolutely give it your best shot any hour of the day or night. You drop everything else. These people are important to us, and we like to think we are important to them," the attorney says, describing a relationship that transcends the typical lawyer-client contact, and becomes a personal symbiosis. Stewart McKelvey has that same relationship with other Maritime families such as the Jodreys and Braggs. It is the mind-meld intimacy of true *consiglieri*.

But as the Sobeys progressed into the 1990s, the two surviving sons were getting on, moving into their 60s, and the supermarket industry was consolidating. They could see the danger of staying confined to eastern Canada as a medium-sized regional firm. The major consolidator turned out to be Loblaws, an old nemesis whose history is intertwined with the Sobeys'. Loblaws too was a family company, but controlled by a different kind of family: the urbane polo-playing and transatlantic Westons, a contrast to the Sobeys, who prefer haggis on Burns Day and backyard barbecues out on the Northumberland shore.

The relationship between the two companies has always been tense and complex. In 1960, when the Sobeys chain had about 20 stores, Frank Sobey's hunger for growth capital caused him to sell 13 per cent of the company to the Westons, which amounted to 40 per cent of the voting interest. The Westons clearly wanted to buy the Sobeys out eventually, but they were blocked by a voting trust set up by Frank. There followed a long period of jousting, which came to a head in 1978, when the Westons blocked a Sobey refinancing plan. It was a marriage that wasn't working, and the Sobeys bought back the 40 per cent in 1980, paying $5 million for shares Weston had bought for $1 million.

Loblaws needed the money, for in those days it was still a pale imitation of the marketing powerhouse it has become today. But Loblaws was also undergoing massive changes that would ultimately restore its fortunes and turn it into the North American role model of supermarket chains. The turning point had come in 1970, when patriarch owner Garfield Weston brought his son Galen back from Ireland to run the troubled Loblaws operation, a staid and unimaginative organization that had lost ground to competitors such as A&P and Dominion. He was told to turn the business around, or possibly to gussy it up for sale. The handsome Galen had cut his teeth in Weston's Irish operations, where he picked up a beautiful wife, Hilary, and a good sense of what an active owner had to do. The company was in tough shape, but Weston collected a formidable troupe of younger managers, including his old University of Western Ontario roommate, Dave Nichol, a brash guy who had gone on to collect a master's degree from the Harvard Law School and had spent time at the McKinsey consulting factory. Nichol himself began to recruit new managerial blood for Loblaws.

David Sobey quickly learned about another member of the new team at Loblaws. David was in England in 1977 on a holiday with his wife, Faye, when they decided to stay over at the Lygon Arms, a historic inn in the Cotswolds village of Broadway, which was used as a stopover by both Charles I and Oliver Cromwell, the bitter combatants in the English Civil War.

After dinner, the Sobeys were invited to visit the Charles I bedroom, where they lounged around the fireplace with their drinks. The maitre d' asked if another couple could join them, and the Sobeys happily agreed. It turned out the husband was the new chief executive of Loblaws who was full of excitement over having sold Weston's drugstore operations to Boots pharmacy chain in Britain. After all, Loblaws in those days was intent on raising cash from divestitures.

The two men had a lot in common: the Loblaws executive, Richard Currie, had been brought up in Saint John, then went off to Harvard and McKinsey before joining Loblaws. Looking back on that day, David Sobey wishes he had never met Dick Currie, that Currie had never joined Loblaws. "I wish he had stayed in the States," David mutters. But over the next 35 years, these men, like Charles I and Cromwell, would joust and parry, as adversaries in the supermarket war. So was it the beginning of a beautiful relationship? "For who?" David chuckles. "I wouldn't go any further on that one. We got along all right. Dick was a little more serious than I am." Indeed, Dick Currie was very serious.

TODAY, AT 66, RICHARD CURRIE is immensely pleased with himself—he is coming home to Saint John. But it isn't to the notorious south end, where he grew up on Duke Street, and where his father worked at the iron works on the harbour. No, Currie has bought a home in genteel Rothesay, the suburban enclave of Saint John's best families, where various Irvings, Olands, and other New Brunswick grandees are domiciled. His house is undergoing massive renovations, undertaken by a Boston firm that has worked on Currie's homes in Florida and Cape Cod. The huge project has become the talk of Rothesay. The house gives him a base to tend to his new duties as chancellor of the University of New Brunswick, with campuses in Fredericton and Saint John. For Dick Currie, it's only a short drive to Rothesay from south-end Saint John, where he grew up, but a long voyage from the bottom of the Maritime social scale to the top of the Canadian establishment.

Saint John's south end is one of those legendary poor neighbourhoods that seem to spawn an inordinate number of ambitious, successful people, as does North Winnipeg and Montreal's St. Urbain. Currie is the product of two very different parents, who represent two distinct strains of the Maritime psyche. His machinist father was a gentle man, a proud working-class guy, who counselled young Dick on the need to always show respect and decency toward people of all classes. "You shouldn't feel like you are better than other people, no matter what you aspire to. It's a journey and we're all going to the same place," he used to tell his son. His mother, meanwhile, was driven to rise to bigger things and was frustrated that her husband, with all his talents, was content to work with his hands. The mother aspired to live as well as the Irvings, the wealthy family on the hill. Her words to her son were "Don't lie, don't cheat, don't steal but don't come home in second place." As Dick got older, he valued the counsel of both parents, his mother for her drive and his father for his democratic decency.

He remembers that in grade 6, students at his public school could write an exam to get free entry into Rothesay Collegiate, the elite private school where the good families sent their male offspring. His father told him that he could certainly write the exam, but if he was accepted, he would still not be allowed to attend. Recalls Currie, "I said, 'Why not?' And he said, 'The world is changing and the people you are going to spend your life with are not the people going to private schools.' I didn't write the exam. He was a very, very, very astute man."

Currie agrees, however, that he has inherited his healthy ego from his mother, an ego that is viewed as a thing of wonder by many of his Maritime friends. "And from my father I got 'Look after your people and your family and give a fair amount of money and set up a scholarship and make sure that ego stays in check.'"

He hopes the ego doesn't add up to arrogance, and he is right—it is more innocent than arrogant, and it seems to stand out more in a Maritime setting than among non-Atlantic business types. In Toronto, where monumental egos are on display constantly, Currie seems almost modest and self-effacing. In the Maritimes, where you are expected to hide your light under a bushel, he is viewed as inordinately pleased with himself, alien to the Atlantic style of modesty and restraint. What's more, Currie, sensitive to his working-class origins, is always a little bit more over-the-top when associating with the Atlantic crowd—and especially with the Sobeys and their friends.

"Dick is an outlier to the average business person in the Maritimes," says a veteran business leader who sits on one of the Sobeys' boards. "I'm not sure if he's caught between Toronto and Saint John. [There is] a bit more ego. I think that any significant show of ego or flash is just not done in the Maritimes."

When he was a young high school graduate, ego and flash were the last characteristics you would associate with Dick Currie. He went to the University of New Brunswick to take engineering and completed his studies at the Technical University of Nova Scotia in Halifax, which is now part of Dalhousie University. When he was at TUNS, he took a course in the social psychology of industry, taught by the head of the psychiatry department at Dalhousie. It was a revelation, a connection between the hitherto distinct worlds of engineering and of management and leadership. It had a profound effect on Currie, who became fascinated with how companies are led and what role he could play as a progressive manager, particularly in working with people.

After graduation and a couple of false starts, he ended up as a process engineer at the big Lantic Sugar refinery in his old neighbourhood in the south end of Saint John. He joined the company in the midst of a huge expansion of the refinery, but the facility was facing major problems in getting production up to meet targets. Currie recalls that the project had sent a number of managers over the deep end, but the young engineer, who grew up in the neighbourhood, was able to get the bugs out of the system and was effectively running the refinery.

Even though he was a success at the refinery and had proven his engineering prowess, Currie knew there were still huge gaps in his skill set. He didn't know a lot about finance and marketing, for example. Also, he was almost 29, married with two children and a third on the way. If he was going to boost his employability, he had to do it now. He applied to Harvard and Chicago business schools, was accepted by both but chose Harvard because of its stellar reputation.

He ended up in a very sharp class, which included such future stars as Peter Herrndorf, a media and entertainment executive in Canada, and Gerald Schwartz, a young Winnipeg lawyer who would become the country's leading corporate buyout specialist. Schwartz became a lifelong friend, who coincidentally later played a significant role, as a major shareholder in Lantic Sugar, in closing down the refinery in Saint John.

In 1968, when Dick Currie went to Harvard, it was a landmark era in U.S. society, the roughest stretch of the Vietnam War. Currie was a mature student even by business school standards, a former sugar refinery manager with a wife and family, but he got caught up in the anti-war upheaval. "All of a sudden, there was this world opening up that was extraordinary, with riots and everything." It is hard to believe today, but there were buses that took students from Harvard Business School to the legendary peace march in Washington. A curious and engaged Dick Currie was on the bus. He remembers that the driver had to slip $100 to a Boston cop in order to get easy exit from Copley Square. In Currie's view, that juxtaposition of idealism and corruption pretty much summed up U.S. society at the time.

When he got out of Harvard, Currie faced some hard choices. It was the moment when the McCain brothers were bursting out of Florenceville, New Brunswick, as global food suppliers, and they were thinking of hiring some sharp MBAs. Wallace McCain came to Currie and offered him a job. But Currie was adamant: He was not going back to New Brunswick. Instead, he took a job with superstar U.S. consulting firm McKinsey, whose research projects for client firms were wonderful training grounds for professional managers.

Currie already had his eye on his ultimate future career. One of his Harvard classmates had been the son of the man who ran Macy's, the great New York department store retailer. At dinner one night with Currie and a number of classmates, the father went around the table asking what each was going to do. Then he summarized by saying that there were no future retailers in the group. "Let me tell you, young men, retailing is the last frontier of the trained mind," he said. That statement changed Currie's life. The message was clear: Until then, retailers were people who didn't work through their minds—retailing was still a touch and feel business. It seemed like rich and uncultivated ground for an ambitious young man who was consumed by facts, data, and results—someone like Dick Currie.

The McKinsey stint was valuable because it got Currie involved in the consulting company's trademark industry studies for clients and taught him how to make effective presentations. He chose to attach himself to McKinsey's Cleveland office because he couldn't afford to live in New York with his family. But he was almost never in Cleveland, and he spent most of his time on the road, working with clients. "I wanted to learn how to present; I knew I could figure out the answers but I had to present them. I knew I could work with presidents and division heads and wanted to assess myself against them to see if I had a future in business."

At McKinsey, he met another young Canadian, Dave Nichol, who had gone to law school at Harvard. The two were thrown together in producing an industry study for the Heinz food company in Pittsburgh. In the middle of the study, Nichol's wife left him, leaving the young man a basket case. Currie's group had to take over the brunt of Nichol's section of the report. When the time came to present the information, Currie coached Nichol and he pulled it off. Nichol couldn't believe someone would do his work and coach him on the presentation, and what's more, didn't tell anybody about it.

Nichol was soon able to repay his debt. During his stint at McKinsey, Nichol got a call from Galen Weston, who had just taken over his family's sad-sack supermarket chain, Loblaws. Weston asked his old friend, and best man at his wedding, to come aboard to help Loblaws. He also asked Nichol to recommend the best person he had met at McKinsey. Nichol mentioned Dick Currie, and Currie was invited to have dinner with Nichol and Galen Weston. He was immediately hired and marvels today that his great career was all driven by the fact that Dave Nichol's wife suddenly left him.

From the vantage point of 2005, it is hard to believe how weak Loblaws was when Currie joined in 1972. "We found dispirited management and decrepit assets," Currie told the *Financial Post* in a 2001 interview. But with Galen Weston's injection of managerial talent, the days of Loblaws as the sick sister of Canadian supermarket retailing were soon to end, and it would rise to become the industry superstar. It had a powerful team—Weston, the engaged but delegating owner; Nichol, the marketing and development genius; and Currie, the strategic mind. According to Anne Kingston, in her biography of Dave Nichol, *The Edible Man*, Galen Weston figured out that Currie's strength was corporate strategy while Nichol had the aggressive personality to shake up management. He named Currie as director of profit development, and Nichol as director of corporate development, and the two described themselves as "the change agents."

In 1976, Currie became president of the entire supermarket company, while Nichol was appointed president of the subsidiary that ran the Ontario operations. The presidency of Loblaws was not the greatest prize in the world—the company had zero financial equity and trailed its competitors in every region of the country. In the Maritimes alone, Sobeys had twice Loblaws' market share. Weston, Currie, and Nichol were working round the clock to fix the company, and it started to generate results. But Weston's elevation of Currie over Nichol was the first crack in the relationship between the two men, although Nichol quickly rebounded to become the marketing and product development whiz, and the public face of Loblaws and its pioneering high-end store-brand President's Choice business.

When Currie became president of Loblaws in Toronto, he found he was working in a much different family business than the top-down Irving empire he had known in Saint John. "I sat in a room with Garfield and Galen Weston and the old man did the talking, of course, and he said, 'Dick, here are the rules: If you want to buy something we want to know; if you want to sell something we want to know; if you want to borrow money let us know. Otherwise, run it as if you own it.' And for 25 years that's the way it was."

In the mid-1990s, when he moved over to run the Westons' holding company, he asked for the same broad rules of engagement, and Galen Weston complied. "So I was in a great position, working for a family like that," Currie says.

CURRIE HAD THE STRENGTHS of the best Maritime managers: He was very good at running things. "Maritimers are good operators," he says. "I think what I brought was I certainly knew how to work, there was a certain sense of pragmatism. If it looks like it, smells like it, it probably is it. I think pragmatism means that once you know the answer, you don't need three decimal places after it. It's either as big as a breadbasket or as a big as a room. You don't have to go on and analyze it once you have the answer. You take it and drive on.

"It's probably a Maritime trait that once you got the answer, you quit fucking around and get on with it," Currie says, thinking back to the days when he got the Lantic Sugar refinery working. There was no time to get fancy, it was a matter of operating and executing.

But he also knew that he had to go beyond his roots. Maritimers, and their companies, were made in his father's mould, highly skilled in a trades and technical sense. They could get things done as builders and operators. They were very good at running businesses built on wood, oil and gas, and farm produce. But when you get outside the Maritimes and travel with the international crowd, you need to tap other skills, in marketing, merchandising, and finance. At Loblaws he was able to do that, whether it was exploiting Dave Nichol's product development genius or chief financial officer Don Reid's capabilities with financial derivatives.

Working with Nichol, he oversaw the launch of President's Choice, the brand that elevated the lowly generic grocery product into up-market status, creating a retail phenomenon that was studied around the world. But as Loblaws flourished, the gap widened between the two old friends, and Nichol, who eventually felt Loblaws was too small a canvas on which to work his magic, left the store chain in 1993 to work for other companies and develop his vineyard in Napa Valley, California. But under Currie, Loblaws continued to thrive, and his legend as a professional manager soared as well. When he left Loblaws in 1996, he could look back on 24 years as president during which the Loblaws stock price had risen 10-fold. In some ways, Richard Currie is Canada's Jack Welch, from the perspective of the management disciplines he forged and the stock market value he created. Like Welch, he was no silver-spoon inheritor but a kid from a hard-scrabble background who became very wealthy because of what he had been able to achieve.

In 1996, after turning Loblaws into the dominant super-market chain, Currie was persuaded by Galen Weston to shift over to George Weston Ltd., the food-processing and distribution side of the family empire. He continued to apply the same rigorous disciplines and analytical skills. He was legendary for his tendency to take a problem and ponder it for a period, but when he made up his mind, to act quickly and decisively. It was a measure of Currie's self-confidence— he never felt he had anything to prove.

When he retired from the Weston organization in 2002, Currie left it in great shape. With the acquisition of Quebec's Provigo Inc. in 1998, Loblaws was now the dominant food purveyor across the country, a company with a market value of $14 billion, up from almost nothing when he took over. And he was not done. He still had a brace of board memberships, including a directorship at BCE. In 2002, he was a central player in one of the most dramatic moments in recent Canadian corporate history: the rise, fall, and departure of Jean Monty, BCE's brilliant, ambitious CEO. BCE under Monty had bet heavily on the late 1990s fashion of convergence and consolidation. He bought a telecommunications network company called Teleglobe at the top of the crazy bubble market of 2000 and watched the investment turn disastrously bad. Currie was a rock of support, but also a central figure in nudging Monty out the door, whereupon he took over the former CEO's role as BCE chairman in 2002. He then became a close counsellor of Monty's successor, Michael Sabia, helping guide BCE's complex $6.3-billion buyback of its own shares from a U.S. telecom company.

For Currie, the early 21st century was a period of savouring the success and rewards of one of the most successful Canadian managerial careers. The awards flowed in: Canada's executive of the year in 2001, inductee into the Business Hall of Fame in 2003, and citation as one of Canada's greatest executives in an article in the April 2005 *Report on Business* magazine. He was musing about writing a book about his years as a superstar manager.

But with all Dick Currie's power and wealth, there is one thing that could still tick him off—that he was always treated as an upstart by the more patrician, intensely private supermarket family operating out of Stellarton, Nova Scotia. Clearly, Currie was not prepared to treat them with the deference and humility that they expected. That was not Dick Currie's style.

People who know him say that has been a tremendous motivator as he marched to the top of the Canadian establishment. According to one former colleague, "Dick always saw himself as a scrapper out of the trailer park. That was a motivation, even though he worked in blue-blooded organizations, such as McKinsey and Westons." Nothing made him happier than taking Loblaws as an also-ran in the Atlantic Canada market and actually vaulting ahead of the Sobeys. "I think Dick looked at the failed Atlantic Canada push and he put huge personal interest in getting it right," the former colleague says. "He wanted to make sure that while Sobeys was expanding outside the region, they were being punished in Atlantic Canada."

Of course, this fierce competition was good fortune for local food suppliers, who now had two supermarket rivals with deep roots in the region. David Ganong, the owner of the family chocolate company in St. Stephen, New Brunswick, says Currie would always argue that he would give Maritime firms a fair chance in Loblaws stores. The Sobeys might go even further, giving a slight bias to the Maritimers. You still had to produce value for money, but it helped to have these guys on your side.

But Sobey family members say they are often mystified by Currie's personal antagonism, which, according to one family member, may have derived from Currie's conversion to uppity Harvard and Toronto ways. "I don't know him, but whether it is because we pissed him off in the past or it comes from the fact he went to a big-time business school and he's a Maritimer." That same family member says that Currie is almost un-Maritime because of his outsized ego. As for his enmity toward the Sobey family, "it was always personal, and I have no idea why. I didn't get that memo."

....

CHAPTER 8

FRESH CROP AT SOBEYS

ROB SOBEY HAS A PROBLEM: His family hates to draw attention to itself. This was actually a great advantage from the 1950s to 1980s, when the Sobeys Inc. supermarket business was a largely Atlantic regional company with regional rivals. Maritimers adhere to a version of the Australian "tall poppies" complex—if you look too big, someone will cut you down to size. Rob's grandfather, the legendary Frank Sobey, used to say it was very smart to be seen as a bit of a hayseed so you could fly under the radar.

But Rob, who manages merchandising and marketing for Sobeys' Atlantic division, wants to fly right into the radar. You can't be modest when you are a national supermarket giant trying to raise your profile in a crowded marketplace, and when one of the world's most successful supermarket companies, Loblaws, and the biggest retailer in the world, Wal-Mart, both want to eat your lunch. It's hard to be humble when you have to imprint your supermarket brand, which happens to be your family name, on the consciousness of millions of Canadians, from St. John's to Victoria.

Rob laughs as he recalls the story of his grandfather Frank, who would buy a new car and then make sure it got dirty pretty quickly because he didn't want to stand out. That attitude suited the Sobeys stores back then, Rob says, but now, the family is facing "world-class marketers, who are very willing and very good at blowing their own horns." In this new world, Rob says, "we've reluctantly had to change—there is a link we cannot avoid between the family and the chain. It's not like it's Smith's department stores, owned and run by the Sobeys. Our name is on the business. We were dragged to the altar with the realization we had to improve the perception of what we do through marketing moves that otherwise we weren't comfortable with."

That trip to the altar was the 1998 mega-merger with Oshawa Group, a deal that tripled the size of the Sobey food empire, made it a national company, took it strongly into Central Canada and the West, and added new brands and store banners, mainly IGA franchise stores, to the Sobeys stable. It was a mismatch of size, culture, and systems as the Sobeys corporate-owned stores merged with the Oshawa Group's wholesale-franchise system. Most of the Sobeys do not mince words: It has been damn hard making it work. And it has caused great stress and family tensions as they try to accommodate their traditional values as modest Maritime entrepreneurs with their new role as national grocery titans.

Those challenges will only intensify in the years to come, if the Sobeys want to continue to be players in the fast-consolidating global supermarket game. When they bought Oshawa Group, family members knew the alternative was struggling along as a largely regional chain in Eastern Canada, which would be unable to acquire and retain key management people. Eventually, the Sobeys believe, the family would have to sell out. After all, the grocery business had been consolidating in inexorable fashion since the 1940s when there were 12 grocery stores on the main street of Stellarton alone. "You have to be a consolidator or a consolidatee—you've got no choice," Rob's father, Donald Sobey, says.

In this role as consolidator, the Sobeys can draw on painful lessons in the Oshawa Group purchase. As they moved their expanded company to a new enterprise software system, they encountered expensive computer systems breakdowns. And the human resources challenges are immense. In some of the most honest words spoken by a corporate executive, Frank Sobey, Rob's older cousin, says the post-merger integration was a dismal failure in a number of key areas. With the creation of a much larger, more impersonal organization, he decries the family's loss of connection with one of its distinctive values—a concern about individual employees. It became just like any big company for a while. "I think we stumbled on that over the past few years, and we have to get it back," Frank says bluntly. "Companies demand loyalty of their employees, but my sense is increasingly they are unwilling to give it back. Their attitude is: What have you done for me today? Historically that has not been a Sobey characteristic. We stumbled, we went through a period of losing good people."

Sobeys Inc. has had to get big in a heck of a hurry, and it has utterly changed things: how the Sobeys see the stores, their employees, and themselves, and how they relate to this 93-year-old family business. And it comes at a time when a new generation is taking over, as Donald and David Sobey, the septuagenarian brothers who built the company from their father Frank's base, slip back into advisory roles, and their children and nephews and nieces take command.

Of all the fourth-generation children in the business, Rob seems to fit least comfortably into the measured, conservative Sobey mould. He is tall, slim, good-looking at 37, sporting jeans and a casual sweatshirt, with a blur of hair extending down the cleft in his chin, the 21st-century version of a hipster

goatee. Like his father, Donald, he loves art and philanthropy; like his uncle David, he is a career retailer. He
remembers that his father's only words of career advice to
him were "Don't be a rock and roll musician." That counsel
has been followed, as Rob has climbed the ladder in the family business. His current job as merchandising boss for the
Atlantic division puts him on the firing line in the competitive
battle with Loblaws and Wal-Mart, which sells food as part
of its huge discount department stores.

In the Sobeys regional headquarters just off the Trans-
Canada Highway outside Stellarton, Rob's office desk is
adorned by classic photos of a pretty wife and two attractive
children on a beach in Pictou County. But otherwise, the
office is all business. He has papered the walls with a chart
showing the relative performance of Sobeys and its Atlantic
rivals, including Loblaws and the Co-op stores. On another
wall, he has tacked Wal-Mart sales promotions for new stores
in Edmundston, New Brunswick, and Yarmouth, Nova Scotia.
They are opening up all over, he marvels, on Newfoundland's
rugged Burin Peninsula and in Goose Bay, Labrador.

Wal-Mart, of course, is expanding its global juggernaut of
big-box stores, although it has yet to enter the Canadian market with its supercentres containing full supermarkets. But
the Canadian Wal-Mart outlets have substantial food sections
containing non-perishable items. That makes Wal-Mart a
formidable rival, even if it never sells a head of lettuce in
Canada. Indeed, Loblaws is taking on Wal-Mart with large
stores offering more general merchandise, in addition to groceries. But the Sobeys stores are pursuing a different tack,
building smaller units with a narrower emphasis on food,
particularly fresh produce.

"Loblaws' strategy seems to be to position themselves as
direct competitors to Wal-Mart," says Paul Sobey, Rob's cousin

and the chief executive of the family holding company, Empire Company. "That's their space and they're doing a good job." Sobeys is sitting a bit off to the side, building on its own strengths in smaller specialized food stores. Not for them the 180,000-square-foot megastores heaped with both dry goods and groceries. They are erecting 45,000- to 60,000-square-foot grocery outlets that are customized for the communities they serve.

The jury is still out on whether this strategy will work. What it does mean is that the Sobeys have to blow their own horns more forcefully in promoting their edge in fresh foods. Rob argues that the Sobeys must resort to more liberal use of superlatives in their advertising and promotion—a concept that is almost anathema to the family and to many Maritimers. In the past, if Sobeys stores were performing well, they would always say the performance was "good," not "very good," Rob notes. "We never wanted to get ahead of reality; we never tried to build perception above reality. But now we realize that, gosh, business is all relative, so how do you deal with this relative to everyone else in the industry." For example, his advertising fliers are more willing to tout the quality of the stores' meat offerings. He is continually pushing his meat managers, asking, "When are you willing to say we have the best meat department in Atlantic Canada?"

He thinks the Sobeys' previous reticence was an outgrowth of small-town life: In small towns, you cannot hide, and the Sobeys' approach to business was flavoured with that attitude. But as the company suddenly got gigantic, the family brought in professional managers from away, who said, "If you truly believe you're good at this, well, let's say it."

Rob's quandary also encapsulates all the pressures and possibilities of the Sobey clan as it enters an exciting and perilous stage. When the company bought Oshawa Group, a company twice as big as it was, there were rumblings of discontent on the family's home turf, and indeed, Sobeys Inc. has suffered in Atlantic Canada, losing the market lead to Loblaws Superstores. But as David Sobey says, they would have had most of their eggs in one Atlantic Canada basket, and they couldn't survive long in that game. The Atlantic market is a low-margin discount business that could not have been sustained on its own. To get beyond that base has meant changing some family habits, such as reticence and modesty.

Rob Sobey also personifies the tensions in the family's new role: He is an owner but he is also an employee. Rob's boss is a non-Sobey, as is his ultimate superior, the CEO Bill McEwan, a Canadian who joined the company from A&P in the United States. Over the past 50 years, the family has moved from owner-operator model (under Frank Sobey Sr.) to the owner-manager model (under Donald and David Sobey) and now to the investor-board-member model (under Rob, Paul, and Frank Sobey, and the 50 or so cousins in their generation). Yet at the same time, the family finds it valuable, even necessary, to have Sobeys working in the company. There is a danger of the family becoming entirely remote from the company, that it will cease to care, that their Sobey shares will become nothing more than a portfolio investment and will be dumped at will. As ownership becomes more dispersed—there are now some 80 adult members in the clan—the fear is the family will ultimately sell out, losing its link to its heritage, and the Maritimes will lose one of its core businesses.

The Sobeys no longer insist on running the company day to day. While David Sobey ran the supermarkets, his son Paul, the brusque, tough-minded leader of the new generation, is the chief executive office of Empire. He is his generation's business leader but he is an accountant and a financial manager, not a grocer. He allocates assets and capital, not the location of stores or the buying of grapefruit. The Sobeys say that the family involvement in the business is focused on Empire, the holding company, rather than the operating company, Sobeys Inc. Empire, whose class B voting shares are controlled by the Sobey family, owns 65 per cent of Sobeys Inc., as well as a massive real estate portfolio and other investments, including a movie theatre chain.

Yet the Sobeys are not entirely done with selling groceries. Rob, the son of Donald, is very much a grocer, a guy who loves to squeeze the oranges and squeeze profits out of stores in Moncton, Yarmouth, and Corner Brook. The retailing genes have flowed through old Frank, to his son David, and now to David's nephew Rob.

Rob is part of a new wave of young Maritime successors who are in various stages of taking over their parents' business: the Bragg children, all in their 30s; various Irvings; the sons of Harry Steele, in their 40s; the children of Ken Rowe, also in their 40s. The Sobeys' standard-bearers are Paul; Frank, the chair of Crombie, the family property company; Rob, at the Atlantic division of Sobeys; Christopher, another Sobeys manager; and cousins Jennifer Sinclair and Jana Sobey, who have both worked in Sobeys' Atlantic operations and were both on maternity leave in mid-2005. They have been the only Sobey women with managerial roles in the family company. This is a critical era for the Maritime Mafia, as this new wave of successors steps up. Will they step back from their parents' companies? Will they still want to own them? Will they still want to keep them in eastern Canada?

Of all the families, the Sobeys have thought the longest and hardest about these questions. They saw the McCains' breakup, and they hired top-notch family business consultants. They have enlisted smart outside managers to senior positions. Their companies, Empire and Sobeys, are both public, both with boards that contain plenty of Sobeys—they believe it is important that family members understand the business. The ranks are also replete with independent directors, although many of these are long-time friends of the family, such as John Bragg, Sir Graham Day, lawyer-entrepreneur Rob Dexter, and Peter Godsoe, former CEO of the Bank of Nova Scotia. They have also created a sophisticated parallel organization that is designed to keep the family engaged in the company. They have family assemblies, family councils, family mentoring programs, and family newsletters. Other business families throughout North America look to them and marvel at what they have created.

Where does this leave Rob Sobey, who may want to be CEO of the supermarket business, but may actually be disadvantaged because he is a Sobey and will have to pass muster with his cousins and outside board members? After all, he has a bachelor's degree from Queen's University, an MBA from Babson College in Massachusetts, and more than a decade of in-the-trenches experience with the stores. Rob doesn't deny he may covet the CEO's job some day, after Bill McEwan's tenure, but he is also measured in his words: "We will take the best person for the job; we can't have it any other way in a publicly traded company." Still, he says the non-family managers of the grocery operations feel it is important to have the family presence in the company. "The flip side is if you had a silly-bugger family manager in there who wasn't pulling his or her weight, that could be very hurtful." The chances of a silly bugger slipping into the management ranks is minimized by the on-the-job training every Sobey must go through. It is accepted that you will have to work night shift and stock and restock shelves. It's all part of being a leader, he says. "There is no way you can go into a meeting with a group of employees and fully understand the situation they are asking you about without going through it."

THE MEETING ROOM at the Hyatt Regency hotel in Cambridge, Massachusetts, is airless, stuffy, and packed with people. Many are consultants who have come to this hotel on the fringe of the Massachusetts Institute of Technology campus to learn about advising their family business clients. This session, part of a conference sponsored by the Family Firm Institute in October 2004, is particularly well attended because it is organized by Kelin Gersick, a New England consultant who is one of the stars of the family business advisory industry. He has brought two of his clients, a leading member of the Sulzberger family, which owns the *New York Times*, and someone less well known to this predominantly U.S. audience. Frank Sobey is a scion of a Canadian retail clan that most people in the room have never heard of. But for Gersick, the Sobeys offer a case study in how to keep a family involved in the business, and how to rejuvenate a family council that has gone stale.

In his low-key way, Frank delivers a fascinating talk packed with insight on how business families keep it all together, even as they enter the fourth generation of their commercial heritage. He describes a pilgrimage that started 15 years earlier with the realization that, as the Sobey generations branched out, the connection to the company was fraying. The core grocery business itself had gone from $800 million to $11 billion in annual sales in 20 years, and was now being largely run by professional outside managers.

He told the story of the journey taken by about 25 family members to Quebec for a retreat and how it changed the way they thought. "It's hard to read people from our area, we are not demonstrative," he explained. "We're unfailingly polite." But at the retreat, people opened up and got emotional. They started talking about their ties to the original Frank Sobey, his grandfather, and what he built. They wanted to keep the links between the family and the company, and they thought hard and long about how to do it.

The family hired Gersick, who advises some of the world's major family companies. The Sobeys decided they wanted to build a parallel organization that would monitor, manage, and nurture the family's relationship to the company. At the head, there would be an elected family council of seven people who would act as the bridge from a dispersed ownership, scattered all over the world, to the business.

"One thing we absolutely agree on: If the family loses touch with the business, it loses the business altogether," says Frank Sobey, talking in his office in Stellarton several months after the conference. "This family council has two real goals: The first is to keep the family in touch with each other, to act as a centre of gravity so that cousins and second cousins know each other." That is done in myriad ways, such as the boating parties he gives in the summer, a bunch of relatives just heading out for a day of cruising, a picnic on an island, and a lot of talk. The socializing happens most often in summer, when the far-flung cousins return to the Maritimes for their annual vacations.

The other important job of the council is to keep the family in touch with the business. The key players in that role are the members who work in the company: Paul, Rob, and Frank himself. It is also done through the annual assembly of 50 or so cousins and other relatives every year, and through constant communications. "It is difficult because the natural direction of things is atrophy, and our job is to energize everybody," says Frank, who has laboured long and hard on this aspect.

Asked if there is a leader of the next generation, Frank says by definition, his cousin Paul Sobey, as the CEO of Empire, is the leader of the family in the business. But in the family council, all members are equal and have an equal vote and equal right to make themselves heard.

In addition, the Sobeys have developed a mentoring mechanism to encourage young family members to get involved with the company early through part-time or summer jobs in high school or university—or perhaps joining the company full-time at some point. It is all part of keeping the family more in touch with the business. Frank told of meeting a young Quebecer one summer who was a second cousin, once removed—his mother had been born in Pictou County but had moved away. But the younger man still had a sense of loyalty and attachment to the company. "He loves the business. That's a connection we want to maintain. If we can hold on to him, it would be a tremendous thing."

But Frank is adamant that while the family will open the hiring door to its members, it won't offer any advantage in moving up the ladder. After family members get into the company, any progress must be on the basis of their personal competence. This policy is laid out in writing, with the understanding of Sobeys' human resources and management people. There are no management positions reserved for the family, but if there is a tie in ability between a Sobey and an outsider, the family member gets the job. Indeed, Paul Sobey is CEO of Empire, but he replaced someone who is not family. The current president and chair of Sobeys Inc. are not Sobeys.

But the role of being a Sobey in the business can lead to a certain tension with the non-Sobey employees. Rob knows that well. "It can be a delicate balancing act," he agrees. "You're working for the guy who in theory is working for you. You have to know when and how to speak; you have to know what hat you're wearing. Is it an owner, a manager? These are two very different approaches and you have to respect that."

It was particularly hard for him when he worked for three years at the national office, where his boss was the non-Sobey CEO Bill McEwan. He admits he has had some misfires in dealing with that. "I wasn't quick enough with changing hats; I went over the line." The ultimate arbiter in such cases would have to be the independent directors, who, he says, the family listens to carefully.

The Sobeys have survived a painful test of their careful balance of involvement and detachment. It involved Karl Sobey, Frank's older brother and a family member with a strong retail expertise, who rose to the leadership of the Atlantic arm. The straight-talking Karl was respected because he learned the business from the bottom up and served as a mentor to Rob Sobey when he entered the business. But the mega-takeover of Oshawa Group saw the retirement of John Robert Sobey, who ran the store chain, and the hiring of a new outside CEO, Bill McEwan, a consumer goods specialist. McEwan wanted Karl to move out of the Atlantic presidency and take on the new role of championing the Sobeys label across the country.

The standard line in the Sobey family is that Karl was tired of the grocery business and wanted to do something else, but David Sobey is forthright on the issue. "Karl didn't agree with [Bill McEwan] and he made the decision to leave," says a clearly saddened David, whom insiders say took a lot of unwarranted blame for the crisis and feels particularly bruised by it all. "We tried to persuade him to take another senior job, but he just didn't want to do that at that time." David now says he wishes Karl had taken more time to think about it, that he might have changed his mind. "Bill just wanted him to focus on the Sobey banner, which is something I think he had the talent to do. I guess it's a different job, and he looked at it as being perhaps not what he wanted." (Karl Sobey did not respond to a request for an interview.)

The incident could have been messy, the Sobey equivalent of the bitter breakup that fractured the McCain family and led to Wallace McCain's banishment. Instead, it only served to reinforce the Sobeys' commitment to the new structure of dealing with a more detached investor role. It was very stressful, one of the family members said, and spurred the calling of a special meeting of the family council. The meeting, the member says, was "tense, acrimonious, and bordered on out-of-control." The council decided to back management, even though the discussion had a polarizing effect on the family. In the end, everyone behaved well—the family, the company, and the board—as well as Karl Sobey himself, who quietly resigned from management while remaining on the Empire board. Says one former board member in the Sobeys' companies, "The interesting thing is that the company, having hired Bill, said, 'You are responsible for this business until we say you are not.' I think that was a very important message, I think it is also fair to say Karl behaved impeccably." The Sobeys dodged a bullet that had brought down many other family companies.

AT 74, DAVID SOBEY'S ROLE now is very much the elder statesman, which allows him to linger awhile longer in Florida each winter, although he still likes to get up to ski at Wentworth ski hill, not far from Stellarton. He spends his time back home playing golf, fishing for salmon with Newfoundland titan Craig Dobbin and Ron Joyce, and slipping into the local supermarkets to catch up on new trends and ideas.

His younger brother Donald is even more absent, but then again, he never felt a need to hang around the office all the time. He is active with art and charities and various board memberships. The closest thing to a jet-setter among the Sobeys, he loves to fly to Paris, spend a few days, and go to the board meeting of the Trader Group, which puts out the fabulously successful *Auto Trader* advertising books. The company is controlled by

John MacBain, a transplanted Canadian and former Rhodes scholar, whose father, a one-time Ontario politician, was born in Stellarton. Donald is also a member of the Trilateral Commission, an elite group of business and government leaders that inspires paranoia in anti-globalization activists. As I caught up to Donald, he was preparing for his annual trip to the World Economic Forum in Davos, Switzerland.

And yet this global capitalist sees no contradiction in the fact that Sobeys national head office remains solidly planted in Stellarton, a town of 5,000 people. For Donald Sobey, the idea of moving the head office is ridiculous, like suggesting the Pope move out of the Vatican or the New York Yankees out of the Bronx. "It is no accident the head office is in Stellarton because the Sobey family is here; I think it's important that the CEO and top-line people be here; they know what the owners are thinking." It does mean that the company leadership, including CEO McEwan, must travel a lot, but they would have to be on the road in any case. There is always talk of moving to Toronto, but Donald says that would be unacceptable. "Our culture is here, it's what we are. If we changed that, it would be very disruptive."

There is another model for a major retail company keeping its head office in a small town that is off the beaten path. Wal-Mart, an organization that makes Sobey look like a pipsqueak, is run from Bentonville, Arkansas. Mind you, Bentonville with 20,000 people is a metropolis alongside Stellarton. But the principle is the same: It is possible to run a big national, even international retail business from a town with no skyscrapers or major airport. In fact, the Sobeys make it all happen with two company jets, which are kept at the airport in Halifax.

The Sobeys have grappled with the decision of whether to move the company to a bigger centre, but have always decided it isn't worth the trouble. As a young man, David

Sobey managed one of the company stores in Halifax and quite liked the city. Then his father called him home to Stellarton to take over merchandising. After about six months, he said to his father, "We should be in Halifax." He explained that Stellarton was mired in a terrible recession and the mines were closing. It was not the place for a growing supermarket chain, but the cantankerous Frank Sobey shot back that "all you guys will be doing in Halifax is going out with our suppliers and having two-martini lunches." David couldn't argue with the logic: In those days in Stellarton, the lunch options were dining in your office or going home. The company never moved out of Stellarton, although David says, "If we were to start all over again, we'd be better off in Halifax than Stellarton."

The purchase of Toronto-based Oshawa Group did change the geographic balance of the company, moving it westward toward Toronto. There was some political pressure in Ontario for the headquarters to move to that province, but the Sobeys resisted. It didn't hurt that they received a $3.5-million payroll grant from Nova Scotia, rewarding them for creating new head office jobs. It is another facet of doing business in the Maritimes: There is always a grant or forgivable loan available to encourage you to do something you would probably do anyway. The Sobeys, like the Irvings, are just good bargainers.

Even with the gravitational pull toward Toronto, Paul Sobey is adamant that the company should never move to the large Ontario city because it is too much of a distraction. Indeed, this is a big theme among the Atlantic firms: In Toronto, there are the investment bankers and consultants who want to nudge you into more mergers and all kinds of crazy, expensive things. But according to Paul, there is simply less loyalty in Central Canada. You might have a hard time getting people to move to the Maritimes, but once they are here, they stay with you and work hard. The Sobeys are regularly targeting émigré Maritimers, such as Paul Beesley, the Empire chief financial officer, a Saint John native who had been the CFO of the *Globe and Mail* before he was lured to Stellarton. He boasts that his commuting time has been cut to five minutes from 45 minutes on the bumper-to-bumper Gardiner Expressway.

But by staying in Stellarton, the Sobeys as a family have had to live with the microscopic attention of being the big fish in a very small pond. They are the constant focus of speculation and gossip. They have learned to pick their friends carefully, choosing people who like them for what they are, not for their wealth or renown. When something happens to them, it is big news. As owners of a public company, everybody knows what the senior Sobeys are paid. Paul has seen the public attention to his highly publicized divorce case whereby in 2000, his former wife was granted $38,000 a month in spousal and child support, and his income of more than $1 million a year was widely reported.

"Just be yourself," Paul Sobey says with a laugh, as he explains his approach to living with such a high profile. "I've grown up here. There is the good and the bad, and the good outweighs the bad. It's like anybody else in any community, the owner of the Ford dealership or any successful business in the community—you are going to get that." But more so, of course, if you are a Sobey.

It does mean you have to modify your behaviour and be careful about what you say about people, Paul agrees. "You can't say, 'Oh, that asshole, it's none of his business! Jesus, he's a jerk.' You have to be very careful about what you say, and cognizant of it. I may have personal views about aspects of the business, but I can't walk down the hallway and say, even about someone in a junior position, 'She is incompetent in what she is doing.' Outside the company, it's the same thing."

It can be especially hard on kids—Paul has six, three from each of his marriages—whose every step or misstep is carefully watched by the community. His cousin Frank, who has three children, says the family has to keep remembering that the community is also the source of their customers. "One of the things I've told my kids is to think of goodwill as a bank account, and throughout your life, make deposits by being responsible, doing what you say you will, thinking about how you run your life."

Frank says that every once in a while when the kids do something wrong, a fender bender or something, they actually say, "Dad, this is a withdrawal."

Asked if it is tough being a Sobey in Stellarton or New Glasgow, Frank doesn't hesitate to say it is. Gossip tends to be more outlandish for the Sobeys than for other families. He and his wife and kids talk about how to handle it. The conclusion is that your true friends don't treat you any differently, and you have to worry about the ones who do.

But your friends and business associates also stick by you, because that is what happens in rural communities, Frank says. "One of the things I've noticed is that urban people are more for the moment: 'What have you done for me today?' They're more ready to ditch and switch. Whether that is because in Toronto, you can leave your job here and go across the street and get another job—it sort of builds a culture."

He says that loyalty to people has become strained in the expanded Sobeys' organization, as it swallowed the Oshawa Group. He wants to get it all back. "There was a period of time when we weren't sure who we were, and I think that's changed and it is starting to spread across the country." That may be the Sobeys' biggest challenge: bringing Maritimes management to an organization that is no longer Atlantic Canadian in its reach, its customers, and its culture.

IF THERE IS A SOBEY standard-bearer in this generation, it has to be Paul, an intense, impatient man with thinning brown hair who seems older than his 48 years. He meets me on a winter morning in his office at Empire Company across the road from the railroad tracks. When the Sobeys are asked what makes their business distinctive, there are the usual clichés about community and commitment. But Paul keeps repeating two words over and over like a mantra: You need passion and drive, passion and drive, passion and drive.

Paul's emergence as the family leader is a result of age, interest, and timing. He also has the benefit of an accountant's training, which has allowed him to take a central role in some of the key turnarounds and reorganizations in the company. He is university-trained—which is not a requirement in the Sobey family—and had a host of good summer jobs, including one stint as a worker for the Loblaws organization until the rival head office found out about it and fired the young interloper.

Paul insists that he was not handed the job of top Sobey on a platter, that he had to earn the CEO's role at Empire. If he doesn't do a good job, he says, "then I won't be here. It's not in my best interests or the shareholders'. You've got to have the drive and passion to succeed or you're not going to be there. The board decides; I go through a review by the hiring committee."

Indeed, the final judgment on Paul Sobey's stewardship will depend on the outcome of the supermarket wars of the next few years and how Sobeys Inc. fares with its acquisitions and smaller-store strategy. The family's old nemesis, Richard

Currie, says the chain faces a major challenge: Its business is spotty—strong in Quebec and parts of western Canada but weak in the key market of Ontario and surprisingly soft in the Maritimes. "They are No. 2 in the food business in the country but not No. 1 in any market. That is their strategic conundrum." It means, he says, that they are continually at the mercy of whoever is No. 1—and in most of the country, that is Loblaws.

Those, of course, are fighting words in Stellarton, where Currie is never seen as an objective observer. The question is whether the Sobeys can challenge for the top spot in some of those regional markets. In July, 2005, they bid more than $1.8 billion for the A&P supermarkets in Canada, but lost out to Metro Inc., the Quebec grocer which offered A&P a package of cash and shares. The Sobeys figured they gave it a good shot. The A&P stores would have given them a stronger hand in Ontario, where Loblaws is so strong. But there will be other buyout opportunities, and the company continues to roll out its smaller-store, groceries-only strategy.

Now that the Oshawa Group merger is under their belts, the family and its managers know a bit more of what they are getting into. And nothing would make them happier than to reclaim the top spot in the bitterly contested supermarket turf of Atlantic Canada.

CHAPTER 9

CLEARWATER RUNS DEEP

IN JOHN RISLEY'S COLOURFUL vocabulary, there is a "shit storm" blowing outside his snow-swept suburban Halifax office. Risley, Canada's leading fishery tycoon and one of its most aggressive investors, is barking that observation into a cell-phone as he paces back and forth in his deserted office lobby at ten o'clock in the morning. It's hard to determine precisely which "shit storm" he's talking about since there are lots to choose from in the world of John Risley, Atlantic Canada's most dynamic entrepreneur. There is the weather outside: The wind is blowing so hard that it feels like Risley's head office building is about to blow off its foundation into the icy waters of Bedford Basin. Or it could be the competitive storm blowing in from China, which is shaking the pillars of his company, Clearwater Seafoods, the world's largest scallop supplier and a powerhouse in the global shellfish industry. Then there is the collapse of the U.S. dollar, which has sliced the value of his sales and has forced the Clearwater income trust to cut its distributions by 27 per cent. Or maybe it is the boardroom brawl over an Ontario company called Environmental Management Solutions, where he and a bunch of new directors have dumped the chief executive officer and are now facing a legal battle. Indeed, it could be the tempest still swirling around FPI, the Newfoundland company that he tried to merge with Clearwater and where his disparaging comments about the Newfoundland work ethic made him the scourge of the island—at least, until *Globe and Mail* columnist Margaret Wente came along. After all, "shit storms" seem to follow John Risley with the relentless intensity of the brutal sou'wester that, on this day in January, has blown up the East Coast from Boston, leaving a trail of ice and snow and school cancellations.

The storm, however, has not slowed down the impetuous Risley, a tightly coiled bundle of kinetic energy who sports intense eyes beneath a solid line of bushy brows. Awake at 4:30 a.m. today like every day, he threw on his jeans, a pink Oxford shirt, and a blue Harvard University sweatshirt and piloted his SUV across icy roads and through whiteouts from his home along the ocean in picturesque Chester, just down the coast from Halifax, to get to his office. Nothing else is moving on the highway. Except for a receptionist, a reporter, and his brother-in-law and partner Colin MacDonald, he is alone in the building, making calls to his business partners around the continent and discussing the latest "shit storm."

As he has been so many times, Risley, 56, is in the eye of a hurricane, an almost constant condition after having emerged from bankruptcy 30 years ago to build first a mighty fish business and, more recently, a network of global business and investment interests. When he fixes you with his piercing glare, it's hard to argue with his contention that Clearwater has been around the fish business for three decades, it's used to the ups and downs of business cycles, and it will survive the current headwinds. The fall in profits at Clearwater is disappointing, but "it's the only company in the industry that is consistently profitable," he asserts. "We've had some horror stories and high-profile bankruptcies in the industry but this company has always been able to run at a profit."

Besides, at his age, he has moved beyond the short term. "Early in your business life your whole focus is around instant gratification—work today, results today. When you reach our age, frankly you don't give a shit about short-term investments; it's all about the long term and the macro trends and how do you position yourself?" Clearwater, he says, simply owns the best fishing licences and quotas in the industry, and "provided that we manage the stocks properly, and we do have a reasonably intelligent management regime, these are great assets to own over the long term."

This unflinching in-your-face credo is the calling card for the man who has emerged as the titan of Halifax, indeed of the entire East Coast. The Sobeys, Irvings, and McCains are still powerful, but all these dynasties are moving into their second, third, and fourth generations, the time when the children start to think about a better life than grinding out 12 hours at work every day. In Halifax, the old establishment has faded, with the notable exception of the Jodreys, the masters of Minas Basin, who still have immense influence and possess some strong assets, particularly in real estate. But they are no longer awe-inspiring, while John Risley inspires not only awe, but envy and resentment. John Bragg, the berries-and-cable tycoon, is also very influential, as is Fred Smithers, a quietly effective marine services magnate, who has cashed in on the offshore oil and gas industry. Joe Shannon, an industrial power in Cape Breton, has a lot of admirers. Newfoundland expatriate Harry Steele is still a force too, although he is delegating day-to-day operations to his sons, who are building the family's Newfoundland Capital into a national radio company. But in wealth and influence, Risley is rivalled by only one other Haligonian, Ken Rowe, the hard-driving aerospace entrepreneur who made his company, IMP, into a major force. Risley is a much more public entrepreneur than Rowe, who only occasionally strides into the glare of public attention. Risley is a flamboyant dealer in companies, homes, land, and sailboats, who has his hand in every pie: in Clearwater, in real estate, in a food nutrients company called Ocean Nutrition, in an investment management company. *Canadian Business* magazine puts his wealth at close to $400 million but such judgments are guesses when so much of it is privately held.

He is also an investment partner with George Armoyan, the brittle Syrian-born vulture capitalist who has an impeccable nose for cheap assets that can be bought, turned around, and sold for a profit. "I am a bottom feeder, I'm not going to apologize. I'm an opportunistic guy and I take advantage of situations," Armoyan says, and Risley is fishing in those waters with him. Risley's hyperactive investment life takes him out of the operations of Clearwater Seafoods, the shellfish company where his brother-in-law Colin MacDonald is in command. These days Risley is spending a lot of time in the telecommunications business in the Caribbean, where he and Armoyan see a huge opportunity in Columbus Communications, a joint venture with flamboyant Ontario mutual fund manager Michael Lee-Chin, a native of Jamaica. "The telecom infrastructure in the Caribbean is where it was in North America 35 years ago," says Risley.

Risley's partnership with Armoyan and Lee-Chin is indicative of his ability to think outside the cramped confines of the Maritime box. Armoyan, he says, has had to smooth some very rough edges, but the two men trust each other implicitly in making investments. When George buys something, he doesn't have to check with John—he just goes ahead and does it. "We more or less have a blind trust in each other," says Armoyan, who splits his time between Halifax and Toronto.

"My style of business is very relaxed," says Risley, who of course is anything but relaxed. What he really means is: I like you if you can make me money, and I don't care who you are. "We don't have to own 100 per cent of everything. The McCains and Irvings will tell you they don't make good partners, and that's a different philosophy. On the other hand, I make a pretty good partner because I'm happy to be in partnership with other people, and I'm happy to make sure we do our part in making sure it is successful."

One of the partners Risley has taken on is Derrick Rowe, the president of FPI, the company once known as Fishery Products International, of which Risley owns 14 per cent. Rowe, a pretty savvy company-builder himself, sees Risley as the ultimate entrepreneur in Atlantic Canada, who keeps popping up in surprising places, such as a seed investment in Garrison Guitars, a St. John's musical instruments maker. "You never know where John is," says Rowe. "He has done so many things that you would never know, and he did it because he believed in the people. If you look at the business plan, you couldn't sign off on it, but if you look at the person he supported you could say, yeah, I understand that. He bets on people, and he is usually right."

But the famous Maritimes understatement, the modesty, the Scottish austerity, does not reside in John Risley. That is not to say he is a boastful man, but he prefers to be judged by his actions, his giving, and to some extent his bountiful possessions. He is not afraid of conspicuous consumption and conspicuous charity. His houses are the stuff of legend, a fine home in south-end Halifax and several properties around Chester, including a stunning 1,000-acre piece of ground called Lobster Point. The house itself, about seven years old, has become a local landmark, perhaps the most spectacular home on Canada's East Coast, a 32,000-square-foot Georgian-style mansion into which Risley has poured about $23 million of cash. He has attacked its construction with both a huge vision and an exacting eye for detail. In fact, he imported a team of about 10 female painters from Britain with expertise in detail trim work for the main rooms. This group became known locally as "the Risley ladies" or, according to Risley, "Charlie's Angels," because of their striking good looks and the leadership of a woman named Charlie. Then there is nearby Lobster Point Lodge with its huge timbers, windows, and fireplaces, plus numerous other buildings, including log cabins, cottages and barns and even a chapel. In one area, he keeps prize horses for dressage, as well as an indoor riding arena; in another, he maintains a herd of well-bred Simmental cattle, which he bought from the Rockefeller family.

He wants to make Lobster Point a public place, an environmental showpiece, and is building greenhouses that would be open to visitors. Risley has been talking to the Rockefellers about how they have approached the paradox of private wealth and public giving, and Lobster Point is his Williamsburg, his Rockefeller Center, the focus of his public legacy. "We do have this wonderful property and consider ourselves lucky to own it," he says. "We tell our children it will never be subdivided or carved up for development; so how do we make it an asset for Nova Scotians and not just for the Risleys?"

Everywhere you look around Chester, a summer and retirement playground for the well-to-do, Risley has put his distinctive stamp. In early 2005, the Canada Reads program on CBC Radio uncovered a Canadian classic called *Rockbound*, author Frank Parker Day's 1928 novel about an isolated Nova Scotia-German fishing community and its parochial, often brutal lifestyle. Eighty years ago, the book's portrait of island life, rife with illiteracy and promiscuity, ignited a controversy on Ironbound, the island near Chester on which "Rockbound," the fictional island in the book, was based. The CBC's elevation of the book to masterpiece status rekindled some of those old resentments. But the dominant figure on Ironbound today is John Risley, who owns an 80-acre farm that takes up more than half of the island.

He is also a leading philanthropist, giving to Dalhousie University, to hospitals, and to other good causes that catch his interest. He says Clearwater is the biggest corporate donor in the Halifax community, but it is not a passive cheque-writer: Risley believes in activist philanthropy, backing things he believes in and where he can play a role. And his giving is contagious. He has encouraged Ken Rowe to become a more active donor, and the aerospace tycoon is now a major fundraiser for hospitals and for Dalhousie. Lately, Risley has caught the bug being passed among many successful Canadian businesspeople: He figures if he can make a mark in business, surely he can solve the Great Canadian Health Care Crisis. He is working with a team of Halifax doctors on a private solution to the public health care system's lineups and surgery delays. Now if he can only persuade the province to go along with it.

And he may just succeed, because John Risley's other great gift is his ability to master just about anything he turns his mind to. "What is interesting to me about John is that he has managed to be the best at a whole lot of things," says one Halifax businessman who knows him well. He recalls when Risley bought a splendid house in the affluent section of South Halifax and launched a massive renovation over a long period. When he finally announced a big open house, the neighbours held their breaths, concerned that this arriviste would have crassly decorated or tastelessly furnished the house. But in fact, it was impeccable in its refinement, the product of high-priced decorating consultants, the finest antiques from England, and Risley's drive for perfection. The neighbourhood relaxed.

Similarly, when Risley became passionate about sailing, he embraced it with style and dollars. He bought the biggest boat around and equipped it with the best crew, tapping the vast reservoir of nautical talent down in Lunenburg, that sacred ground of *Bluenose* sailing, just across Mahone Bay from Chester. He refuses to say how many sailboats he now owns but the number is substantial. He has sailed on the Fastnet circuit, the celebrated race from Ireland to England. He has been heavily involved in two of the elite America's Cup teams, including the unsuccessful New Zealand contender in 2003. Risley happily admits he is cut from different cloth than the more austere Maritime Mafia: He gets great joy out of owning a fine boat and is not going to hide his passion. "It's just stupid, what's the point? I'm not interested in driving a Rolls-Royce, it's too flamboyant and not what I am. But am I willing to spend millions of dollars on a boat? Yes, I am, because a boat can be a great business tool and it can be a great investment." Above all, it is an outlet for his competitive energy and has given him a chance to sail with the world's best. "You always learn from champions. I just enjoy being on the water, it's hugely relaxing, and my business is the water."

At times, Risley's flamboyant consumption and charity suggest a more West Coast, Silicon Valley style of capitalism than is associated with the titans of Canada's East Coast. But his roots are reflected in his sailing and his office and boardroom decor, which is dominated by the nautical paintings of artist Jack Gray, a folk-art scene of Lunenburg, and coastal maps and prints. Indeed, Risley has a typical Easterners' attachment to real assets: the forests, the sea, and the land. He believes that hard physical things are the most enduring and resilient targets for any investor. "Over the long term, if you own coal or oil and gas, or forests, these are wonderful assets, because you're not going to wake up some morning and find that some guy in Silicon Valley has made them obsolete. Or some guy in China has stolen your business out from under you because he has figured out how to do it at a much lower cost. These are assets that are going to have value 50 to 100 years from now. They're all renewable assets that have been there 100 years and will be there 100 years from now." You can argue all you want about whether coal, or a scallop, for that matter, is renewable, but John Risley is unshakeable in his beliefs.

At the same time, he is ready to use high technology for trading and investment programs in financial derivatives, an area where Risley is considered a master. This derivative trading is done both as a currency hedging strategy for Clearwater and for his own personal pleasure and profit. Purdy Crawford, a Clearwater board member, says Risley knows more about these specialized financial instruments than most trading professionals, and he attacks it with his usual obsessiveness. As for Risley, he says, "I invest personally in derivatives. I have a real interest. I understand the difference between intelligence and luck, and I have been very lucky."

In two hours with John Risley, you will be entertained, you will hear a lot of opinions and a lot of cursing—all delivered in a non-stop staccato. His straight talking, he says, comes from the fact that he is a man in a hurry. "I don't want to waste time. I think the best way to get people to expose themselves to you is to expose yourself to them. Talk straight to people and you can expect the same back. Talk in circles and what do you get back? I want to know right away, can I do business with this guy? Is there an opportunity here? Is this worth my putting energy and time into? Let's get on with it. I make a decision right away, and you will too."

JOHN RISLEY HAS ALWAYS been a man in a hurry, and he has the windburn to show for it. The middle-class son of a Halifax insurance adjuster, he went to Dalhousie for two years but dropped out because English, history, and biology seemed to have nothing to do with making money. He admits now it was a huge mistake. If he had stayed in school, pursued a law or business degree, he might have learned a bit of discipline.

Instead, Risley learned it the hard way, through bankruptcy and humiliation. Indeed, John Risley's drive and hunger are built on his total failure as a young capitalist. In the late 1970s, he bet heavily on real estate, made money in the inflation spiral, and then lost it all when the market went flat. "When you're young and naïve, you tend to think you're real smart and you're not—you're just benefiting from macro-economic conditions," he says. "Then money got tight and interest rates went up, and inflation went out of the system; the men got separated from the boys, and I was left behind."

He was a young married man with a baby on the way and no money to pay the weekly grocery order of $20. "And if you didn't have it, you were in shit. The rent at the end of the month you could worry about then, but how do you buy groceries now?" It was a difficult but valuable education—the bouncing cheques and the worries about responsibilities—which he regrets his own two children will never experience.

The value is it teaches you to be a fighter. "If you don't go through that, when you get in trouble, you give up," says Risley who regularly gets approached by people whose businesses are in trouble and need investment money. He finds that it is not that the ideas are bad, the problem is that the people behind those ideas have never learned how to fight.

Risley learned to fight the day the telephone company came in and ripped the phone off the wall. It led his wife, Judi, to complain for years about the decorating challenges of having a big bare spot on the wall. But, he says, "it's not fun and when you are ambitious, as I was, these are big setbacks. But it's like getting in the ring—the guys who end up winning the fights are the guys who understand how to get knocked down and pick themselves back up again. It's a very, very valuable experience to get knocked down a few times."

Still, Risley had to find a way to get up off the canvas, and for that, he credits two defining moments. The first was when his older brother, Robert, a successful restaurateur, asked him one day when he was going to figure out how to get out of this mess and make some money. John saw the remark as a "shame on you, clean up your act and stop embarrassing me and the family."

The second moment came on one of those fateful Fridays when he went for his $20 grocery order at the local Sobeys store. He tried to pay for his groceries with a cheque and the cashier stepped away to consult with the manager. She returned and showed him that his cheque from the previous week had bounced. She wasn't going to make the same mistake again. Leave the groceries on the counter, she told him, in a sobering moment for a man who would later become a director of Sobeys. He took a big breath and said to himself, "Look, this has got to stop."

It helped that he got lucky. At his most desperate moment, he was approached by a friend in the real estate business, who had acquired a seafood restaurant along the Bedford Highway. The friend, a mentor of Risley named Malcolm Swim, told him he could take over the restaurant and just run it, and start paying him rent when he got it rolling. Risley was not a restaurateur, so he turned the place into a retail store for lobsters. He would drive his rented truck 250 kilometres north to the Northumberland Strait to bargain with lobster fishermen. He got Colin MacDonald, a university biology student and his wife Judi's brother, to give him a hand. "I needed someone who wasn't looking for a paycheque on Friday and was prepared to work as hard as I was. That was a huge plus and then as the business grew, and we had ambitions to grow aggressively, the timing in the industry was right to receive growth."

Soon, MacDonald and Risley were carting lobsters off to New England for sale, and when that market slowed, they were airlifting the crustaceans to Asia and Europe. To maintain his lobsters in good shape the whole year, he came up with the idea of the dry-land pound, a storage operation in which lobsters could be maintained in ideal conditions and at the right temperature all the time. The lobsters are kept safe in separate compartments, in a kind of lobster hotel. It was Clearwater's first big innovation in the lobster business that set it apart from the rest of the pack. It developed two such pounds, one in Arichat on Cape Breton, and the other at Clark's Harbour on the southern end of the province. Clearwater was able to exploit big shifts in the fish industry, as a lot of the old family businesses that plied the Atlantic waters came up for sale. In a two-year period, the two brothers-in-law bought 10 East Coast fish companies. Clearwater rode the ferocious cycles of the industry and the crazy spirals of oversupply and overfishing. The regulatory climate was changing to help an ambitious guy who wanted to consolidate the industry. Although he cut his teeth in lobsters, by the 1990s, Clearwater was taking its revenues equally from lobsters, scallops, shrimps, and clams, and it was growing into a $350-million business.

In the late 1980s, in a bid for expansion capital, Risley sold a 50 per cent equity stake in Clearwater to Hillsdown, a British food company. There were plans to launch an initial public offering, but the market was not conducive, and Risley and Hillsdown parted company, with Risley and MacDonald re-acquiring the Canadian operations. But that didn't slow him down. Risley envisaged creating the major global fishery company, a vertically integrated giant that would span the distance between shipping fleets and branded products, and amass annual sales in the billions of dollars. His model was not the typical Nova Scotia fishing company but Smithfield Foods, the integrated southern U.S. pork giant whose businesses spanned hog barns to branded packaged pork chops.

In the late 90s, Risley looked across the Gulf of Saint Lawrence to the Newfoundland equivalent of Clearwater, a company called Fishery Products International. FPI, as it became known, had survived a series of hard knocks from the time it was privatized from federal-provincial ownership in the mid-1980s. Under Vic Young, a smart former public servant, it emerged from government hands, prospered for a while, and then endured the cod fishery crisis, in which a deteriorating supply of fish forced the temporary shutdown of that industry and sparked the continuing concern that it would never recover again. Young had undertaken a dramatic downsizing that had seen the company's workforce reduced to 2,000 people from 8,000, and ultimately moved it back to profitability. It was a smaller company, more focused, but still a Newfoundland icon and part of the social fabric of the province, with its operations dotted among the small villages and outports. But Young's spectacular salvage job only made FPI an enticing target in John Risley's grand plan for a fishery juggernaut.

It was John Risley's one great defeat, and it still rankles bitterly. Risley, along with a group of partners, launched a

hostile takeover bid for FPI in 1999. It failed, but he accumulated enough shares in the company to come back two years
later with a proxy fight that ousted FPI's board, installing former telecom entrepreneur Derrick Rowe as chairman and
dumping Young, the company's long-running CEO. Young,
whose measured, conservative style contrasts vividly with
Risley's bold thrusts, contends that FPI's shareholders were
enticed by the prospect of a share-price gain that was always
very dubious, given the economics of the industry. At the time
of the proxy fight, the stock was valued at $12 and, Young
says, "we mainly lost because of the promise that it could be
a $20 stock, and we could make no such promise—we knew
it was a very uncertain industry and couldn't make those
kinds of profits." As of late June 2005, the price was still
down at $7.50. But of course, the Risley team never got a
chance to exercise its grand blueprint for the fishery.

That blueprint became evident in 2001 when Risley and
Rowe unveiled a plan for the much bigger FPI to acquire
Risley's Clearwater in a deal valued at more than $500 mil-
lion. Finally, the dream of a fisheries mega-company seemed to
be within Risley's grasp. But the plan got entangled in the particular culture of the Newfoundland fishery, accusations of
secret plans and betrayal, and John Risley's shoot-from-the-
hip personality. It underlined the inability of outsiders, even
Maritimers like Risley, to understand this very separate island.

The Risley group unveiled a plan for the Newfoundland
fish plants that would see massive investments, but also a
downsizing of 600 jobs in small communities. What would
be left, he said, would be real jobs with real incomes, not a
patchwork of seasonal labour and employment insurance.
There were charges that he had not disclosed these plans
when he launched his proxy fight and installed the new
board. In fact, critics said, the Risley group committed itself

to no layoffs. Risley shot back that he had unveiled his plans in meetings with the Newfoundland premier Roger Grimes before he went public with them. But Risley's off-the-cuff remark that Newfoundland's fish industry amounted to a culture of milking unemployment insurance doomed any chance of success.

In the end, the government, as custodian of the public's interest in FPI, said it would exercise the legislation that prevented any single shareholder to vote more than 15 per cent interest in the company. The Risley-Rowe group was stymied, with effective control of the company's board but no way to engineer the massive reorganization needed to change the industry. Since then, they have remained in a kind of limbo, as FPI continues to rationalize its operations in an attempt to control costs and contend with the new threats of low-cost fish processing from China and a rising Canadian dollar.

It was one of those galvanizing moments that intrigue and exasperate people who follow the Newfoundland experience. Some Newfoundlanders backed Risley in the need for change, including the former federal finance minister John Crosbie, who was part of FPI's new slate of directors and who stumped hard for the Clearwater merger. In Crosbie's view, "Risley is the leading East Coast fisheries businessman, the clearest thinker, and the most intelligent operator with a wide vision. I thought FPI and Risley had the potential to become the leading fishery company in the world." But the problem with Risley, he says, is "he wasn't politically sensitive." Fishing is not just an industry in Newfoundland, Crosbie says. In fact, it contributes less than 8 per cent of the province's gross domestic product. But it lies at the core of the culture, the arts, and the social safety net. It is, he says, what the island was founded on, and politicians are loath to tackle its underlying economic challenges.

Risley concedes he did a poor job of selling the industry reorganization but insists that the short-term thinking of the province's political class is dooming the industry to a slow and painful death. His dream was to create the necessary adjustment that would carry the industry out of its role as a social safety net and into a truly productive sector, thus ensuring the survival of the small rural communities through the continuation of fewer but better paid jobs. "It's just a great shame to see politicians fighting that and saying, 'Oh no, we need to preserve this, we don't want to let elements of the real world creep in here, we want to use your industry as a mechanism by which we enter the social safety net of the country.'" The government, he says, is deluding people into thinking that everything can remain the same; that people can continue to work only 12 to 14 weeks a year, get their EI benefits, and patch together a half-decent household income. "But I tell you these communities are emptying out," he says. "It's tragic."

He argues that FPI, which injects a payroll of $55 million into the communities of rural Newfoundland, should be allowed to operate like a true company. "If it's not allowed to operate like a true company, I promise you that in 10 years time it will be lucky if we are putting $10 million in wages into rural Newfoundland. And there is no one who remotely comes close as a comparable employer. Forget other companies. You try to talk to these [politicians] and they say, 'Whenever we beat you guys up in the media, our ratings go up.' So we say, if that's what you're going to do, we'll pick up our marbles and play somewhere else."

Risley had failed in his biggest test and was still holding a 14 per cent stake in FPI. He took Clearwater public in 2003, which generated $45 million for his treasury and created an income trust for the fishing assets. In a move that was both symbolic and substantive, Clearwater acquired the fishery operations, including valuable scallop licences, of High Liner Foods, the other major Nova Scotia fishing company, which had evolved into a branded processor of seafood products. But while his dreams remained alive, John Risley had made the transition from fishery entrepreneur to investment tycoon, making deals with a wide range of friends and partners.

WHILE JOHN RISLEY spent much of his early career on the ropes, George Armoyan came up through the school of hard knocks—literally. For a period during the 1980s, Armoyan, a young engineering graduate of Dalhousie University, supplemented his nascent real estate career by managing a couple of professional boxers in Halifax. "I thought there was money in it—I thought guts and ignorance were supposed to be a good combination," Armoyan recalls. But it turned out to be one of the few failures of his unusually successful business life. He lost a few thousand dollars and hung up the managerial gloves. The funny thing is he couldn't stand to watch the fights. "I'm not much of a fighter," he says.

In fact, George Armoyan is very much a fighter, if not in terms of fisticuffs, at least in business and life. He is the kind of guy that John Risley was destined to discover and to go into business with. The boxing bit was a typical career move for Armoyan, who has become a multimillionaire by playing the kind of bare-knuckles game that most Maritimers find unseemly.

"I have a saying that if you want to make an omelet, you have to crack a few eggs," says the 44-year-old investor. "People in Nova Scotia are concerned about being controversial, being in the limelight, and to a certain degree, I agree with that. But if I were to do everything very quietly, it just goes against my grain."

"George has an amazing appetite for work, and he's got a very quick mind," John Risley says of his partner. "He retains everything he hears and reads, a very quick study, and he has polished himself up a lot. He needed a little polishing, because he was rough at the edges."

When told that Risley once saw him as "rough around the edges," Armoyan snaps that "I'm still rough around the edges even today." He sees his combativeness as a natural response for someone who was born in Syria of Armenian parents, in a world of violence where it was hard just to survive. "People don't appreciate how lucky they are to be born and raised in countries like this, you know. It's easier not to be rough around the edges when you were born and raised here."

It's a typical comment from Armoyan, who still sees himself as an outsider in the persistently Anglo Halifax establishment, where people with names like Jodrey, Risley, Smithers, Bragg, and Rowe still call a lot of the shots. The defiant Armoyan clearly sees this as a privileged club to which he would not accept membership, even if it were offered. Asked if he has a house in Chester, that playground of the Risley crowd, he says, "That's for the classy people, and I'm not one of them."

But he does see himself as the vanguard of a new multicultural group of entrepreneurs—Armenian, Lebanese, Egyptian, and Chinese—who are changing the complexion of the Nova Scotia establishment, particularly in the area of real estate development. In fact, Armoyan argues that 75 per cent of the new apartment buildings in Halifax are being built by people who were not born in Canada.

Twelve years younger than Risley, Armoyan moved to Boston from Syria with his family when he was only 12 years old. When young George was ready for university, his parents looked around and decided Canada was a good and affordable place to attend school. So George became a civil engineering student at Dalhousie University, and soon his entire family had joined him in Halifax, including his equally resourceful brother Vrege.

After university, he started investing in student digs and graduated to residential construction—along with his side trip into the world of boxing. He once appeared on CBC TV's *Venture* as a hot young entrepreneur. That led to a number of invitations to work with other business people, and he accepted the invitation of an Armenian-Canadian businessman based in Toronto. He learned a lot, but his mentor moved back to the Middle East. Armoyan returned to be with his family in Halifax and resume his house-building career. Over the years his company, Kimberley-Lloyd Developments, became the major residential house builder in Atlantic Canada, known for building affordable units and stirring up controversy.

Armoyan would cut down trees, ignoring the concerns of local environmentalists; he trampled on a historic trail beloved of local history buffs. "Critics say that his companies have a reputation for brashly clearing land and making money by crowding homes into subdivisions," *Globe and Mail* reporter Kevin Cox wrote in a 1997 column on Armoyan's takeover of a bankrupt German-owned spa project at Chester. Cox noted that the same day he was bidding for the spa, "residents of Cow Bay were urging city politicians to reject plans for an Armoyan Group subdivision that they said would ruin their semi-rural way of life on the Dartmouth side of Halifax Harbour."

George admits there is truth in this reputation, which he describes as the natural product of impetuous youth and his aversion to bureaucracy. "I wasn't the most patient guy around," he admits now. "I was a young guy just trying to survive. My cash flow when I started in business was day by day and I found it frustrating the way people can hold you up for a month or years." He insists he didn't break the law, but there are things he now wishes he hadn't done. "Youth leads you to do things you sometimes regret. A lot of these things happened, no ifs, ands, and buts, they did happen." In short, he says, "I became infamous." But he adds that he was portrayed in the press as much worse than he actually was, which caused hurt for his children. "I do make mistakes but do I deserve all these other things? I don't think so."

The uproar hasn't ended as he has moved into his 40s. In recent years, he has incited controversy as the owner of Scotia Learning Centres, which negotiated with the province to build and run 13 new high schools in the province. The $200-million construction project has been a lightning rod for educational activists who worry about the injection of private capitalism into the public school system.

As Armoyan was rising in the Halifax business world, he left the real estate operations to his brother and began to build a reputation as a savvy vulture investor. He joined the Atlantic chapter of the Young Presidents' Organization, a remarkable breeding ground of entrepreneurial talent, attracting membership from both old families and young strivers. It is where Armoyan got to know John Risley, and the two decided to go into business together. They first partnered to buy the venerable Lord Nelson Hotel in the Public Gardens area of central Halifax. That project worked out nicely, they sold it, and the two decided to start something more formal. The result was an investment company called Geosam, an amalgam of George and Sam, which are his two sons' names. Armoyan and his family own 60 per cent, and Risley along with two other Halifax movers and shakers, Carl Potter and Hugh Smith, own the rest.

They started out in that ultimate bottom-feeding game— buying non-performing loans from banks at deep discounts and wringing gains out of them. But as they moved up the food chain, they began to take a run at a number of under-performing public companies. For example, in 2001, Geosam launched a hostile takeover of the national moving company, AMJ Campbell, which sparked a management buyout that netted a nice profit for the group of investors.

In early 2005, Geosam was the largest shareholder in eight national public companies, including Clarke Transport, real estate company Royal Host, and Halterm, the under-performing owner of the Halifax container terminal. The name for what Geosam does ranges from "private equity" to "vulture funds" to "catalyst investing," but the idea is the same: defining under-performing assets and capitalizing on them. It suggests an aggressive, confrontational stance that is very different from the low-key Maritimes model. Armoyan is not satisfied with safe 5 to 7 per cent annual returns, but is aiming for 18 per cent or more. He says that from 1997 to 2005, Geosam has averaged returns of more than 20 per cent a year. "One of these days I will have a bad [investment] and I just hope it will not be catastrophic," Armoyan muses. "But so far we haven't lost money in anything; it has just been a matter of how much return on my money."

Recently he has shifted more of his focus to Toronto, where he lives part of the time in his parents' house. The shift is inevitable for any successful Maritimer, he says. "It reminds me of a baseball player: Once you become good in the minor leagues, you go to the major leagues. I think Maritimers are very good business people and once they do well, they try to expand their wings outside the Maritimes. Look at the Sobeys, the Jodreys, the Irvings."

He has big hopes for Clarke, a company with Maritime roots and a recent Toronto address, whose headquarters he is moving back to Halifax. But he has hit hard times at Halterm, which has lost ground in the battle for North American shipping traffic. He argues that management had done a good job in turning it around, but it was inevitable to have some bumps along the way. "The container business is going to boom worldwide and hopefully Halifax will benefit." But he adds that he does have a limited amount of resources and "you have to balance which ones will give the best return on [your] investment."

There is no time for hobbies in George Armoyan's world. There is only work and family. He works 16 to 17 hours a day, six to seven days a week. "To me, making deals and thinking about how to do these things is my hobby. I read a lot of financial reports but I try to meet people and talk to people."

He says he and his brother intend to build something to pass on to their children, a goal in which he feels a certain kinship to the more established Maritime plutocrats. In 50 to 100 years, when people talk about the great Atlantic Canada families, they will talk about the Irvings, McCains, Sobeys, and Jodreys, but also about the Armoyans, he pledges. That is one club that George Armoyan clearly lusts to join.

So if he sniffs at the idea of buying a place at Chester, in another breath he talks about converting the spa property he owns there into a home for himself. But his most dramatic gesture is his recent purchase of Oland Castle, a landmark of downtown Halifax, a century-old pile built by a member of the beer-making family. But Oland Breweries was sold to Toronto-based Labatt's in the early 1970s, and the only beer-making Olands are in Saint John. So George Armoyan is renovating the house, and it will become his Halifax home.

It is the most visible symbol of the changing of the guard in this slowly changing city. Yet Armoyan argues that outside of John Risley, John Bragg, Joe Shannon, and a few other people, most of the dynamism, particularly in real estate, is being provided by immigrants.

"I think immigrants are hungrier for success than people who were born here," he says, adding that he doubts his own children will be as hungry as he is. Immigrants are risk-takers who come to Canada and figure they have nothing more to lose. "You start with nothing and you know it's hard to go worse than zero."

But those who know Armoyan say he is changing as he rubs shoulders with the likes of Purdy Crawford, with whom he sits on John Risley's board. Purdy has known him for only two years and is impressed with his investment record. "He has a different style and, who knows, he's evolving," Purdy chuckles. "He may become more Maritime over time." Armoyan agrees that "there is no doubt working with John and the others has helped me quite a bit." Then, he adds, "But there is no doubt, I will always be an outsider."

JOHN RISLEY INSISTS he is not some crazy workaholic but a man who has found an equitable balance of work and play. He still gets up at 4:30 a.m. and hits the office by 6 a.m., but he is out of there by 3 p.m. He spends the rest of the time at Chester with his golden retrievers and Yorkshire terriers and his horses and cattle. The truth is that after about 90 minutes of exercise, he is back to work again in his home office. He spends a fair amount of the evening on his computer, handling the barrage of e-mail from around the world.

He says he will never really retire. "I'd drive my wife and my kids crazy." The future of Clearwater's management, he says, is in the hands of a board dominated by independent directors. "They will decide whether Colin [MacDonald] can run the company or can't, and if he can't, it will make a change," he says with classic Risley brusqueness. He seems relieved that choice has been, to some extent, taken out of his hands. He quotes Donald Sobey, who told him that one good reason why Empire was public was that it took these wrenching management succession issues out of the hands of the family.

But the one area where he feels less confident is predicting the future of his own children, both in their 30s. His son, Michael, is a Hollywood actor who was lured out of the fish business when he appeared as an extra in the Sandra Bullock movie *Two If by Sea*, which was made in Nova Scotia. He has received solid reviews for starring roles in two low-budget movies, *Revolution#9* and *Nowhere Man*, but nobody much saw these flicks. Risley's daughter, Sarah, is a fashion journalist in London. In the past, John has jokingly dismissed them as artsy-fartsy types but clearly enjoys their career risk-taking, which parallels his own experience. Asked why he did not pressure them to join the company, he says he knows his own limitations as a mentor and parent. "My children were much too worldly and independent and were going to make up their own minds. I probably would not have been a very good teacher for them. I think it takes a unique kind of personality, and you tend to be harder on your own and that's tough."

But, then again, John Risley's successors are everywhere in Atlantic Canada—among the new brand of entrepreneurs, who like George Armoyan are not afraid to look, act, and spend like tycoons.

CHAPTER 10

THE MARITIMIZATION OF KEN ROWE

KEN ROWE SAYS HE'S RICH enough to drive a Rolls-Royce, but he prefers a simple Jaguar to ferry him around the neighbourhoods of conservative Halifax. "When you're one of the richest guys in Nova Scotia, you don't want to go around just showing off," says Rowe, 71, whose privately held IMP Group is a transportation juggernaut with $500 million in annual revenue and tentacles into every corner of the Canadian economy.

Rowe's IMP Group has been the Nova Scotia equivalent of what the Irving companies mean to New Brunswick—privately owned, secretive, tough-minded, and oblivious to the need for positive public relations. But Rowe's lone-eagle image has softened over the years, as he has reached out to the Halifax community and sought a higher profile as a philanthropist and fundraiser. His choice of a Jaguar—"the poor man's Rolls," in his words—is further testimony to his total immersion in the Maritime business elite, more than four decades after he first came to Halifax as an aggressive young manager for a British fishing-equipment company. Unlike his friend John Risley, who stands out in the Maritimes for indulging his passions for houses and boats, Rowe shuns ostentatious displays of wealth, and that has helped him gain acceptance. Part of the reason, he speculates, is that he is British, which makes him naturally conservative. "I fit into the Maritime cult fairly easily," he says. "I think I am respected from a business point of view and, personally, I'm not expensive or flashy. I have nice homes and a nice car—anyone would expect that—but I am not extravagant, whereas they know I could be if I wanted."

Despite his early reputation as a bit of a loner, Rowe is convinced that he melds into the Halifax landscape as comfortably as the historic Citadel that looms over the downtown area. In fact, Rowe says bluntly that "I'm the head of the Maritime Mafia," and, really, who's to argue with him? This British immigrant, after 41 years in Halifax, has become a philanthropist whose name graces the new $25-million business faculty building at Dalhousie University. His IMP Group is a dominant presence at the Halifax airport, with extensive aircraft maintenance operations and as the base for its new national airline, CanJet. He is a massive investor in public companies across Canada and the largest individual shareholder of Canada's biggest financial institution, the Royal Bank of Canada, from whose board he recently retired after 18 years.

The Maritimization of Ken Rowe has extended to his friendships among the local elite, people such as Allan Shaw, a member of the old Halifax building products family and a colleague in Dalhousie University fundraising, and Risley, the only Haligonian who probably outdoes Rowe in wealth and influence. Risley and Rowe were both outsiders at one time, and both have gained acceptance, but these are two very different creatures. "John is more of a passionate guy," Rowe says, describing his friend's up-and-down entrepreneurial career, which has taken him from early bankruptcy to dominance in shellfish, to selling part of his company at one point and then buying it back. "I admire him for his guts and street smarts, what he's got and learned. I've been more private, and quieter."

Quieter, perhaps, but Rowe is no less street-smart than Risley. Ken Rowe is possibly the edgiest, toughest, and most pugnacious Maritime business leader of them all, and, most strikingly, he revels in showing that side of himself, even when it seems to go against his interests. He has built a public persona around being hard-nosed, combining the imperious manner of a naval officer with the truculence of an expatriate Brit on the make. Before Donald Trump's *Apprentice*, there was Ken Rowe. "He's got skin as tough as a rhino's hide," an unidentified former IMP manager told *Report on Business Magazine* writer Michael Salter in 1987. "He likes to make the rules, not follow them. And he's always threatening to fire you." In that same magazine article, he was cited as one of the country's toughest managers. But popularity is not what motivates Ken Rowe. Like the Irvings, he is willing to risk negative press and hard feelings in the name of making a business point. He is constantly getting into scrapes, which, some observers say, raise questions about his business judgment. More often than not, though, he gets out of them through the art of confrontation and the nerve of a cat burglar.

The most dramatic example came in 1998, when he obtained a court order to have an Aeroflot plane impounded on the tarmac of Dorval airport in Montreal, because, he said, the Russian airline owed him $8 million in a legal dispute stemming from their co-ownership of a Moscow hotel venture. He got the money, but the hotel adventure grinds on, now with a new cast of dubious Russians. Not many Maritimers would have the balls to take on Aeroflot; indeed, not many Canadian business people would have found themselves as part owners of a Russian hotel in the tricky early stages of market capitalism in that former Communist country.

Nor do many members of the Maritime Mafia display the bare-knuckles investment style that Rowe has demonstrated time and time again. Take the case of Spar Aerospace, the former Toronto aviation company. Rowe was part of the group of investors that threw out the company's board in 1999 because of what it alleged was poor performance. He claims it is the first such case of total board overhaul in recent Canadian history. Rowe then tried to buy Spar, which would have fit nicely with IMP's aerospace operations, but his offer was rejected. Along came a U.S. firm with a richer price, and Rowe was ready to sell his own stake for a big profit. Such cool detachment is typical these days, he says. Over the years, "we've become unattached, unemotional with our businesses." Yet, in the same breath, he points out that he is uncommonly loyal to some of his core operations.

In recent years, Rowe has also been the largest shareholder in an aviation repair and overhaul company called Vector Aerospace, a company spun out of Newfoundland helicopter tycoon Craig Dobbin's empire. After Vector went public, Rowe was part of an investor group that in 2003 kicked out Vector's top managers, including the CEO, Mark Dobbin, who is Craig's son. As of early 2005, there was still litigation looming between former management and the investor group, led by Rowe, who has a 19.5 per cent stake in Vector. There is no love lost between the Dobbin and Rowe families, who along with several other parties are like hungry animals circling little Vector. Mark Dobbin's only comment on Ken Rowe is that he is not well liked in the aerospace business.

Inside IMP, Rowe is known to rule with an iron hand and a tight fist on expenses. As he built the company, he had his nose in every business decision. He is the ultimate entrepreneur whose company is an extension of himself. "It is a very personal business," says John Chamard, who teaches entrepreneurship at Saint Mary's University in Halifax. Chamard says the challenge for IMP has been moving from an entrepreneurial "hunting and foraging" enterprise to a larger, mature organization. Rowe himself says he has had to change as the company has grown. He leaves the day-to-day operations to president and chief operating officer Stephen Plummer and the five divisional heads, who include his three children.

One Halifax businessman who has worked with Rowe on charitable ventures says the reality of the man is far more complex than the tempestuous public image. "Ken Rowe has a reputation for being hard, for being tough on labour, but in truth, he has a soft interior," the business leader insists. "He is a generous man, but puts up this gruff exterior that sometimes gets in his way." He has a love affair with airplanes, the man says, and Halifax has benefited mightily from this obsession. And he has worked to become a leader in charitable giving, although he still lags behind Risley, who had urged him to open up his pockets and his horizons in philanthropy. Indeed, there is an element of self-satire in Rowe's tough-guy nature—he clearly loves to put people on.

Chamard, the business professor, says Rowe was also a forerunner in the transformation of the once home-grown Maritime business elite. The Maritime Mafia used to be a largely rural phenomenon, whose ruling families had their roots in the sea, natural resources, agriculture, and the Atlantic countryside—the McCains in Florenceville, the Sobeys in Stellarton, the Jodreys in the Annapolis Valley, and the Braggs in Oxford. The Saint John-based Irvings built their original business on the forests, and even John Risley created his massive wealth from the sea. But Ken Rowe is an urban phenomenon, whose arrival signalled the transformation of Halifax into a metropolis with its own self-contained economy that was quite separate from the surrounding region. The major elements of his business do not depend on the land, the forest, or the sea—although he did get his start in marine supplies and is still a big player in that sector. Other urban entrepreneurs have followed in his wake, including the flurry of real estate magnates, such as Ralph Medjuck, Richard Homburg, and George Armoyan.

These days, it is a good time to be Ken Rowe. While the Russian escapade rumbles along in the background, Rowe is enjoying good fortune at home. He has been buying medical supply companies across Canada, the latest thrust in his steady diversification. His little airline CanJet, with its ten leased Boeing 737-500s, is starting to look like a winner, meaning that Rowe may finally succeed in the airline business in his fourth shot at it and may at last extract a measure of victory in his 25-year dogfight with Air Canada. An early attempt at a small commuter airline failed. He bought Air Atlantic, a feeder line to the former Canadian Airlines, but shut it down after two years. Then he founded CanJet in 2000, but ran into a tough market, as giant Air Canada undercut rivals in what Rowe insists was an abuse of its competitive power. He won injunctions against Air Canada's deep-discounted fares but couldn't make any money. In early 2001, he sold CanJet to another discount rival, Canada 3000, but it collapsed in the fallout from the 9/11 terrorist attacks in New York. Two years later, he revived CanJet with a mission to expand it gradually as a national airline, one city at a time.

CanJet did well serving its largely Atlantic clientele and then benefited from the insolvency of Jetsgo, a discount airline that was chasing market share by selling tickets way below cost. With Jetsgo removed from the market, CanJet has continued its expansion from its East Coast base, moving into the West with service to Calgary and Vancouver. If it succeeds, it will be Ken Rowe's crowning achievement—the ownership of a national consumer brand and a small incursion into hated Air Canada's dominant position.

So one might think that Ken Rowe is immensely pleased with his 42-year-old daughter Julie Gossen, who heads the CanJet operations. The entrepreneur harrumphs: "All my senior managers, some of whom have been with me for 20 to 25 years, are still all on probation, including my daughter." Then he softens a bit, observing that Julie is a good people person, which is an essential trait in a service business like airlines.

Julie Gossen, a funny, self-deprecating woman, laughs when she hears the probation comment. It is typical of her father, she says, who can be tough-talking one minute and compassionate the next. But she also admits it can be hard working for such a demanding boss, who happens to be her dad. She is always relieved when he begins his annual summer sojourn on his cabin cruiser. When he is on the ocean, she says, he is, for the only time of the year, truly gone from the business. The rest of the time, he is totally engaged.

Asked if he is still one of Canada's toughest bosses, Rowe says, "I can be very tough when it needs toughness. But you very seldom hear of anyone leaving IMP in management. The toughness is required in a leader when you have a tough problem to solve. You don't do it by committee."

Rowe is the product of a business-oriented family in England—he was the son of a railway manager father and a mother who ran the local general store in the Essex community where he grew up. But instead of heading off for university, young Ken went to sea, joining the British Merchant Navy, where he studied to be a navigator. He rose to become an officer, and for a while entertained thoughts of a sea-going career. But he has been quoted as saying that he noticed that it was the ship owners, not the ship officers, who made the big money. He left the merchant navy to train as a commercial secretary, which was the equivalent of a British professional manager. Employed by the Great Grimsby Coal Salt & Tanning Co. Ltd., then Europe's largest manufacturer of commercial fishing gear, he was sent to Halifax to develop the export market for the firm's equipment. He liked the city and saw an opportunity to get into business for himself. In 1967, he mortgaged his house and bought the assets of a bankrupt foundry. He called his new company Industrial Marine Products and built it into a manufacturer, importer, and distributor of equipment for fishing fleets. Even today, it is the leader in that market, although the sector itself is not growing. Later, he shortened the name to IMP Group as he diversified into aerospace, airlines, hotels, medical supplies, and other areas.

As he built his marine business, he ran into a typical Maritime obstacle, the same that has confronted John Bragg and John Risley. "Down here in the Maritimes, when you are building a business and become successful at it, you run out of market share to acquire," Rowe says. As the marine business hit the point of local saturation, Rowe diversified into aviation and into other parts of the country. He has reaped a lot of success in servicing military aircraft for clients such as the Canadian Forces and the U.S. Navy. He became a master of buying and turning around undervalued public companies, such as Innotech, an aviation service and management company in Montreal. "There is nowhere to go once you have become the dominant person. You've got to get into other things or other areas of the country," he says, pointing to the experience of the Bank of Nova Scotia and the Royal Bank of Canada, which had their roots in Nova Scotia but had to seek growth elsewhere. Today, nearly half of IMP's operations lie outside the Maritimes, although it remains a force in Halifax, employing about 1,000 people at the airport alone. That is where it performs its repair and overhaul business for clients such as the Canadian and U.S. military.

While he built the business across Canada, he maintained the IMP headquarters in Halifax because he likes the lifestyle in his adopted hometown. Although he has eschewed the Maritime Mafia weakness for gargantuan sailboats, he does keep a 42-foot Sea Ray motor yacht. "With the increase in communications, you can manage the company from here," he says. If he were still a hired gun for a British company, he would probably be living in Central Canada and not having nearly as much fun.

But geographical expansion has also landed Rowe in one of his trademark scrapes. In the early 1990s, he was attracted by the opening of Russia to market capitalism. He learned that Aeroflot, the big Russian airline, wanted to build an ultramodern hotel and office building in Moscow, and Rowe, who owned a Holiday Inn in Halifax, stepped forward as its partner. The $100-million hotel, known as the Aerostar, was developed by Aeroimp, a joint venture of the two companies, which leased the building from a state agency.

But the hotel quickly turned into a nightmare. In 1995, the Russian-appointed boss of Aeroimp unilaterally annulled IMP's contract to manage the hotel. IMP accused Aeroflot of trying to squeeze it out of the venture and took its case to an arbitration court in Stockholm. The Canadians won a $22-million settlement but the award was ignored. It was the nonpayment of this award that spurred IMP to impound the Aeroflot airliner at Dorval airport in March 1998.

Over the past decade, IMP has invested $45 million (U.S.) in the Aerostar, but Rowe has had to fight like a tiger to protect his investment. While IMP retained its hand in management, the Russian ownership of the building changed hands as a result of bankruptcy proceedings, putting a murky company called Aviacity in control. In mid-August 2004, Aviacity produced documents saying it owned the building and had IMP managers and 150 guests thrown out of the hotel. Since then, the Moscow prosecutor's office has alleged that a fraudulent bankruptcy gave a small group of conspirators control of the Aerostar and numerous other state-owned assets.

"There's been a criminal investigation into this whole gang in Moscow," Rowe thundered in early 2005, as he pressed his case with the Russian prosecutors to recover the hotel. "The investigators have found firm evidence this was a premeditated bankruptcy." Rowe's contention was that the new owners had taken over the assets using a valuation figure that was a fraction of the real market value. That gap justifies the prosecutor, under Russian law, to return the assets to state ownership, he argued. Meanwhile, in civil courts, IMP had launched a $58-million claim. "We're not just going away as they thought we would. We're trying to fight this," Rowe said, as he lobbied for the support of the Russian public prosecutor. In his view, Canada should be pressing the Aerostar case as a litmus test for any further Western investment in Russia.

But while Rowe's commercial life remains as eventful as ever, he has found some contentment on the philanthropic front. That is partly because of Risley, who has emerged in the past 15 years as a leader in the Halifax fundraising community. Rowe openly admits Risley, in his fiercely single-minded way, arm-twisted his friend into opening up his wallet and his horizons. Rowe had traditionally confined his giving to the health field, such as the Grace Maternity Hospital and its related institution, the IWK Health Centre, where he and his wife Dorothy have sponsored an MRI clinic in their names. The Rowes were also big contributors to the mental health field as patrons of the Nova Scotia mental health foundation. But Risley urged him to open his wallet more and move into educational giving. "I had been more and more involved but he pressured me—John's influence was really putting me toward education and Dalhousie."

For his part, Risley says that "Ken had never really come to grips with the fact that he was worth a lot of money and he really needed to start thinking bigger about his philanthropic horizons and he needed to start making some big gifts." Rowe, he said, had always been very generous with his time, sat on a number of boards and advisory councils, but never saw himself as one who would step forward with the big gifts. When the Dalhousie business building was being planned, Risley pointed out to Rowe that if he came up with a big gift, he would have a sense of pride every time he drove by it. Rowe came up with a $3-million donation toward the building's $25-million cost. "I don't think you can look to the community to support you in your business activities without saying, hey, I owe something back," Risley says. "That's the whole theory of charitable giving."

Also influential in Rowe's transformation was Risley's lending him John D. Rockefeller's 1906 autobiography, *Random Reminiscences of Men and Events*, which had been important in developing Risley's own thinking. For Risley, anyone who wanted to balance his private fortune with public philanthropy should tap into the thinking of the legendary U.S. investor and builder of companies and endowments, such as his $80-million gift to the University of Chicago. Now Rowe is considered one of Dalhousie University's major givers and fundraisers. It's a role he has taken on with some misgivings. Halifax is a small corporate community and inevitably fundraisers keep going back to the same group of friends. "You stretch your personal friendships and associates because you feel your community needs it," he says. He has also been a major contributor to the Pier 21 project in Halifax, which commemorates the Canadian immigrant experience. The Kenneth C. Rowe Heritage Hall provides space for group functions. His daughter Julie says her parents have always given considerable money to good causes but Ken has widened his interests. Instead of just being the target of arm-twisting, he is doing a lot of the twisting. Above all, friends say, Ken Rowe's higher profile as a philanthropist, supports his self-image as a leader in the community.

Another source of satisfaction is the rising role of his family in the business. Julie runs CanJet, although observers say she operates on a very short leash from her father. Indeed, she makes no secret of this: She reports to chief operating office Steve Plummer, but she can count on calls from her father in the evening after work. Ken, on the other hand, insists he is stepping back as the discount airline continues to prove itself. His two accountant sons oversee other key parts of the company: Kirk heads the Innotech operations in Montreal, and Stephen manages commercial operations in Halifax.

Julie, who has a bachelor's degree and an MBA from Saint Mary's, says she concluded very early in life that she would always work in the family business. After all, she says, it made sense to want to work for yourself, instead of somebody else. She spent time in the trenches, labouring as an assistant for Steve Plummer at head office for a while. When "CanJet One," the family's first try at the national airline, got started, she was only peripherally involved. But one day two years ago, Ken took her out to lunch at Tim Hortons—he is famously opposed to expensive lunches—and said, "I've got a job for you." When he explained he wanted her to run "CanJet Two," she was game, but "absolutely overwhelmed" by the tight deadlines. Her team put the airline together in two months, largely because she was able to reassemble the team from the first CanJet, even though a number of key members were working elsewhere. They were drawn back by the challenge and the ability to live in Halifax, which has a huge appeal to Maritimers. It has not always been easy because Gossen is a divorced mother of two teenaged sons, and she is loath to be away from home too long. Her former husband, David, is an executive vice-president for IMP. "No, we didn't fire him [after the divorce]," she says, laughing.

Julie's credible performance creates a happy dilemma for Ken Rowe. He is reticent about discussing the future ownership of the company, conceding only that it is tied up in estate planning. But who will replace him as CEO? He insists it will be the best person for the job, whether he or she is family or not. Chief operating officer Plummer, a 50-year-old former air force brat born in Trenton, Ontario, has worked with him for almost 30 years and is a natural candidate to succeed him, perhaps as a bridge to one of the children.

It would be delicious irony if Ken Rowe, often portrayed as the toughest manager in the Maritimes, eventually installs a woman as his CEO. Female bosses are rare in the Maritime elite, and Julie herself knows of few other women leaders outside the professions. Rowe says Julie's ascendance is always a possibility, because she is a very capable executive and a 20-year corporate veteran, in addition to being the boss's daughter. "She's a contender," he says, but there is a board of trustees that, if he got hit with a truck, would decide how succession would proceed. Meanwhile, Julie, with a disarming candour, makes no bones of the fact that she would like to step up and replace Steve Plummer as COO some days and perhaps ultimately rise to the CEO's job. As for her two brothers, she doesn't know what they want, but she expects they have higher aspirations too.

But family management of IMP is not a sure thing. "It's a family-owned company but it isn't run like one," Ken says, and it starts with the CEO and chairman. He insists he works in the business in much the same style as if he were just a hired gun. "I don't work like an owner," he maintains.

Still, he can no longer be the totally hands-on manager that he was as a younger man. "At over 70—a bit like a boxer—I work smarter. I don't travel as much as I used to. I've got a bunch of senior managers who do a lot of that." He lets Plummer and his division heads do their thing, reporting to him every quarter on operational issues. Meanwhile, he keeps absolutely informed, relying on what he describes as excellent management information systems to find out what is going on, which allows him to "bore down," if necessary, on what he calls "hot spots"—areas of immediate concern or urgent importance. "In other words, when my managers see a lot of me, they should start getting concerned." In recent years, the Moscow hotel upheaval and the startup of CanJet have been the major hot spots that have seized Rowe's attention.

That ability to focus keeps employees on their toes. "He's the type who, when he sees a problem, he is on it, on it, on it, on it, until it gets solved," says Julie. Inside the company, there is an expression that some division of the company is in "ICU—the intensive care unit—when the owner is devoting his highly focused attention to some issue or problem there. It's something that no division manager wants to experience, but Julie shrugs it off as a fact of life. When told that Ken considers CanJet to be out of the ICU now, Julie wryly observes, "In his mind." In reality, she expects the monitoring and the daily phone calls to go on for some time.

In addition, Rowe and the IMP chief financial officer look after the company's large investment portfolio, which is heavily weighted to chartered banks and other financial companies. And, of course, he commandeers the strategic orientation of the company, such as its recent push into the medical supply business across Canada. "When you're younger, you go on the front line," he says, "but when you're the general, you're considered more valuable and don't stay on the front line."

Rowe clearly lives for his business, as well as his regular matches of hyper-competitive tennis. "For release I play tennis all year, I ski, I golf, and I boat," he says, adding that "I can still beat the hell out of the boys on the tennis court." He is bemused by his friend Risley's adventures in conspicuous consumption. "I keep telling John, 'I don't know why you keep buying these houses and boats.' That's his style and he's a very intense guy and that is how he releases himself. If I want a bloody big boat, I just go and rent it. It's a pain for me to keep it."

Still, he speaks of Risley with great affection, as someone who shares his love of the business game. "He's a great fellow for building all those things and wanting those things, and that's fine. It's his money and you can't say he doesn't give to the community.

"I just can't be bothered. Someone asks why don't you have a house down in Florida and I say that's the last thing I want. I just went to a five-star hotel, and it's lovely to be looked after."

Still, he does have four houses around Halifax, including a nice modern Halifax home surrounded by trees and beside the water. He has a summer place at Saint Margaret's Bay, just west of Halifax, which includes a three-bedroom guesthouse. Also, he and a partner are building a new condominium development, and Ken will have the penthouse unit.

And he's not done in the business game. He has plans for IMP to double its revenues in three to five years, rising to a billion dollars in annual sales through a combination of acquisitions and organic growth. He could, for example, buy Vector Aerospace, which would immediately add $300 million to the top line. But Rowe, true to his new ethos, has remained coolly detached about Vector. Someone will certainly buy it, he says, and, if not him, he expects the new owner to pay a handsome price, thus providing a nice win for IMP under either scenario. He is immensely proud that while many of the Maritime Mafia have taken parts of their business public, he owns the largest entirely private company in Nova Scotia, the Halifax equivalent of the Irvings, only much smaller—at least, for now.

He also betrays a certain fascination with George Armoyan, another Risley friend who, like Rowe, has been an outsider and who has a reputation for shrewd dispassionate investments in undervalued stocks. Syrian-born Armoyan, he says with some admiration, "plays at the edge of the envelope, it's his style." But it is no longer the style of IMP, which, he says, has become almost too institutionalized with its systems, controls, and policies. Those were things he didn't have at the beginning, "when you could sort of do what George is doing."

In the beginning, as a younger man, "I used to bet the farm. I don't do that any more. Too many people work for me, whose jobs depend on it, and you can't be cavalier with a company our size. You have to run it like a public company but without all those bells and whistles that are all costs and time without getting any return. Being private suits me and my style of management—we have very little hierarchy."

As for the future, Ken Rowe looks forward to when he and Dorothy can give up their house and "downsize" to the penthouse condo. But his lifestyle will never really change. He will come into the office regularly and do what he likes to do—make money at business. "I'm not a big spender, I enjoy making it and winning in business," he says. And, these days, this self-styled tough guy also gets a kick out of giving it away.

CHAPTER 11

....

CASTING THE NEWFIE NET

FROM HIS OFFICE HIGH up on Harvey Road in St. John's, Mark Dobbin can watch the whales frolicking in the blue Atlantic just beyond the Narrows, the sliver of a channel connecting the ancient harbour with the ocean. It is a $3.5-million view, the kind that the Dobbin family fortune can easily afford in this city that sits on the edge of Canada. This is where Mark, 45, invests some of the dollars amassed over the past three decades by his bumptious, larger-than-life father, Craig, the world's major commercial helicopter entrepreneur. In St. John's, a huge private fortune like the Dobbins' stands out like the tower that looms over the Narrows up on Signal Hill.

The Dobbins are the Irvings and McCains of Newfoundland, all wrapped into one sprawling Irish-Newfoundland clan, whose various members have become leaders in the wave of post-Confederation entrepreneurs—which in Newfoundland's case, means after 1949. Craig Dobbin, now 70, has been brutally exposed to the challenges of life here: He survived several near-bankruptcies, an almost fatal chopper crash, and a brush with death from lung disease to build a rare global company out of the thin soil of the Rock. The size of his fortune makes "Danny Millions"—a.k.a. Premier Danny

Williams—look like a piker, notwithstanding the $230 million or so Williams got when he sold his cable TV empire to Ted Rogers of Toronto to launch his political career.

The Dobbin empire is in transition: Craig has officially left the city, moving his major company, CHC Helicopters, across the country to Vancouver, and has sold off his big St. John's apartment portfolio. He has homes in Vancouver and Florida but no longer in St. John's. But the Dobbin influence hangs over this city like a dense pea-soup fog: his brothers Derm and Basil, among Craig's ten siblings, own a lot of real estate in the city; his nephew Brian is a major resort developer on the west coast around Corner Brook; even Craig still owns lots of undeveloped land, some fishing lodges, and part of a Junior A hockey team with brother Derm. All of Craig's five children live here, and Mark continues to expand the family profile as a private equity investor. His new enterprise, Killick Capital, was already creating a stir by buying up shares in Vector Aerospace, a company that had once fallen under the Dobbin umbrella but had been wrested away by non-islanders.

Craig Dobbin is not particular about where he makes his money. He always felt the need to move beyond Newfoundland's small market, but he will never emotionally leave the island. "You know what they say, 'The savage loves his native shore,'" says Craig on the phone from Oxford, England, where he has jetted in for a weekend to visit friends.

But what happens after Craig? Where is the new Newfie money? There are some nice dollars being made in providing oil services to the big offshore projects (although it is the multinational oil companies that rake in the big bucks), there is mineral exploration, and there are still some fisheries magnates, despite the emaciation of the cod stocks. But the breed of entrepreneur who strikes it rich in the wider world, who builds large global concerns, is noticeably absent here. "Unlike Nova Scotia, Newfoundland doesn't have that big powerhouse league because we haven't created the super-entrepreneurs. There was no big, big money made, maybe except for the Dobbins," laments Derrick Rowe, who co-founded satellite services company Stratos Global, Newfoundland's one high-tech comet, who became a millionaire but admits he falls short of the titan league. He now finds himself labouring to save FPI, a company whose potential has been hamstrung by its role as a social safety net and a political football—and more recently by the emerging competitive threat of China. "We had our little run with Stratos, but that money kind of got dissipated," Rowe says sadly, "and then there was no big one to follow."

The "big one" may not be evident, but not for lack of trying by the entrepreneurs who grapple with life on the Rock, an isolated island of a half-million people, separated from the mainland of Canada by the Gulf of St. Lawrence and a bigger gulf of misunderstanding. Newfoundland is of course not the Maritimes—it has an entirely separate history extending up to 1949, when it entered Confederation, an event still as contentious today as it was 56 years ago. Its tumultuous relationship with Canada has been fuelled by Upper Canadian condescension, Newfoundland insecurity, and the residue of one-sided resources and power deals. The resentments and anger boiled over in 2004 with the battle between Danny Williams and Paul Martin over offshore oil revenue. This chasm is reflected in the business class, which sees itself as quite distinct from that of Central Canada, or even Halifax. Indeed, business in Newfoundland is a kind of extreme sport. Entrepreneurs here seem edgier and crazier than those in any other part of Canada, perhaps reflecting the monstrous difficulties of actually striking it rich in a place where the population is small, capital is hard to raise, taxes are high, and travel to anywhere else is an extremely long distance. As in "New York, New York," if you can make it here, you can make it anywhere—if you can find the financing. "You have to be tougher in Newfoundland," says John Crosbie, the former federal finance minister and a Newfoundland political icon. "The fact we have no Irvings or Sobeys indicates how tough it is. Business people are just as capable here but it's not possible to be of any size."

"We are at war," says Rod White, the cerebral high-tech iconoclast who helped build Stratos Global with Derrick Rowe and is now the éminence grise of a small tech company called Consilient Technologies. He says the immense challenges facing Newfoundlanders, as far as attracting capital and being taken seriously by the rest of Canada, create a warrior mentality in many of its business people but also a tremendous drive to find creative solutions. "If you travel or read, you do feel under an additional stress or inferiority complex in Newfoundland. Anyone with any go is just going to go harder. I feel extra motivation—anyone with entrepreneurial feeling does."

So it is not surprising that Newfoundland has spawned Danny Williams, a Rhodes scholar, successful lawyer, and truculent hard bargainer, who is determined not to give an inch to the mainland sharpies, whether it is Paul Martin or the Bay Street crowd. "I am a tough negotiator," Williams told *Globe and Mail* columnist Roy MacGregor in the middle of the offshore revenue row. "Just ask Ted Rogers." Indeed, Rogers's first offer for Williams's cable company, Cable Atlantic, came in at $90 million, but ended up at $230 million.

"We're emotional in Newfoundland," says John Steele, son of the legendary entrepreneur Harry Steele and president of the family's extensive broadcasting interests on the island.

"If we love you, you can do no wrong; if we hate you, you can do no right." He adds that business is extremely informal because it is such a lightly populated place. "If you don't know someone directly, you know loads of people who know that guy, so you have a good sense of pretty well everybody." And business and politics here are tightly intertwined.

Newfoundland has in fact generated several big waves of wealth and capital investment. First were the merchant families, many of them English, who built fortunes as middlemen in the fishing industry, serving as suppliers and customers for the strongly Irish-settled outports. These trading families give rise to the so-called Water Street Merchants—the derisive label attached by Joey Smallwood—names like the Ayres, Crosbies, Collingwoods, Lundrigans, and Hickmans, some of whom are still powerful in the St. John's economy. But many have faded. John Crosbie, the former cabinet minister, puts it frankly: His late brother Andrew "came a cropper" in the 1980s, sinking under heavy debt. Andrew's sons, while doing well, are relatively small players compared with the former Crosbie glory days.

Since World War II, another wave of entrepreneurs has emerged to thrive off the province's development in energy, transportation, and forestry. The leader is Dobbin, but the other key players include Ches Penney, a powerful but little-known titan owning a bundle of companies with $600 million in annual sales, and Harry Steele, whose interests have spanned hotels, newspapers, radio stations, car dealerships, and airlines but who now bases his empire in Dartmouth, Nova Scotia. His heart is still in Newfoundland, though, and the Steele holdings include radio station VOCM, a veritable daily town-hall meeting of the province, most of whose citizens seem to be calling in daily to its live on-air programs. "We're all political junkies here," John Steele explains. This post–war era produced perhaps the wildest, most innovative Newfie entrepreneur—a charismatic oddball named Geoff Stirling, who owns NTV, an eccentric local TV outlet. Now 84, this former anti-Confederation activist dabbles in movie-making and reincarnation theory. "I am whole, I am perfect, I am unlimited," he told *Report on Business* magazine.

Now, a new entrepreneurial wave is emerging, which might be called Danny and the Juniors—younger players who have made their money in cable, technology, and oilfield services. Other members of this group include Danny's partner and friend, Dean MacDonald, now president of the cable company Persona; Brendan Paddick, another former cable czar who works with John Risley in the Caribbean; Derrick Rowe, Rod White, and Trevor Adey, all of whose roots are in Stratos Global; and Mark Dobbin himself, who has had a career in and out of his father's aerospace interests. The newest member is 31-year-old Chris Griffiths, who owns Garrison Guitars, a four-year-old company that makes acoustic guitars. Garrison has just turned the corner into profitability—thanks to a large investment from John Risley, whose reach knows no bounds.

There is still money being made from the fishing business, some very serious wealth—for example, the Barry family of Corner Brook has been involved in fishing for 100 years. The leader of the current generation, Bill Barry, another sometime partner of John Risley, is controversial and outspoken. Other major players include the Quinlan family and the Daley brothers, who are also no strangers to controversy.

But St. John's is where it is happening in Newfoundland, and the economy has been on a tear. According to many St. John's people, the real catalyst is not the vast Hibernia energy field, but the cultural scene, a blend of music, drama, and the irrepressible Newfoundland comedy, led by such national television stars as Mary Walsh, Rick Mercer, and Cathy Jones.

"We're a resource-based province but our biggest resource is actually our culture," says Dean MacDonald, the cable TV president. In MacDonald's view, arts and culture are driving a lot of the economic development in St. John's but are now starting to have their impact in rural communities, where the depopulation of young people has reached crisis proportions.

It could be called the Great Big Sea Economy, based on the popular roots band whose members still live in the Avalon Peninsula. It finds its strongest expression in the tourist-packed bars on George Street in St. John's, places like O'Reilly's, the Fat Cat, and around the corner on Water Street, the Rose and Thistle and Erin's Pub. There is great irony in that Great Big Sea is such a source of riches, while the real great big sea is such a source of worry, with vulnerable fish stocks, imperilled jobs and communities, and a looming threat from China. But where else in North America is there a viable music industry built on a population of 513,000 people?

Newfoundland is truly different, with its outsize problems—capital access, size of market, population, and distance—but also its innate resourcefulness. To make it in rural Newfoundland, you have to be shrewd and flexible, which applies to Ches Penney, 74, who since the 1960s has spun out a classic Newfoundland conglomerate. To make it big in Newfoundland, you can't be in just one thing, the province just isn't big enough; you have to be involved in a bunch of activities, and Penney owns assets in construction, concrete, car dealerships, tanker ships, fish plants, real estate, and a host of other endeavours. He is a partner in about 50 companies on the Rock.

Penney comes from Carbonear, a small community made famous by Margaret Wente's take on Danny Williams in the *Globe and Mail*. In a column that enraged Newfoundlanders, she questioned "why it's a good idea to keep picking the pockets of Chinese dry cleaners and Korean variety store owners [in Scarborough, Ontario] in order to keep subsidizing the people who live in Carbonear, no matter how quaint or picturesque they are." That brings a smile to the ruddy, tanned face of Ches Penney, who is neither quaint nor picturesque nor a deadbeat. His father owned a small service station in Carbonear and Ches, after high school, went to work in the bank. He liked the work and rose to branch manager, becoming in his mid-30s the youngest Bank of Commerce manager in the country. But he resented the cheap salary, figuring he was making about the same as a lowly labourer at the local paper mill in Grand Falls, where he lived. So he quit and went into the retail auto parts business and then added a supermarket, which he then sold to an expansionary Frank Sobey.

He used the Sobey proceeds to bail out his struggling construction business, but in 1969–70 he lost everything to bankruptcy. He realizes now that he was too much of a party animal to pay close attention to his business. He came out of that period at the age of 38 with seven children to feed and no company. He watched bitterly as Lundrigans, a construction company controlled by one of the oldest Newfoundland families, bought up his assets. He was determined it would never happen again. "Fear can be a tremendous motivator," he says.

He focused his attention, managed to buy back some of his equipment, and built up the construction business, helping to pave the province's roads. He moved into oil tankers and car dealerships, often in partnership with someone else. Then 25 years after going bust, he achieved a measure of satisfaction when he acquired many of the assets of Lundrigans when that company cratered. In his office, prominently displayed on the wall, is a framed picture of a road construction site that he took from among the assets in the Lundrigans office. "Look at it, that's my crusher," he says, pointing to a piece of equipment featured prominently in the photo. It's a reminder of how far he fell and how far he came back, and of the hubris that comes with the proudest of corporate empires. "The point is that I went bust and they were the heroes. Then 25 years later, they went bust too." Construction, he concludes, can be a rough game.

His answer has been continuing diversification outside construction and increasingly outside Newfoundland. "In Newfoundland, the work is not here and you can't create it," he says. He has ready-mix concrete in Nova Scotia, a fish plant in Prince Edward Island, and a new joint venture with an Alberta company to build trenches for pipelines. He has also been a busy investor, including a stake in Consilient, the high-tech company run by Trevor Adey and Rod White. In all cases, he has been comfortable being in partnership with other people, including some of his ten children, who work with him at the car dealerships. He has teamed up with a Norwegian company, J.J. Ugland, in providing tankers to carry crude oil from the big rigs on the Hibernia and Terra Nova oilfields off the Newfoundland coast. Now in his later years, he is content that he has truly recovered from the trauma of bankruptcy. In early 2005, the kid who went to Memorial University for just a term out of high school was given an honorary degree by the university.

But in Penney's eyes, he is a bush leaguer compared with what Craig Dobbin has done, building a global helicopter business out of St. John's. Indeed, Dobbin built much of his fortune outside Newfoundland, overcoming the limitations of his home market with sheer ambition, personality, and bluster. "It was a parochial society in Newfoundland, and there was no market there. I had to move," he says. The descendant of Irish immigrants who came to St. John's in the 1750s,

Craig's father was a manager for the Harvey family's lumberyard, and he had to struggle to feed his six sons and five daughters. As a young man, Craig got work as a professional diver, then branched into house-building, making money through the time-honoured pattern of erecting a house, living in it, then selling it quickly and moving on before it was finished. In his first two years of marriage, he and his first wife lived in 13 places. The children remember going to bed by climbing ladders in half-finished homes that were about to be sold under their feet.

He took his act to Ottawa and Montreal, where he built houses, but also developed a business in erecting free-standing department stores for Kmart around Canada and into the United States. He made enough money to head back to St. John's in the mid-1970s, where he befriended Frank Moores, the Conservative premier of Newfoundland and a golfing enthusiast like Dobbin. Moores got into salmon fishing, and he hooked Dobbin on that hobby too. "I fell in love with it," he says. The two men would take off for Newfoundland's and Labrador's isolated salmon pools in government helicopters. But Dobbin's work schedule was keeping him in St. John's a lot, so in 1976, he bought his own chopper so he could fish whenever he wanted. The sociable Dobbin admits he never learned to drive one: You can't be a pilot and entertain guests at the same time. He soon found that a helicopter is a very expensive toy, so he went into the charter business, buying several machines. That business, called Sealand Helicopters, was the beginning of CHC. Soon he was running seven or eight commercial helicopters, the origins of what became a $600-million business. The offshore energy scene was starting to rumble, and he was able to capitalize with a fleet of modern choppers.

But his darkest moment came in August 1979, when he was touring out in Clarenville, Newfoundland, with a couple of his bankers and the president of Memorial University. As the pilot ascended into flight, suddenly the engine power died and he started the emergency auto-rotation process. But the machine approached some power transmission lines, and the pilot had to abort the flight to avoid the lines. The chopper spun down into some trees in an isolated wilderness. The pilot and Dobbin's bank manager were killed. The others were badly hurt and Dobbin, his sternum crushed and his face torn, was the only one who was mobile. He climbed out of the wreckage, took off his shirt to wipe the blood from his head, and stumbled a couple of kilometres till he encountered a railway track. He had the presence of mind to drag a log onto the track to mark his access point, and began to stagger up the line. After walking a distance, he began to hear chainsaws, and encountered a team of loggers. Using Dobbin's marker, the loggers were able to retrace his steps back to the crash site and helped the survivors make it to hospital.

Dobbin insists the near-death experience had no impact on his zest for helicopters. Within a week of getting out of hospital he took a chopper ride with his brother Pat, a doctor, and the pilot went through a number of stunts just to test Craig's nerve. He passed that test. Still, his son Mark, who was 19 at the time of the crash, says his father considered exiting the still young and still pioneering helicopter business. "He was worried about being in a business that would be killing people over time." But Craig snapped out of his angst with a stronger dedication to safety. "It haunted him," Mark says, "until he decided not to sell it but to take it to a more professional level." The crash was later determined to be the result of a mechanical defect.

Through the 1980s and 1990s, he built the company into a force in the offshore helicopter services. He survived the vicious cyclical nature of the business, which rode the peaks and valleys of the resources industry. In 1986, he bought a

Toronto company that diversified his reach into air ambulance services. He waged price wars with other Canadian chopper services, until he consolidated a large part of the Canadian industry with the takeover of rival companies, including arch rival Okanagan Helicopters, which resulted in the new merged entity, called CHC, going public in the late 1980s. All the time, he was supported by the Bank of Nova Scotia with its Maritimes-rooted executives, such as Cedric Ritchie and Peter Godsoe.

While CHC has its roots on the Rock, it did not confine itself to the growing oil services work spurred by discoveries at Hibernia and other fields. In the 1990s, it built a large repair and overhaul business, and pushed out onto the international stage, buying companies in Britain, Norway, Holland, and South Africa. Son Mark joined the business as a globe-trotting salesman and brought his Colombian-born wife back to St. John's.

When he bought the British company, it gave Dobbin entry into the rich European and North Sea energy market. To own a European chopper licence, he had to carry a European Union passport, which he was able to accomplish by obtaining honorary Irish citizenship—the work of his good friend, then Canada's ambassador in Dublin, Mike Wadsworth. One of the costs of citizenship was a chair in Canadian Studies, which Dobbin funded at the University of Dublin. "They gave me a passport and a university degree," he says. "It was the best million pounds we ever spent. We made the company on the back of that."

Dobbin says the company really started to come together when he bought Helicopter Services Group of Norway. He credits CEO Peter Godsoe of the Bank of Nova Scotia for going out on a limb and lending him $750 million. "I want to tell you, he was on the end of the diving board when he did that, but he's got big shoulders and he put faith in me and we repaid it."

But by the mid-1990s Craig Dobbin was a very sick man, who was having trouble breathing. He was diagnosed with idiopathic pulmonary fibrosis, a degenerative disease, often with genetic origins, that scars the lining of the lungs and eventually proves fatal. The only cure, he found, was a lung transplant, and lungs were in short supply and heavy demand. As well, not all hospitals would perform the procedure for someone in his early 60s. Dobbin figured he had little time, and he and his second wife, Elaine—his first marriage ended in 1987—planned his transplant strategy. He would set himself up in a geographically central place, from which he could easily reach as many of the U.S. transplant hospitals as possible. He chose Birmingham, Alabama, and put himself on the waiting list in 16 hospitals, all of which he could reach by air within two hours—the minimum for status as a preferred "local patient." Equipped with a leased Gulfstream jet and a team of pilots, he rented two little houses near the Bessemer airfield in Birmingham, one for himself (at $3,500 a month) and one for his rotation of four pilots. And he and Elaine waited.

At one point, in 1997, he was permitted to fly out to his vacation house in Florida, where he got a pager message from Alabama that there was a lung available. He and Elaine prepared to rush to the hospital, only to discover it was a false alarm. A crestfallen Dobbin drank the good part of a bottle of whiskey that night and was feeling no pain at 4 a.m. when the call came on the red telephone: There was a lung in Philadelphia. "I had to get my half-drunk ass out of bed and we got up there in time and I got a transplant after eight to nine hours," he says. "I said to the nurse, 'I've had a few drinks, is that okay?' And she said, 'We don't do sobriety tests around here.'"

The lung transplant took very well, and Dobbin, then 62, was back in business in no time. "I was just off the ventilator and was on the phone calling to see what had happened to the stock," he recalls. "I'm not ready for the Boston Marathon, but I'm okay." His son Mark says the family thought Craig would slow down and smell the roses, but instead, "he took a second kick at the can. He created more value after the transplant than before." He went back to his work and his hobbies, including his regular mid-June jaunts to the best salmon fishing streams in eastern North America. He brings along a varied bunch of fishing pals, including David Sobey, Harry Steele, and the former president of the United States, George Bush Sr., who fell and almost drowned as a guest of Dobbin in the early 90s. Friends who travel with him to northern Quebec marvel at how Dobbin jumps out of the sack early in the morning and plunges into a nearby ice-cold stream, wearing just undershorts, to try to catch a couple before breakfast. "It's tough at first but you feel invigorated when it is over," he chortles.

But like many entrepreneurs, Dobbin ran the company pretty much the way he wanted, without much regard for the niceties of corporate governance. Over the years, CHC delivered good returns for investors but also rewarded the Dobbin family with healthy compensation and paid millions of dollars to companies controlled by the family for office rent, hangar construction, and helicopter repairs and loans. The CHC board had become a cozy club for Craig, family members, and friends. The new post–Enron era, though, ushered in new stock exchange guidelines that, in turn, prompted CHC to overhaul its board. A *Globe and Mail* article in early 2005 written by Jacquie McNish and Janet McFarland reported that the family deals were being phased out, because, new director Jack Mintz said, Craig and the new independent

directors understood that investors were increasingly intoler-
ant of transactions between the company and related parties.

Craig Dobbin says he is now a convert to the new corporate governance spirit, and he has been changing the company
in other ways too. He had built a network of international
country units, each with its own overhead and infrastructure. In 2004, he decided to consolidate the operations,
cutting jobs in many of the units and centralizing operations
under a single headquarters. That one place is not St. John's
but Vancouver, a city that Dobbin had come to love and was
already the home of his international operations. So he
closed the St. John's head office, with the loss of about 20
jobs, and moved it across the country. It seemed to be a grievous psychological blow to the city that spawned Dobbin and
CHC, but it was surprisingly uncontroversial. For one thing,
it got lost in the uproar over Paul Martin's alleged treachery
on offshore oil revenues. Also, Newfoundlanders accepted
Dobbin's rationalization that he had to do this for efficiency
reasons, and they were used to the fact that CHC was a
global business with a St. John's address. It is a sign of
Newfoundland's sophistication that not much was made of
the move. Besides, there was little evidence that the Dobbin
family had turned its back on St. John's: The names of Mark,
Brian, Basil, and Derm Dobbin were in the local newspaper
all the time.

As for Craig, he insists he is not done yet. He gave up the
CEO's job in late 2004, handing it over to his long-time operational boss, Sylvain Allard. As executive chairman, Craig
was free to roam the world looking for a takeover that would
launch CHC into a new line of business. "I'm the entrepreneur, not the operating guy," he explained to me. The
company, now trading on the New York and Toronto stock
exchanges, had just hit $1 billion in market capitalization,

and "I want to make it a $2-billion and a $3-billion and a $4-billion company. So I'm leaving the operations. Not totally—I am still the largest shareholder and executive chairman and I'll be carrying on getting my daily reports on what is happening in the company. But my main thrust is I'm out looking for a deal."

WHEN DERRICK ROWE talks about Craig Dobbin, it is with a mixture of admiration and sadness. Like Dobbin, Rowe, a lanky red-haired bundle of extroverted energy, embodies the entrepreneurial moxie and the business challenges of Newfoundland. Rowe was a high-tech entrepreneur who built a fine company, a global leader, just like Craig Dobbin, but that company—Stratos Global—didn't make him incredibly wealthy, and he eventually left the company with regret at what might have been. Through a twist of fate, he has found himself running an ailing fish company that represents the very heart and soul of this island. He has, in a sense, done the entrepreneurial thing in reverse—from high tech back to primary resources and processing.

Long before he was running FPI, Rowe was a young kid playing guitar in a St. John's rock and roll band and trying to decide what to do in life. After a couple of years at Memorial University and a technical course at a local college, he wandered into a job with a small company doing communications work on the offshore oil rigs. There he met up with a bright young Memorial physics grad named Rod White, who had been working for a local phone company, and they made an important observation that would change their lives. "Really, the opportunity became obvious," Rowe recalls. "There were a lot of people working offshore who couldn't make phone calls. A really simple concept: If I wanted to make phone calls from an oil rig, there was no mechanism to do it."

He and White started a company to provide radio services linking the oil rigs to the mainland, with Rowe as the customer man, and White as the technical guy. "We just had confidence, no fear, and we became good at what we were doing. We put $500 each into this, and just did it." It was rough for a while and Rowe had to depend on his mother for decent meals, and he sold off his beloved guitars. But the company grew.

White says the partners soon discovered that Teleglobe, the former Crown corporation that held Canada's membership on the Immersat satellite consortium, was letting a lot of money fall off the table by employing foreign systems and not using Canadian companies. "We just started our mission—that we had to get hold of this revenue," Rowe recalls. That set off a series of acquisitions and partnerships that culminated in a deal whereby Stratos Global wrested the Immersat signatory status away from Teleglobe, while Teleglobe got Stratos shares. Today, Stratos is the largest Immersat member company in the world.

Rowe sees something noble in what he and White built, a real rags-to-riches story. It's not in the model of Danny Williams, a lawyer who struck it rich in the cable game, which is basically a monopoly bestowed by the government. Rowe agrees that Williams was very smart on the cable business, was very astute in selling his unit for big money, and has proved a tough negotiator. But that's different than starting a business where he had to sell his beloved guitars and cadge dinners off his mum. Rowe doubts that Williams ever faced a situation like he did in 1994 when he learned he was a finalist in the Ernst & Young Entrepreneur of the Year award in Halifax. He was in Washington at the time and told organizers that he couldn't justify leaving the job he was doing unless he knew he was the winner. "Well, I don't want to be disrespectful," he said, "but I'm in a lot of shit down here, a lot of problems." The organizers hinted broadly that he probably would find it worthwhile to head up to Halifax for the awards dinner. He got to the Halifax hotel with a rumpled suit and a shirt that had been worn for several days, and everyone was decked out in black tie. He went into the hotel sauna, took off all his clothes, and hung them up, as a startled hotel guest looked on. "I threw some water in the rocks and got some steam, put the clothes back on and went off, and the other fellow must have been thinking, 'Jesus, who is this guy?'" He won the award.

Rowe also faced the traditional Newfoundland problem of lack of access to capital. "We did pretty well, but our biggest problem—it's unbelievable—our interest kept being diluted because capital here is very expensive. I once sold 30 per cent of the company for $500,000. I became a millionaire, very wealthy in Newfoundland, but if I had done it anywhere else it would have become hundreds of millions. That's why you don't get the big hits here."

Rowe is very thankful to the local entrepreneurs who forked out venture capital to keep his company growing. A lot of those people too made more than a million dollars with very modest investments. Rod White left fairly early, having made some money and seen the company grow beyond his comfort. Soon, Rowe too was ready to make an exit. He was 24 when he started, and 38 when he got out. The company had simply gone through too many amalgamations and ownership got diluted too many times for him to keep control.

Today, Stratos focuses on the global market, and its operational headquarters is in Bethesda, Maryland, which is close to the headquarters of the U.S. communications establishment. That's fine, says Rowe, because you have to be where your customers are. It still maintains a back office staff in St. John's. But Stratos was, in a way, a lost opportunity. It did not spin off big money for Newfoundland or a high-tech industry, although both Derrick Rowe and Rod White remain active in the St. John's business world with two very different ventures.

Having left Stratos, Rowe played the role of high-tech investor himself. He got whipsawed in the dot-com bubble and lost some money in an on-line music venture. In 2003, he was approached by John Risley, a man he scarcely knew, to become CEO of FPI, in which Risley was the largest share-holder. It was an odd choice for a tech guy but he figured, why not? Here was a chance to build something important in the province's most storied industry. Then Rowe got caught in the buzz saw of Newfoundland politics, snared in the middle of the controversy over the proposed merger of FPI with Risley's company, Clearwater. Newfoundlanders were up in arms when they discovered that the game plan included a rationalization of the fishery. They felt betrayed, and the government nixed the deal, using an amendment to legislation governing the former Crown corporation. His opponents had the lines down pat, Rowe smiles bitterly. "It was 'Close the loophole, get rid of the asshole.' And 'I see Derrick Rowe's lips move and John Risley's words coming out,' and they swore they would have my head and his head on a stake."

It was a signal to Rowe that government interference was going to be a constant reality in this company, and he has had to live with that. The defeat of the Clearwater deal has not halted the harsh economics of the fishery industry, which has forced FPI to continue closing plants in small communities. Each time, there was the inevitable uproar and talks with the government. When FPI decided to make an income trust out of its U.S. division, it set off another round of talks. In early 2005, Rowe was a tired, frustrated, and angry man.

He had some hope that a business-oriented premier might show some support, perhaps by calling a free legislative vote on the status of FPI. Meanwhile, there is a slow attrition of fishing plants, and no more hope of a quick solution.

"This is a prime example of why we don't have more success," Rowe says, explaining that he came to the company with the dream that he could make it a bigger success than Stratos ever was. "We started with the best assets of the business, and this should be a three- or four-billion-dollar company, the dominant player in the world." But it isn't happening because of government interference, he says, adding that "treading water is a slow way to drown." FPI, he says, is "the saddest business story in Newfoundland," instead of what it should be—one of the most exciting business stories.

Rowe at the time was facing a huge backlash from FPI's closing of a fish plant in Harbour Breton, which once employed about 350 people in a village with 2,000 people. The controversy over Harbour Breton created one of the saddest spectacles in Newfoundland's corporate history, the image of FPI slinking away to Toronto to hold its 2005 annual meeting in a lawyer's office, rather than face the fury of unemployed fish plant workers protesting in St. John's. "We didn't want to have a riot," Rowe said, explaining the move. It was not the way Derrick Rowe dreamed his business career would unfold.

THERE IS ANOTHER LEGACY of Stratos Global, and it can be found in an office building in a St. John's suburb, not far from Derrick Rowe's FPI headquarters. That is where you will find Rowe's old partner, Rod White, working with 50 software engineers in a start-up called Consilient Technologies. While Rowe is voluble and expansive, White is a distant man, a wiry coil of intellectual ferment. He left Stratos earlier in the growth process, went back to university, and pursued a PhD in philosophy and lives in a big house out by the sea. He also teamed up with a younger colleague at Stratos named Trevor Adey, who was a talented salesman. The company is a developer of software for wireless communications devices, including the ubiquitous Blackberry.

White and Adey come with a desire to avoid all the mistakes of Stratos, and indeed of past Newfoundland ventures. They carry a powerful strain of Newfoundland nationalism, insisting that their business destiny has been blunted by Confederation, which made it too easy for Newfoundlanders to pursue their dreams elsewhere. White explains that he was conceived as a Newfoundlander, but born a Canadian, right after Confederation in April 1949. "It's really been the story of my life," he says. Now, to build Consilient, he and Adey say they have had to look outside Canada, to Silicon Valley, an area they see as more generous to Newfoundlanders than the canyons of Bay Street.

I met them in St. John's, during the fever pitch of anger and anticipation that, in January 2005, had built up around Danny Williams's brinkmanship with Paul Martin, a time of disappearing Canadian flags and Margaret Wente columns. On that snowy day, Adey and White were angry men who shared the typical Newfoundlander's deep resentments at the island's lot in Confederation, where they are portrayed variously as village idiots, welfare bums, or the quaint simple folk. Even business people, normally rational and deliberate, have an emotional response to the stereotypes they encounter.

Adey still gets mad recalling when he was 15, competing in the Canada Games as a racquetball player in Chicoutimi, Quebec. In the opening ceremonies, televised on CBC, the Newfoundlanders were suddenly pulled out of the parade.

There wasn't enough time in the broadcast to show all the provincial teams, so Newfoundland was the province selected not to walk around. "I mean, that is how we are looked at by rest of the country."

It's a dismissive attitude, which he says he still encounters when he goes to a business meeting in Toronto. Someone immediately tells a story about the music on George Street or how nice Newfoundlanders are, and the talk diverges from the business issues that brought Adey there. Yet whenever he goes to meetings on Sand Hill Road in Silicon Valley, where the venture capitalists hang out, he never faces that condescension. "Why waste my time dealing with that stereotype when I can go to other parts of the world and not deal with it?" White says it wouldn't be so bad to be dismissed as a unique and funny little island if the economy were performing better. But when the economy is a constant struggle, he does not find much joy in the quaintness—however many tourist dollars it might bring to the island.

For high-tech entrepreneurs in Newfoundland, it is an uphill battle. They can recruit good people trained at a fine university, and these recruits want to stay in the province. But the problem is the lack of a critical mass of other companies with people who have experience in product development, and marketing around the world. For St. John's to leverage its people and their knowledge, it has to create a cluster in the technology industry of the kind it has nurtured in its music and cultural scene with Great Big Sea, Figgy Duff, Mary Pratt, George Street, and Ron Hynes. Ironically, the very enterprise that Adey and White find so demeaning—the mass-marketing of Newfoundland's quaint culture—contains the lessons for where they have to go.

Actually, the two men are optimistic: They have obtained seed capital from local Old Economy entrepreneurs, such as

Ches Penny and Chris Collingwood, the descendant of an old merchant family. Now, the province is eager to kick-start a labour-sponsored venture capital fund. Will Consilent be the "new big thing" in St. John's, the spiritual successor to CHC Helicopters and the progenitor of a new wave of technology start-ups? Or just the next chapter in a long volume of promise and perish?

CHAPTER 12

BEER AND CHOCOLATE

NEW BRUNSWICK IS the hardest province on your waistline, a danger zone for Atkins aficionados and South Beach zealots. Start with the world's biggest french fry maker, McCain Foods in Florenceville, and the fourth-biggest fry maker in North America, the Irvings' Cavendish Farms. Move on to Pizza Delight in Moncton, where Bernard Imbeault and his franchisees have built a quarter-billion-dollar fast food business in Canada. Then wash it all down with beer from the Oland family's Moosehead Breweries in Saint John, the second-largest Canadian-owned independent brewery. Then top it all off with rich chocolate confections from 130-year-old Ganong Brothers in St. Stephen, which has added the manufacture of the Laura Secord brand to its sweet arsenal. There goes the diet.

New Brunswick is the home of the independent family food business, a rare cluster of family companies that survive in a tough global industry. These companies come out of the province's Old Economy past, its rich trove of family companies, and a legacy in agriculture and food processing. Add to that a proclivity for treating the nearby U.S. market as part of its home market, an even more natural place to sell and succeed than Central Canada. Each of the players is at a critical point, where the entrepreneur is thinking about moving on, and the children must decide to pony up or take off.

IT'S TEN O'CLOCK IN THE MORNING at Moosehead Breweries, and a team of workers is hoisting a new fermenting tank, with the help of a truck from the neighbouring Irving pulp and paper mill in Saint John. Derek Oland looks on with the keen pleasure of a man who appreciates the little things that make his brewery succeed when other Canadian-owned counterparts are under attack. Oland is a survivor in a consolidating global industry. Molson Brewery, a giant competitor based in Montreal, is now morphing into Molson Coors, the product of a merger with U.S. giant Coors of Golden, Colorado. The other half of Canadian beer's Big Two, Labatt's, a company whose history is intertwined with Moosehead's, is now owned by InBev, the world's largest brewer, which is based in Belgium. Among the surviving independents, there is Sleeman Breweries, a publicly traded family company in Ontario, and Moosehead, which enjoys a strong regional market, a growing contract-beer operation, and a cult following across North America. A recent *Jeopardy* question asked: What Canadian beer comes out of the city of Saint John? The TV panel didn't get it but many U.S. beer drinkers would. If they didn't know Moosehead, a favourite brew among discerning U.S. barflies, they would know the names of other beers brewed there: Moosehead has contracts with British food and beverage giant Diageo to brew the Irish lager Harp and Guinness stout for the U.S. market, and makes Carlsberg products for Canada.

Parts of the Moosehead brewery in Saint John are more than 100 years old, but they have been folded into successive stages of expansion to create an ultra-modern brewing machine.

It includes a nifty packaging unit that employs robots to pass around cases of beer like little toys in their mechanical hands, and a super-fast assembly line in which bottles march through like hyperkinetic soldiers.

Overseeing it all is Derek, 65, the fifth generation of beer makers in his family. In the Maritimes, Oland is synonymous with beer, and Derek's family branch is just one strain of this tumultuous, often-divided clan of booze makers. Derek is not the rough-and-ready beer guy you might expect, but a tweedy, thoughtful, gentle man with a neat speckled beard and the look of some Ivy League professor. For the past decade, he has been chairman of the company, having stepped back from day-to-day operations, handing it over to president Bruce McCubbin, a professional manager with a long pedigree in consumer products. He admits that McCubbin's presence has turned around the company, which in the final years of his presidency had been drifting under his operational oversight. Now, Oland keeps an eye on strategy and future leadership, which means grooming the next generation, his two older sons, Andrew and Patrick, both in their late 30s and employed in the company. "I am chair and Bruce is president and runs the company day to day," Derek explains. "We're talking a lot all the time; my thinking is more long term but also my interest is developing and ensuring future leadership."

If Derek is professorial, he is no less competitive. He likes where his $130-million company is sitting. "I don't want to be the biggest, I just want to be around for a long time, and hand it on to the next generation in better shape." He is dismissive of the strategy of rival Sleeman, led by another family brewing scion John Sleeman, who has gone the public-offering route and amassed considerable debt to buy up a number of smaller breweries. "Sleeman has grown but look at the debt he accumulated, with the little wee facilities he is buying." Although Sleeman has passed him in dollar sales, he is running just behind the Ontario brewery in beer volume because of Moosehead's contracts for Harp, Guinness, and Carlsberg.

Like the Sleeman name, the Oland legacy flows through the history of beer in Canada. The family emigrated from England in the 1860s, and a matriarch named Susannah Oland is said to have concocted a recipe for brown October ale in her Dartmouth backyard. From those origins, the Olands rose to bestride the Atlantic beer markets like titans, in an age when interprovincial trade of beer was forbidden and locally owned breweries could flourish. Then in 1933, Derek's great-grandfather, beer baron George C. Oland, divided his empire, leaving the bulk of his Nova Scotia-based brewing operations to his older son, Colonel Sidney Oland, and control of a much smaller operation based in Saint John to his other son, George B. Oland. The Saint John Brewery grew into today's Moosehead, which Derek Oland, George's grandson, now controls.

From the moment of that geographic split, the two factions of the Oland family were at "lagerheads." To exacerbate things, the Halifax Olands still owned 20 per cent of Moosehead, as well as another Saint John brewery called Red Ball. The bitterness was intense. Because it was forbidden to ship beer from one province to another, Moosehead opened its own Dartmouth brewery in the 1960s, adding more salt to the wounds. Derek ran that brewery and moved his family to Nova Scotia for a while. This aggressive interfamilial rivalry was a contributing factor in forcing the Halifax Olands to sell out in 1971 to John Labatt Company, the Central Canadian beer and food giant. One distant member of the family told me that his mother until her dying day blamed the other faction. In fact, Derek's second cousin, also named Sidney, became a prominent executive at Labatt's, rising to president of the company in the late 1980s.

As Derek moved into a more senior post, he had more and more influence, urging his father, Philip W. Oland, to go after the big U.S. market in the late 1970s. Moosehead made great gains in the U.S. import market as a kind of cult premium beer with a wonderfully rustic northern name, and Labatt's followed suit. For a time, it created a media stir, with two Oland cousins, Derek at Moosehead and Sidney at Labatt's, fighting it out for the U.S. suds stakes. What makes it even more piquant is that even today, Labatt's maintains the Oland name as a regional brand in Nova Scotia, a rival to Moosehead.

Even the Saint John branch had its share of family tension. Both Derek and his younger brother Dick worked in the company, and both wanted to be president. But the old man decided Derek should have the prize. Dick left the company in 1981 to run the family transport company, which has since been sold, and still owns a piece of Moosehead. "I was just looking for opportunities, and if they weren't present in the existing system, I had to leave," he told the *Financial Post* in 1992.

These days, Derek seems to reserve most of his competitive fire not for other Olands but for Molson Coors, which he accuses of heavy-handed discounting of beer in the Maritimes. His rage deepened in late 2004, when the New Brunswick government provided $6 million in forgivable loans and grants to support a new Molson brewery in Moncton that would create 40 jobs. What's more, the new brewery would give Molson immediate status as a domestic provincial supplier, thus avoiding the steep tariff on beer brought into the province. To add insult to injury, the new plant, to open in 2007, would take over brewing Molson Canadian for the Maritimes, which is currently being produced on contract by Moosehead. "We think most New Brunswickers would question why the government is subsidizing a multinational corporation in a way that harms a company that has been employing New Brunswickers since 1928," Oland fumed at a press conference.

For Derek Oland, it is just a continuation of the great Maritimes government tradition of pushing dollars down from on high, hoping that some of the investment will seed much-needed jobs. He says Moosehead, in recent years, has been blissfully free of this kind of top-down subsidy, the kind that flows regularly from the federal Atlantic Canada Opportunities Agency. "I think the money could be better used creating more entrepreneurs than dumping it down, whether it's worth it or not. What happens in ACOA is there is someone doing reasonably well and someone else comes along with an idea directly on top of it and they'll fund it, putting the first person out of business, which will disturb the market." And disturbing the market is what the New Brunswick government did by supporting a new Molson plant in his backyard.

Still, Derek feels he is doing very nicely in Saint John, where the company maintains marketing and promotion activities that, in other firms, are often relocated to Toronto. He says he can hire high-quality people in Saint John because of the relaxed family lifestyle, although it is a challenge to attract couples who are both professionals. It may sound sexist but it is a fact of life: The best candidates are couples with full-time mothers looking after the kids. "There is nothing like the Maritimes for finding the ideal place to live—fresh water, salt water, mountains," he says. Indeed, managers can do very well coming to Saint John from Toronto, but if they plan to go back to Central Canada, they risk losing their status on the promotion ladder, as well as their place in the real estate market. They have to think about it.

Derek and his wife Jaqueline have four children in all, including Andrew and Patrick in the company, Mathew who is with Procter & Gamble in Toronto, and Giles, a young high-tech entrepreneur in Halifax. The challenge now is to give his two Saint John sons a range of experience and credentials to prepare them for senior roles. In 2005, Patrick was on leave getting his chartered accountant designation so that he can play a financial role; Andrew was moving up on the marketing and sales side. Derek says frankly that leadership is the biggest challenge for the company, but is careful not to tip his hand on how it will work out. For advice, he depends strongly on his duo of outside directors, Sir Graham Day and Courtney Pratt, a human resources specialist who is president of Stelco, the Hamilton Ontario steel company.

"The family company is only as good as its professional management," Oland says. "If you don't have professional management involved, with the ability to become president, you don't have a good viable business." In other words, he says, it is important to keep non-family like Bruce McCubbin interested. Moosehead follows a different model, he says, than his neighbours, the Irvings, who take a highly centralized approach, with the family assuming key operating roles. "They live the business and they work it very hard. It is a different paradigm with them; I just don't think it's my paradigm. I enjoy having that guy [McCubbin] there. That's their style; what they do they do very well, but I get my satisfaction from that old definition of a manager, getting things done through other people. I think I added 10 years on my life when Bruce came in."

If his own succession seems closely guarded, at least he has a plan, a working board of directors, and 140 years of history to rely on. His major concern is that the Maritimes seems to lack a ready supply of enterprising company-builders beyond the old families like his. "Part of the problem is we don't have enough entrepreneurs, no question about it." He saw some promising young players emerge in the dot-com bubble years of the late 1990s, but a lot got out when the bubble burst. Now, he says, New Brunswick and the Maritimes don't do enough to encourage them. For one thing, he says universities are stuck in a traditional approach to business training. "They are not really looking at how businesses are formed, how you need enough guts and intelligence to make it work." He would like to see courses in, for example, how to go to a bank for financing and present your business plan. "I'm frustrated with universities that they continue to teach the same way as when I went to school—generally by professors who have never run their own businesses, turning out good technicians but not putting it all together."

Unlike others in the Maritimes, he doesn't see the lack of availability of financing as the key issue. "I think if you're prepared properly you can convince shareholders and government and bankers of the validity of the idea." But he adds that "when we grow this business, we pretty well stay away from government. We've never gone for grants and the reason is that companies, once they get going, should exist on their own. We're not going back to the trough."

Famous last words. When the dust settled on the Molson subsidy controversy, Oland was able to reveal that the provincial government had agreed to provide equivalent incentives for Moosehead's own capital expenditures. He explained that if the government was going to dole out assistance for his out-of-province competitor, he was determined Moosehead would have its share—even if it meant violating his principles.

Perhaps such pragmatism is just part of being resilient, which is a key to long-term survival in the Maritimes. Another is family succession. While Andrew and Patrick are being groomed to replace him, Oland is just as proud of Mathew in Toronto and of the entrepreneur of the family, Giles, a 28-year-old tousle-haired techie living in Halifax.

I catch up with Giles in downtown Halifax, where he and a team of young technology workers are gazing at computer screens in an open-concept office, strewn with coffee cups and fast food. One of Giles's colleagues is seated at a computer screen, which takes him by virtual means into a customer service centre in Truro, where telephone attendants are trying to persuade *Toronto Star* customers in Central Canada to keep their subscriptions. Giles and his team can keep tabs on the length of calls, the amount of time spent talking, the success rate—an amazing intensity of data. Giles is a 30 per cent partner in the company, called ECRM Networks, which provides technical support for call centres.

Giles was a student at Old Dominion University in Norfolk, Virginia—a member of the crack varsity sailing team—when he got interested in industrial technology. When he came home, he didn't want to get tied down in the family company, which already had two of his brothers well established. "Giles, you do what you want," his father said. So he lit out for Nova Scotia, where he worked as a computer technician for Maritime Steel, an old economy icon that was trying to burst into the 21st century.

After some interesting projects, including setting up a company intranet, he realized that he didn't enjoy the workplace culture and left to join ECRM. Now he likes what he is doing, enjoys Halifax, and has bought into the company, but he admits that sometime in the near future, he could find himself in Toronto. It is hard to resist the drift of jobs and career opportunities to Canada's biggest city.

But at lunch in a restaurant beside Halifax harbour, Giles's genetic makeup becomes evident. When the waitress comes to take the beer orders, the young Oland starts grilling her on the availability on tap of the family's Moosehead and Alpine beer, and how much she sells of the stuff. He does that a lot, he admits. After all, beer is thicker than water.

AT FIRST GLANCE Bernard Imbeault would seem to have little in common with Derek Oland, except perhaps the natural pairing of Imbeault's pizzas and sandwiches with a pitcher of Moosehead draft. While Oland is a fifth-generation beer baron, Imbeault is a first-generation company-builder, the son of a stable master in the lumber camps of Gaspé. While Oland reeks of old Anglo Maritime money, Imbeault is an adopted son of Acadia. He left the Gaspé to study at the Université de Moncton in the 1960s and became part of the cultural and commercial blossoming of that city's francophone community in the past three decades.

But like Derek Oland, he is at a crucial point in his career and in his life: Although blessed with thick black hair and a dark bushy moustache, he is 60 years old and is grooming his children to take over. Also, he is confronting the challenges of growing from a New Brunswick base and moving beyond his regional haven into the U.S. market.

Imbeault's major restaurant brands are Pizza Delight and Mikes Restaurants, which together constitute the largest eatery chain in the Maritimes. He has built a franchise system with total sales of about $235 million a year, with the bulk coming from the Maritimes. But at 250 outlets across the country, it is still a small slice when compared with Tim Hortons's 2,500 Canadian outlets. Imbeault wants to double system sales in the next five years, and then double it again to a billion dollars. The conversion of the business into an income trust gave him $45 million to retire some debt and a bit of capital to buy something, but he's finding a shortage of targets in Canada. Many of his potential acquisitions have already gone the income trust route, taking them out of contention. A Maritime-born lawyer based in New York is looking for prospects in that neck of the woods.

His mission is to build a business that he can leave for his children, who have shown keen interest. He has six children, two of whom work in the business: One son works at Mikes Restaurants in Montreal and another is running the family granite business, a further cornerstone of the Imbeault empire. A daughter is getting human resources training and will likely join the family business; yet another daughter works in arts and film.

Unlike the five Oland generations, he says, "there is nothing behind us. I came from a family of 15 children and no one had ever been in business. We owned a small grocery store and my father was a stable master who looked after the horses in the forest industry." Yet he harbours the same dynastic dreams as the Irvings and the Olands, to build a company for future generations. "The second generation will take over in the next 10 years and we will try to go from there. I hope I can build it to the level that is exciting to them."

Despite his humble origins on the Gaspé, he was an early convert to capitalism. At 15, he was already operating a vegetable business, selling to the iron ore camps on the north side of the St. Lawrence River. Even with his high produce expenses, he was able to undercut competitors by his low transport costs, moving the products by ferry across the St. Lawrence. It was a lesson in logistics that has served him well: "I wasn't selling vegetables, I was selling transportation."

In the 60s, the ambitious Imbeault came to Moncton to take a short course in English at the university. He took to this city with its strong Acadian community, so he stayed to get his degree. It was a time of upheaval, with the city polarized in battles over bilingualism, fanned by a divisive anglophone mayor named Leonard Jones. Despite the strife, Imbeault sensed that something important was happening—the awakening of an Acadian nationalism. Some of that nationalism materialized in the commercial sphere. One watershed event was the decision of Canadian National Railway in the late 1980s to close down its Moncton maintenance yards, tearing 1,000 jobs out of the local economy and leaving a commercial void. But a wave of entrepreneurialism filled the emptiness, much of it coming from an Acadian business class, of which Imbeault was now a part.

Imbeault quickly learned there was something special about doing business in the Maritimes, a kind of connectedness in a culture where everybody tends to know everyone else. These connections are not formal and they don't really change the final business decisions. But it is much easier to get information when you know the other party's family.

"We need that because we are far from major markets or where financing decisions are done; there is often the perception that faraway markets are not as viable. We are discounted when we present a project to a financial institution. We need something else and, thank God, we have those direct relationships between Maritimers to help."

As a student, he and a buddy bought an option to purchase the nascent Pizza Delight chain from a couple of university professors, and they were able to exercise it. They started expanding in New Brunswick through a number of businesses, including a combined Irving service station and Renault car dealer in Moncton. But the new tycoons had plans to open a Pizza Delight in Bathurst in the Miramichi region, and knew about a site owned by Irving Oil. So Imbeault put in a call to the Irving organization, and he was connected with K.C. Irving himself. "No time to talk," the old industrialist said, "but call me back between 9 and 10:30 tonight." "I did, and I got him at home," Imbeault recalls. Irving found out what the young man wanted and gave him a contact in Bathurst. The Irvings had a site where they planned to put a bus station, but they found room for Imbeault's pizza shop on the same lot. "They made an exception for us," Imbeault recalls, and he put up his fourth Pizza Delight.

It was an introduction in how contacts worked, and he never forgot. It was a lesson in the value of playing the Maritime card, and, for K.C. Irving, it didn't matter whether you were Anglo or Franco as long as he liked you.

Later, as he built his company, Imbeault got to know Harrison McCain and became convinced that there is a different style to business in a sparsely populated region like the Maritimes. Business is more direct, more informal, less pretentious, more honest. Several years ago, Imbeault recounts, he had a trademark problem with the McCain's organization that involved teams of expensive Toronto lawyers on both sides. He picked up the phone, called Harrison, and explained that his company owned the Pizza Delight trademark and now McCain's was trying to register "Delite Pizza" for their frozen pizza. How could we avoid an expensive wrangle? Imbeault wondered. The McCain chairman's reply was "I do not want to walk on a New Brunswicker's toes. If it were Dominion Stores or someone else, I would fight them to the death. But I don't want to trouble your company with that." McCain's withdrew its application and changed the product name.

Imbeault has watched a lively coterie of francophone entrepreneurs develop in the Maritimes—particularly in construction, forest products, and fishing. But except for Pizza Delight, there have been few breakout companies that have grown beyond the small to medium size and taken on a national market. He has trouble figuring out why, because there is no shortage of entrepreneurial spirit. It may be that it is too early in the process. But it could also be an Acadian mindset that a medium-sized company is big enough. The tendency is to sell out, rather than build a company for future generations. He also is concerned that many founders get too big for their britches; they feel their success is attributable entirely to themselves and not to their workers or community. He says Pizza Delight knows where it comes from.

Donald Savoie, a professor of public administration at the Université de Moncton, says it is important to remember that until the 1960s, when Louis Robichaud became the first francophone premier, the Acadians were still "a clergy-dominated rural backwards people with little education. We worked on construction sites, we fished, farmed, and so the business community was completely foreign to us." He remembers the local priest continually emphasizing that it is harder for a rich man to go to heaven than for a camel to pass through the eye of a needle. But the Church's influence began to wane in the 1960s, and New Brunswick Acadians in 1963 were given a university of their own in Moncton. The first business and engineering degrees from the Université de Moncton were awarded in the late 1960s and early 1970s. "We're the first generation of business," Savoie says. He would argue that the entrepreneurial class in Moncton is now dominated by Acadians, and the next generation will take it higher, perhaps creating some national players, just as the second generation of Irvings produced the formidable K.C.

That's certainly what Bernard Imbeault would like, to see his children run a major company from Moncton. He thinks the family can somehow build on its expertise in running multiple-unit businesses, not just in food services but perhaps in hotels, in office maintenance, or cleaning. The Irving expertise is in manufacturing; the Sobeys' is in retail; the McCains' is in processing. The Imbeaults, he says, can run large service operations with many units or franchises. "We can expand this business and branch out too," he says.

MUCH IS RESTING ON the narrow shoulders of Bryana Ganong, the 31-year-old standard-bearer for a 130-year family tradition in chocolate-making. Sitting in a downtown Toronto hotel restaurant, she is winding up a tour of Western and Central Canada where she has played her role as the public face of the company, involved in product development and marketing. She is also the key liaison with Laura Secord, the iconic Canadian chocolate brand with 65 to 70 products, of which Ganong is the new contract manufacturer. "She is kind of the meat in the sandwich, and she is doing a great job," her father, David, beams.

Bryana does concede that she has become much more hands-on at the company, but that is about as definitive a comment as she makes in a half-hour interview. There is a reluctance to venture beyond the bland and superficial, which may reflect a nervousness and lack of experience in dealing with the press. Still, inside the company, her father likes what he sees: "She is more tough-minded than I am, which is what is needed." But he also acknowledges that it is too early to pass judgment on any of his children: Bryana, Nick, who works in the planning department, or Aaron, who works in the hospitality business in Western Canada.

The company is an anachronism of local ownership in a world gone global. The Ganong family, which came to New Brunswick as United Empire Loyalists in 1783, has always run the business out of St. Stephen. David's grandfather, Andrew, is credited with creating the first chocolate bar in the world. For years, it was Whidden Ganong, David's uncle, who commanded the business. Then in 1977, Whidden felt he had had enough and suddenly handed the top job over to his nephew, David, a graduate of the University of New Brunswick in his early 30s. He was, he now admits, too young to be running a business. "I ended up in the job too early; I should have had five or more years more," David says now. But his uncle couldn't hang on any longer, and unlike Derek Oland, wouldn't appoint an outsider as a transition manager to hold the fort until David was ready. It's something he pledges not to do himself. "As soon as you put in a family member who is not competent you lose your professional management."

As he learned the business, he has grappled with Ganong's limitations as an aging business stuck in a remote region. Under his leadership, Ganong has become a contract packager of fruit snacks and other items, in addition to the company's branded chocolate business. He has been on a determined drive to add bulk and economies of scale to the operations. For help he has relied on an active corporate board, which includes both family members (including his wife, Diane) and outsiders such as Purdy Crawford, Bernard Imbeault, and the octogenarian former chief executive of the Royal Bank of Canada, Rowland Frazee, who is a St. Stephen native.

David Ganong knew he needed to expand the business aggressively, but he was saddled with an ancient factory building. As he developed a plan, he relied heavily on the advice of his peers among the Maritime business community. The Atlantic chapter of the Young Presidents' Organization was a valuable source of guidance, particularly a mechanism called "the forum," in which young CEOs would bounce their challenges off a group of peers. His own forum contained the best and brightest of Maritime business people, including a Sobey and a couple of Risleys—restaurateur Robert Risley and his hard-nosed fish magnate brother John. "The guys listened and got updates every month on how business was doing," David recalls. "I said we were going to expand it and add some features. John Risley looked me in the eye and said, 'Get with it, David, you can't make that old five-storey building work. Build a new one or you're going to go broke. That's a stupid idea, David.'" So Ganong went away and thought, "I don't like what he said, but he's right."

With that in mind, Ganong built a new factory that revolutionized his company. It also set him on a single-minded drive to expand. One of the solutions emerged a few blocks away, for the U.S. border crossing can be viewed from his office in St. Stephen. He targeted the U.S. market, and it has paid off. As of late 2004, Ganong Brothers had doubled its sales since 2000; David was determined to double it again in the next few years. "The second double will be a lot harder than the first," he admits. The United States contributed about a third of its business, not so much in chocolates but in contract packing and fruit snacks.

With this expanded business, the company has been able to buy entire rail cars of glucose and sugar, which pull up on a rail siding to the factory, off the New Brunswick Southern Railway. Like so many things in the Maritimes, the railway is owned by the Irvings. As of early 2005, Ganong Brothers employed 400 people, an increase of 125 in 12 months, which makes it the largest employer in little St. Stephen.

Another turning point came with the financial troubles of the Archibald Candy company, the Chicago firm that owned the Laura Secord brand of chocolates. (It is delicious irony that Laura Secord, named after a Canadian icon who raised the alarm on a U.S. invasion during the War of 1812, has spent most of its recent history in U.S. hands.) As part of a reorganization, Archibald decided to outsource its Laura Secord production in Canada, and David Ganong went after this business. But in the middle of it all, in January 2004, Archibald sought bankruptcy protection. Most of the outsource candidates bailed out, but not Ganong, although David admits his own team lost interest. "I said, 'Wait, it's a perfect fit and we have to figure it out.' At business school, they didn't teach us how to negotiate a long-term contract with a company you knew was going to file Chapter 11. We spirited our way through that." Ganong got the Laura Secord contract and the Laura Secord business was later sold to Gordon Brothers, a U.S. private equity firm. So why didn't Ganong step up and buy Laura Secord itself? David Ganong says he was approached but it would have cost a lot of money, and his company had no expertise in retail stores such as those Laura Secord operated. Also, he wasn't sure how customers such as Loblaws and Wal-Mart would take to Ganong becoming a direct competitor in their retail candy business. It was far safer just to do Laura Secord's contract manufacturing.

The Laura Secord contract has been a big boost to the top line, filled up more of the plant's capacity, and refocused the company's sales efforts, at least momentarily, on Canada. It also opened up a new liaison role for Bryana, who had been working for the family company for seven years. David was saying he'd like to see his children run the company, but acknowledges it is too early to know if they have the royal jelly. To qualify for ownership, he believes they should be competent senior managers first. That kind of managerial engagement is important for good ownership. If the family owners become too detached, the company would likely be sold. And David Ganong sees his company very much as a Maritime public legacy.

If Ganong Brothers were sold to Cadbury, Nestlé, or Stover, these companies might make initial commitments to keeping employment in St. Stephen, he says. "Maybe it will last five years or 10 or six months but sooner or later someone will rationalize it and move it out." It's the same with Moosehead if Derek Oland were to sell to Molson or Labatt's: The company and the jobs would be the next to go. "Our company has had an enormous commitment to community for 130 years. I share that. As soon as the ownership of Ganong Brothers goes, the jobs will go. So what do you do?"

What you do if you are David Ganong is set in place an intricate—and unusual—succession plan that maximizes the chances of keeping the company in St. Stephen, even if he were to die suddenly. First, he has insulated the company from having to be sold for taxes by setting up an estate freeze, a widely used strategy that effectively freezes the value of the firm for tax purposes. The disposition of his voting shares on his death is entrusted to a team of high-profile Maritimers: Rowland Frazee, John Risley, and David's brother Gordon Ganong.

His instructions are that if one or more of the Ganong children are in senior management and considered competent by the trustees, some or all of the voting shares can be passed on to one or all of them. But he emphasizes that they have to be competent and in senior management. Alternatively, the trustee can wait to make that decision, or indeed, David Ganong could make that same decision at some point during his lifetime.

If none of the children are capable, competent, and interested, he has instructed the trustees to sell the shares to the employees at a discounted price. Whether the price is $2 million or $30 million, he insists his wife, Diane, doesn't need the extra money to live comfortably. "The importance of the business to the community carries a lot of value," he says. He insists that the trustees not try to maximize value and not bring in an investment banker to conduct an auction. If the company can't be sold to employees, it should be sold to the province of New Brunswick, still at a discounted value. Only as a last resort should the deal be taken to Toronto and marketed for the best price possible. "Most people would say I have lost it," he admits, "but I'm not sure that maximizing a few million dollars is what I've worked all of my life for. If Bryana or Nick is interested and wants to move forward, I've created a situation where the share ownership can move from one generation to the next."

As for managing the company, he is not committed to having his children play that role, at least not right away. He would love to see it but Diane tells him not to force it on them. After all, she says, "it took a lot out of your life. I don't want them to feel obligated." Of course, he also wants to make sure that if they do run it, they are the best possible people. He admires what Bryana is doing but she is still in her early 30s. He suspects that the next president of Ganong after him will be the first non-Ganong in the company's history, a transitional leader like Bruce McCubbin at Moosehead. But that wouldn't be too bad, as long as St. Stephen remains the sweet spot of the Maritimes.

CHAPTER 13

FELLOWSHIP OF THE RING

IT'S A CLEAR COLD DAY in early December in Antigonish, Nova Scotia, and Trudy Eagan is experiencing her proudest hour. She is standing before the graduating students of her alma mater in the chapel of St. Francis Xavier University. The students have assembled for the defining moment of their university career, even bigger than graduation itself—the annual X-ring ceremony when they receive the ring that inducts them into a special club. It is "the cult," in the words of John MacDonald, the telecom executive who came from Cape Breton but chose Dalhousie for his university training.

Eagan, now 57 and a retired newspaper executive who attended St. FX in the 1960s, is the keynote speaker. In front of the students, faculty, and the school's energetic president Sean Riley, she gives a warm, inspirational 19-minute talk. Blond, petite with a plain-spoken manner, Trudy talks straight to students on her lessons for life, the things you have to do to get ahead, like show people respect and send thank you notes for acts of kindness. When she is done, she basks in a standing ovation. As she makes her way across the stage, the students are still yelling, and Eagan makes an exaggerated bow from the waist. "They hooted and hollered and I just thought, 'I want this moment to live on for a long time,'" she recalls. When the X-rings are handed out, her skin tingles with emotion as the throngs of students bang their rings on the back of the pews, a traditional outburst in one of the most powerful ceremonies in Canadian academe. "You can hear this wonderful sound throughout the chapel. It's the metal on wood and all these young vibrant people are doing it at once. Then they all pour out of the chapel and the parents are waiting for them."

Eagan went to St. FX for two years in the 1960s, never graduated, and gained her own X-ring only by dint of an honorary degree. But she lobbied hard for this honour of keynote speaker, as intensely as she had for any job at the Sun Media Corp., the feisty Toronto-based tabloid newspaper company that made her a top executive and ultimately a millionaire. She had risen from a shopkeeper's daughter in St. Stephen, New Brunswick, to the highest-ranked woman in Canadian newspaper publishing. But here she was in 2004, absolutely humbled by giving the top speech in the ceremony that cements much of the Maritime Mafia.

Afflicted with rheumatoid arthritis in her hands, she doesn't wear her X-ring very much, and it has been specially tailored to fit around her swollen middle finger. But whenever she wears it, or even mentions her St. FX roots, she elicits a knowing comment or wins a new friend or business contact. People will leap across an airport lounge or a corporate boardroom to shake hands with someone who, like them, wears a St. FX ring. Kevin Francis, a computer executive in Silicon Valley, says, "I have had people in Tokyo, Germany, France, and Ireland spot an X-ring and come lunging over to me, regardless of age. There is this natural bond like none other."

At St. FX, the ring sums up an entire experience, a potent fusion of myriad elements: the hothouse atmosphere of a small university in a small town, the intense bonding at a formative time of life, the rich athletic tradition, the Catholic idealism and cooperative ethos, and the ghosts of the Highland Scots who settled that region of Nova Scotia.

But the St. FX phenomenon is just part of a broader phenomenon—the networks for life that arise out of the university tradition in Atlantic Canada. There is the esteemed Dalhousie Law School, which produced Purdy Crawford, Graham Day, John Crosbie, and James Palmer, a venerable Calgary lawyer whose great-grandfather was a Father of Confederation in Prince Edward Island. St. Mary's University's Sobey School of Business has turned out U.S. natural foods tycoon Irwin Simon and aerospace executive Julie (Rowe) Gossen. Indeed, the Sobeys have adopted St. Mary's as their focus for university donations and board memberships. The University of New Brunswick produced many of the boffins at NBTel, such as Lino Celeste and Gerry Pond. The Université de Moncton feeds the growing Acadian business and professional cadres. But probably the strongest branding has been achieved by a trio of undergraduate liberal arts universities, Mount Allison, Acadia, and St. Francis Xavier. They were once primarily the training ground of Atlantic Canadians, but their quality and cohesive spirit have made them powerful magnets for young people from across the country. *Maclean's* rates St. FX as the top primarily undergraduate university in Canada, with Mount Allison and Acadia right behind it. The schools work hard to cop those rankings, which is how they sell themselves to the increasingly broad Canadian and international markets. For many Americans, they have been a high-quality, lower-cost alternative to a U.S. college or university.

"One of Atlantic Canada's greatest resources is its universities," concludes a 2000 study for the Atlantic Provinces Economic Council and the Association of Atlantic Universities.

The report points out that the region is home to 17 degree-granting institutions, nearly a quarter of Canada's total, and they attract full-time total enrolment of 64,000 students, the highest proportion of youth enrolled in university programs anywhere in Canada. The universities generate more than $1.1 billion of annual spending in the region, and yet the provincial spending on universities is constrained, leading to some of the country's highest tuition rates. The report identifies many reasons why this trend should be reversed, including the need for skills and research and development in the region. But it does not mention one of the quiet underestimated strengths of the Atlantic universities: Relatively compact by North American university standards, they foster unusually strong lifelong networks, which form the basis for business alliances, investments, job creation, and university fundraising. These old school ties are the Maritimers' unnatural advantage.

All three of the liberal arts institutions feed hungrily on the prestige of their alumni groups, among the most powerful segments of the Maritime and Canadian business class. Mount Allison, a red-brick haven in Sackville, New Brunswick, just south of Moncton near the Nova Scotia border, is where Wallace McCain met his future wife, Margaret Norrie. Today, John Bragg, the blueberry-cable titan from nearby Oxford, Nova Scotia, serves as chancellor and Wallace and Margaret's son Scott McCain is on the board—as is Monique Imbeault, the lawyer wife of Pizza Delight's Bernard Imbeault. At Acadia, Arthur Irving is the chancellor and the Irvings are major benefactors of a university that still celebrates its Baptist roots and traditions. Other prominent donors are the Jodreys, whose fortune began in nearby Hantsport.

But no university has built networks as brilliantly as St. FX, and no other university experience is so transforming.

The university is a tiny powerhouse of just 4,000 students in sleepy Antigonish with its quiet main street, a few student bars, and a nice restaurant or two. It has been the breeding ground of a powerful unholy trinity of political bosses: Allan J. MacEachen (known simply as "Allan J."), the Liberals' wily intellectual political tactician of the Trudeau years; Brian Mulroney, who came from Baie Comeau, Quebec, to attend a university steeped in Catholic activism and went on to be a Quebec labour lawyer and a controversial Conservative prime minister; and Frank McKenna, current ambassador to Washington and the man who created an economic revolution as Liberal premier of New Brunswick. These three men have attracted constellations of advisers and associates, many of them drawn from their alma mater. But these networks have also reached across into Canada's business class, particularly in the case of Mulroney and McKenna, who have leveraged political careers into directorships and executive roles.

One of the reasons for the resilience of these relationships is the natural bonding of young people, often rural Maritimers, as they are separated from their families for the first time. They are looking for a new feeling of family away from home, says St. FX's current president Sean Riley, adding that "students are looking for personal meaning that goes beyond the classroom." St. FX, with its students thrown together in a small town, allows that feeling to ripen over four years. "Relationships aren't immediate or automatic or hot and cold," he says. "They mutate in intensity over time."

By the time the kids graduate, the network has taken hold. This network extends to Korea, to Calgary, and to Toronto, and if anything, it gets stronger and more entrenched. Riley believes the Antigonish culture makes people "networkable, a little more geared that way." It breeds the adaptive human skills of people like McKenna and Mulroney. "What they got here is their ability to operate," he says.

Today, St. FX is a favourite destination of students from across Canada, of all faiths, who are drawn by the aura of quality and school spirit. Almost half the student body is non-Catholic. But its alumni base remains heavily populated by people who came out of the small-town Catholic environment of Atlantic Canada. That role comes from history: The university was founded in the 1850s by exiled Highland Scots to be their own cultural greenhouse and training ground. Liberated from their Anglo overseers in the British Isles, they built St. FX as a Catholic rural counterpart to Dalhousie University, then the elite urban training ground of an Anglican establishment. "This was the Scots' chance to make their stand," says Sean Riley. It was the university for the farmers, priests, and teachers of the villages within hailing distance of Antigonish and northeast into that stronghold of Highland nostalgia, Cape Breton Island.

Over the decades, this role metamorphosed into new variations. It became a practical training ground for Nova Scotia farmers, artisans, and craftspeople in the 1900s—and an academy to produce Maritime professionals, intended to stem the tide of out-migration. It welcomed back the children of those out-migrants, now living in the United States, who sent their progeny home to get Catholic training and a taste of Nova Scotia life.

In the 1920s and 1930s the university's focus moved outward from its tribal Highland roots, as it became the home base of Catholic social activism when a charismatic priest named Moses Coady created the Antigonish Movement of community development and economic progress. That in turn spawned the Coady International Institute, which now takes community leaders from the Third World and gives

278 | THE CODFATHERS

them a crash course in commerce, micro-lending, and credit unions. In many ways, the university is the emotional and spiritual centre of the credit union movement in the world.

St. FX thus became a perfect expression of the tribalism–globalism tension that is Atlantic Canada's great strength and its challenge. Like the Irving family, with its forest and energy operations, it is torn between inward-looking isolation and global engagement. Certainly, its special role in the rural Catholic Maritimes gave it a kind of cocoon status, drawing a very smart and engaged but homogeneous student body. For generations, the brightest and the best from all the little towns ended up being directed to St. FX by the local parish priest. In the 1960s and 70s the Coady Institute pushed St. FX out into the wider world by providing specialized training for leaders in development organizations in Asia, Africa, and Latin America to come here and work on community development, self-reliance, and cooperatives. "If I parachuted you into Cairo or elsewhere in the developing world, you'll find someone in 24 hours who knows about this place," Riley says.

That globalism did not entirely overshadow the tribalism, which was reinforced by the fact that an education at St. FX has become a family tradition through the Maritimes. Kevin Francis, who grew up in Cape Breton, is the product of two parents who went to St. FX, and his son and daughter-in-law are graduates, as are his sisters and uncle and aunts.

Annette Verschuren, now president of Home Depot Canada, is the daughter of two Dutch immigrants who as a young couple in their 20s joined the post-war exodus out of Europe and ended up in Antigonish. Her father, who had worked as a dairy specialist, became herdsman on the St. FX university farm, while her mother worked at the nearby convent. They eventually scraped together a down payment on a dairy farm in North Sydney on Cape Breton Island. So when the time came for their daughter Annette to go to university, she went down the road to that familiar family sanctuary at Antigonish.

Trudy Eagan was the daughter of a good Irish family in St. Stephen, the New Brunswick border town where the Ganong chocolate factory and a major paper mill were located. David Ganong, now the family company's president, was just another kid in school. Her father was a butcher and grocer who helped guide the community through rocky economic times by giving credit to his customers. When the time came to go to university, she too chose St. FX. For two years she had a great time—her first roommate was Julie McKenna's sister—but Trudy in those days was not into studying. She needed a bit of adventure. So she hit the road, working in Bermuda for the burgeoning new mutual fund business and for a charismatic rogue named Bernie Cornfeld. Then Cornfeld moved her to Luxembourg, where she made enough cash to join a group of friends travelling across Europe by van. Out of money, she made her way back to Canada, where she ended up searching for work in Toronto.

She applied at the new tabloid paper, the *Toronto Sun*, where she got a job as a secretary for another loveable rogue, the *Sun*'s pioneering publisher Doug Creighton. "Doug hired me and said, 'I'll give you enough rope to climb it or hang yourself,'" she said, and he was true to his word. She rose out of the secretary's role and climbed to vice-president, a formidable woman in the testosterone-drenched world of the *Sun* with its Page Three babes, its full-throttle sports content, and its red-meat right-wing politics.

She became a rare woman on the board of the Canadian Daily Newspaper Association. Before she was introduced to the board, she bet a friend $20 that when she entered the board's meeting room, some of the macho board members would assume she was just a gal there to get coffee. She stepped into the room, and the board member who was speaking stopped in mid-sentence: "Great, can I have a gin and tonic?" Trudy said to her friend: "Twenty dollars please." So she rolled with the punches in this male world. "When you get sure enough of yourself, you enjoy that," she says. "Male culture is the same everywhere."

Trudy almost became publisher of the *Toronto Sun*, and partly because of the St. FX connection. After the *Sun* was sold to Montreal's Quebecor Inc. in the 1990s, Brian Mulroney as Sun Media CEO asked her to take the job, which would have been a revolution: the *Sun* being run by a woman. But she turned it down because of the challenges of working with the new owner. She had become a millionaire in Sun Media's initial public offering and Quebecor's takeover, and retired to do good works, including the endowment of scholarships for women business students at St. FX, a group that has become known as the Eaganettes. And she continues to come back, drawn by the aura of this unique university and what it has come to mean in the world.

INDEED, ST. FX HAS an almost irresistible pull for its former students, and no one embodies that more than Sean Riley, the current president, who was literally born to run the place. About the same time as Annette Verschuren's parents were scrambling to leave the Netherlands, Riley's father, a Quebecer, was demobilized from the Canadian Army. He had read about Moses Coady and the Antigonish movement, and like many of his generation, headed to that small Nova Scotia town, where he would spend the rest of his life. He met his future wife, a graduate of St. Bernard College, at that time the women's college associated with St. FX, who was working in Moses Coady's office. Sean was born in Antigonish, and his father worked first for the credit union league and when they created the Coady Institute, he did some graduate work and taught there. "I grew up mainlining it straight into the veins," Sean says.

Riley, who at 50 still has the air of the boyish athlete scholar, has spent his whole life alternately rejecting and embracing the whole Maritimes shtick. It is one of the reasons he is so effective in his job; he is both part of it and outside it. He went to St. FX, graduated with high honours, was male athlete of the year, was awarded a Rhodes scholarship, and got a master's degree in International Relations at Oxford. He started his doctorate but, like many St. FX grads, ended up working in Ottawa, first for Senator John Stewart, and then for local hero Allan MacEachen, who was foreign minister at the time. That experience began a decade in Ottawa that appeared to set Riley on a career path in government. But as a friend of Sean Riley points out, he has an inclination toward unorthodox career moves. It's as if he identifies his weakness and then moves toward that flaw, with the goal of making it a strength.

In 1981, Riley found himself cleaning up after the disastrous federal budget, when the normally sure-footed MacEachen, now finance minister, suffered a grievous political miscalculation. It was a radically reformist and disruptive budget in the middle of a major recession, which left the Trudeau government at bitter loggerheads with the business community, including many of its own supporters. It was Riley's job to filter every public statement that MacEachen made to ensure that it did not fan the already angry flames. "We were in such a mess and damage control," he says. "We had released the budget and in four to six weeks, [MacEachen] had to stand in the house and say we goofed on this and we goofed on this and on this. I wrote that speech. In the midst of a recession with 23 per cent interest rates, you were not likely to get a real warm reception."

In a funny way, that was the making of Riley's career path. He was doing consultations with businesses on the next budget, when he was hit with a severe bout of entrepreneurial ambition. He decided he could do the business thing. "I wanted to get away from people telling me, 'What the hell do you know?' I had never met a payroll. There is a very robust antagonism toward government and academic people among the business community." He figured he could stay in government or academics forever, but at 31, he had a hunger to learn what business was all about. After all, he said to himself, "the worst thing that could happen is I self-destruct."

There were a few times over the next decade when he indeed thought he was self-destructing. He realized the best place to get a crash course in practical business was in a bank. He purposely did not apply at the Bank of Nova Scotia where Maritimer Cedric Ritchie was in charge, and where a friend, Nova Scotian Peter Nicholson, was working. His wife was a Montrealer, he wanted to work in a bilingual culture, and he decided to tackle the National Bank of Canada.

He went straight to then CEO Michel Belanger and asked him to take a chance. Belanger was reluctant for he could not pay the young Maritimer a salary at the level to which he had become accustomed. So the cocky Riley made a proposal: In 12 months, Belanger would either pay him a salary he could live with, say $60,000 or $70,000, based on Riley's performance, or he could let him go. "I basically bet him that I was going to jump six or seven steps in the hierarchy." He went into the corporate finance department at half his targeted salary and a year later, they were paying him the full amount he desired.

Still, it was a humbling experience going from G8 summits with cabinet ministers to a cubicle in National Bank's back offices. It was a place where "being a Maritimer doesn't cut it. I left my complete network to do this." After some success in corporate finance, he was put in charge of institutional services, which was the money market and foreign exchange trading division for inter-bank trading. He was a complete disaster at this job, he admits, and asked to be moved back to corporate finance, where he continued his education.

But he also came to the conclusion that he could not stay in the bank, that he was not psychologically equipped to spend another 15 to 20 years rising to become a senior officer in a giant corporation. The entrepreneurial spirit was stirring again; he had learned some things and made some money and now he wanted to get out and pursue his dream. He joined with another former Rhodes scholar, John MacBain, who had been working at Power Corp., and together they went looking for something to buy. Eventually MacBain found his calling, a collection of classified advertising magazines, including the popular *Auto Trader*. And in east-end Montreal, Riley also found his unlikely target, a dishwasher and kitchen cabinet maker named Belanger Laminates Inc. Backed by the Royal Bank, he bought the company, but the timing in the late 1980s was the worst possible. It happened just as the economy was cratering. The education of Sean Riley took a terrible but equally instructive turn: He had to struggle to keep the company out of bankruptcy by learning to cut costs, service customers with just-in-time speed, work with restless unions, and beat the competition.

"We came as close to going under as you can imagine," he recalls. He had to become an expert in all kinds of things he never dreamed of, such as the logistics of moving products across the continent. He had labour troubles and lived in fear that he might be in personal danger. But he kept the business alive and the company began to recover. "I now conclude if I had not had a lot of entrepreneurial instinct, it would have died for sure. We went through hell and back, got the business cranked up, and started to take market share."

Finally, he was paid the ultimate compliment—his competitor wanted to buy him out; the offer amounted to a small profit but no windfall. He was sitting in his factory one day and the call came from a friend: What did he think of the St. FX job? Riley had no idea what he was talking about. The friend said some of his colleagues thought Riley should come back to become president. "You can't imagine how far I am from that," he replied. He went home and talked to his wife. She wasn't eager to leave Montreal, but the company was close to being sold and there was pressure to join the new owner in Detroit. At 42, he was going home, at last.

It was no picnic. He moved into a turnaround situation that was not as severe as his counter-top venture, but challenging in its own way. The St. FX board was dealing with renewed pressure to consolidate the Nova Scotia universities and concerns about government funding, which had been under increasing pressure in the province. "They were looking for a different style of leadership, someone to get up on a white horse and ride off into the world to fight the good fight for the old institution." And who better than a new president for whom St. FX was literally embedded in his DNA? "I knew that I had this thing in my blood, so I actually decided I would do it."

While Riley was a product of St. FX's glorious past, he also felt somewhat imprisoned by it. "One of my main concerns was that I had the sense that everything good was in the past. There was a genuflection to the past, a sort of driving in the rear-view mirror. I needed to know whether the board wanted a forward offensive strategy or wanted someone to play defence. I told them I wasn't the right person for the status quo."

As in manufacturing, a lot of the things Riley did were little things, designed to achieve small palpable wins. St. FX started to climb in the *Maclean's* ranking, and the momentum began to build. But his biggest challenge was attitude, which may seem surprising in an attitude-heavy place like this. He wanted to take what was an intense culture in its solidarity, but "a little under-gunned on the can-do side. It wasn't a world-beater culture." He said his idea was to create a strong sense of confidence by a series of initiatives to build momentum.

Indeed, after eight years, Riley is credited by a number of alumni for turning the place around. He got the board behind him to undertake an ambitious physical renewal, a $75-million project that involved new student residences, a new school of business, and a $20-million science building that doesn't stint on facilities and appearance. The aim is to "upgrade to quality," he said, a watchword that he kept repeating as he gave me a quick tour of the university in the late fall of 2004. Riley had just come from watching a soccer game on the athletic field and still gave off the air of an intensely bright, voluble grad student in his jeans, St. FX ball jacket, and his Oxford sweatshirt.

Riley admitted that he is constantly thinking about the essential challenge of St. FX. The beauty of the place is the cocoon, he says, and the challenge of it is the same cocoon. With its geographic remoteness and unique culture, it is a great environment for undergraduate students to study, play, and make lifelong friends, away from the pressures of the world. "But at the same time you have to work very hard to build connections out of the region," he says. "To my way of thinking, a whole set of networks out into business and public affairs communities helps sustain it."

In building those networks—and finding the money for his grand vision—he has made ample use of his businessman's experience and the old Maritime Mafia. One case study of the network's broad reach is his funding of a new school of business and information technology. The business school is being driven by a donation from corporate buyout tycoon Gerry Schwartz, a native of Winnipeg, a graduate of Harvard business school, and a Jewish Torontonian, who now finds himself giving millions—the exact sum is undisclosed—to a Catholic school in rural Nova Scotia. "Here's a great Catholic college and a Jewish boy like me, with the business school named after him," Schwartz observes with a chuckle.

Schwartz had come to St. FX for an honorary degree and was impressed by the cross-disciplinary nature of the curriculum, which merges business strategy with the new technology. Riley began to hear from key alumni, such as Frank McKenna and Brian Mulroney, who suggested Schwartz might be willing to make a tangible contribution to the school. And Schwartz was not new to universities, having served on the boards at the Harvard Business School and the University of Toronto.

Riley makes it clear it was a team approach. "Let's just say it probably didn't hurt to have Frank McKenna involved— both McKenna and Mulroney were very high on Gerry. Brian said I was moving the place forward and that didn't hurt." When the announcement came, it was in the middle of a takeover bid for Air Canada by Schwartz and his Onex Corp. Cynics suspected that it was a ploy to buy support for Onex's bid in the skeptical Maritimes, but Riley said the timing was purely accidental. As it was, the Schwartz bid for Air Canada failed.

Ironically, one of his lingering challenges lies in what is often touted as St. FX's strength: its brand. "I'd say I am only 60 per cent to where I'd like to be on the brand," he admits. He rhymes off all the elements of the school's brand: East Coast, Catholic, sports, politics, Mulroney, football, X-rings, network. But he also knows that the recognition is stronger in the government and public service than on the street, and he also worries that there might be a perception that St. FX is deficient in quality education.

When he took over in 1996, "I looked at our curve of applications and we were in freefall. I was scared to death that I was going to get here and be short a bunch of students and start slashing budgets. That was the reason for going out to the market and seeing what advantage we had. We were actually making a mistake at the time: Other schools were saying quality, quality, program, program and yes, you might have a decent time and make a couple of friends. We went out and said St. FX, we love each other, God we love each other, I had a great time, and by the way, academics are pretty good, not bad. We had to reverse the approach."

With the *Maclean's* ranking, he believes he has a tail wind behind him now. The brand has moved up to the point where there is an appreciation of the quality of education, as well. "We've now got a brand where you are starting to get a real interesting combo of academic quality and bonded community, total experience and personal development, all that stuff." To add to this, St. FX's athletic programs in hockey and basketball are traditionally near the top in the country, which builds excitement in the brand.

Now he wants to take it higher, and for that, he plans to reach back to another part of its heritage: the Coady International Institute, and its dimension of sustainability, micro-lending, and the Third World. There are some strong names associated with the institute, including the British actress Vanessa Redgrave. "In three years from now, if this doesn't come up as part of our brand, then I've failed," Riley says.

It is all about delivering an experience that is unique and of high quality, not just in the classroom but outside. He shows me plans for a new $20-million dormitory, with marble in the front hall and air conditioning, but with a design that would fit into St. FX's classic collegiate decor. It is a building that would blow the minds of the dour Scottish Highlanders who founded the university in the 19th century. But St. FX is part of a global community now, and the competition from other institutions is fierce. Says Sean Riley, "If you're sitting in a rural town in Nova Scotia and you're mediocre, you're dead, completely dead."

The challenges are ongoing. There is continuing pressure to integrate Nova Scotia's disparate universities, to get some critical mass behind the largest concentration of post-secondary schools in the country. Observers say that these are fine little schools, but the Maritimes doesn't have a world-beater in any one single area of instruction and research. Purdy Crawford and John Bragg, both prime alumni movers for Mount Allison, talk of more cooperation among the liberal arts institutions, with one school providing instruction in its strongest subjects to students of all three. This is possible now with the Internet and video teaching. It also makes sense in a world where Atlantic governments are hard-pressed to keep up their university funding, but it is sure to hit resistance from loyal alumni who believe in being true to their schools.

That school spirit, plus a legacy of muscular Catholicism, athletic prowess, and international networking, are embodied in Bob Shea, whose relationship with St. FX was forged 55 years ago, when he and his brother were recruited from Boston high schools to play football for the school. They had never been in Nova Scotia before, but they found Antigonish to their liking. Shea made good friends, such as Al Graham, a future Liberal fundraiser and senator from Nova Scotia; Lowell Murray, a future Conservative senator; and a garrulous young kid from Quebec named Brian Mulroney. "He was a very bright young affable guy," he recalls of Mulroney, who was six years younger. After graduation in 1956, Shea went home to Boston and made a lot of money in insurance. He and his brother were among the first in a wave of Bostonians, mostly good Catholic kids, to attend St. FX and he figures they started a parade of 1,000 St. FX grads over the years—their cousins, their own children, and their friends' children. "The educational quality was very high, and the cost of going there, compared with American universities, was substantially less," he says.

But as he built his business, he didn't have much officially to do with the university until 1976, when on a sales trip to Rio de Janeiro, his family contacted him to say his name had been put forward for the school's board of governors. "I was a Boston guy and they were going to try to raise some money in the U.S. and I had done fairly well in business." Indeed he has raised a lot of money for his alma mater.

When he joined the board, Shea went back to St. FX where he reconnected with his old buddies, such as Mulroney, who was also on the board then. He was amazed to discover that the young men he had known in the early fifties had done well in business and politics. "Guys who I knew when I was there had risen to the top." When Mulroney became prime minister, Shea found himself invited to the White House during one of Mulroney's state visits with Ronald Reagan.

The reconnection with St. FX drew Shea into the Maritime Mafia. He helped found the New England–Canada Business Council to promote commercial and cultural ties. He started investing in Atlantic companies and going on their boards. Since 1982, he has been a director of National Sea Products, now known as High Liner Foods, and has watched its transformation from a fishing company to a branded food company under CEO Henry Demone, a Lunenburg fishing captain's son. He joined an advisory council of Massachusetts business people and officials who provide input to Nova Scotia Business, the organization mandated to raise the province's commercial profile.

Now 72, he pilots his motor yacht to Nova Scotia in the summer months. When he docks at Maritime marinas, his big boat always needs a bit more electrical juice than the local vessels. But everyone is happy to oblige because, after all, he is one of them. He has the ring.

CHAPTER 14

LIFE AMONG THE UP-ALONGS

IT'S THURSDAY. ALMOST midnight, in the Saint John Airport and Geoff Flood is part of a band of road warriors staggering off the last flight from Toronto. For Flood, there is exhilaration amid the exhaustion. He will see his wife and family again, after three days working in Central Canada as the president of a fast-growing computer services and consulting company. He also knows he will be back in Toronto on Monday or Tuesday, fulfilling his duties as boss of T4G Ltd. This has been his pattern of life for some time now—three to four days at home in Saint John, often working in the local office of his company; the rest of the week in the east end of downtown Toronto where T4G is based. He has a weekly commuting schedule that makes the daily rush hour from Barrie to Toronto or from North Vancouver to Howe Street look like a walk in the park.

"I love Toronto but I felt my kids should know their family," explains Flood, a lanky, serious-looking 55-year-old from a prominent construction family based in the Saint John suburb of Rothesay. He enjoys the fact that his sons can live in a community where his father and grandfather built many of the houses. "We have a large family in Saint John and no need for them to be distant."

Flood is part of a new twist on an ancient theme, the Atlantic Canada brigade of long-distance Maritimes commuters, who are Air Canada's best customers and most knowledgeable critics. In the most extreme example, they commute weekly from Halifax, Saint John, or St. John's; others grab bits and pieces of time at home in Atlantic Canada, when their work schedules allow. In summer, the flow of airplane commuters swells to a torrent—one spouse and the children go to the ocean home and the other visits on weekends. The reasons for this movement centre on the family: to allow their children to grow up in the saner confines of small towns and cities, or to really know their cousins, grandmas, and grandpas. Often, there is the assumption that the move to Toronto, Ottawa, or Montreal is a short-term career-boosting move and they will get a posting back in Atlantic Canada. Sometimes they do, but most often they don't. Also, there is simply the pull of the sea, the land, or the forests, the kind of thing that has pulled Maritimers back home for a hundred years from the Boston states or Toronto.

There is another factor that burns brightly in their motivation: They don't want to give up on the Maritimes, as so many Central Canadian critics have done. They believe that the Maritimes will return to the mythic past glory of the 19th century—and when it does, they will return for good. Like parts of the Prairies, this is Tomorrow Country, where tomorrow never seems to come.

The sad irony is that any bright tomorrow will be hard to achieve as long as Atlantic Canada suffers a continuing migration of these same professionals, managers, and entrepreneurs to Central Canada, the West, and the United States. To put it in numbers, the population of three of the four

Atlantic provinces declined between 1996 and 2001. In Newfoundland, the number of people fell to 513,000 from 552,000; in New Brunswick to 729,000 from 738,000; in Nova Scotia, to 908,000 from 909,000. Only Prince Edward Island gained people, and it is the smallest province with 135,000.

To make matters worse, people with a university education are the most likely to leave their home provinces and seek opportunities elsewhere. While this mobility of the well-educated is a common phenomenon everywhere, it is devastating for some of the Atlantic provinces, particularly Newfoundland. From 1991 to 1996, Newfoundland lost 8 per cent of its university-trained population to other provinces, a massive erosion of knowledge and skills, according to a 1999 study by the Royal Bank of Canada. Nova Scotia in that period lost almost 4 per cent of its educated people. The only province with a substantial net inflow of university graduates was British Columbia. Lise Bastarache, the Moncton-born Royal Bank economist who wrote the report, said the solutions to this outflow are not obvious: "Stronger job creation . . . is linked to more dynamic regional economic development, for which, unfortunately, there are no quick fixes." Not that there aren't attempts. New Brunswick actually has a program to "repatriate" émigrés by finding them good white-collar jobs.

It is difficult to calculate the magnitude of Maritimers and Newfoundlanders who work in top executive jobs outside the region. It is safe to say that it numbers in the thousands. As I researched the book, I kept uncovering new examples and, in fact, the search could have gone on forever. I discovered Cynthia Trudell, the New Brunswick engineer who runs the Sea Ray yacht company in Tennessee after a stint as leader of U.S. carmaker Saturn, and Lawson Hunter, the

Florenceville native and corporate lawyer who is Canada's former competition watchdog and now handles BCE's regulatory issues in Ottawa. And Mark Binns, the Prince Edward Island native and son of the provincial premier, who is the general manager of Mezzanine, an up-and-coming management consulting firm in Toronto.

As this white-collar migration from the Maritimes swells, the long-distance commuting of well-educated, well-paid people becomes more frenzied and frequent. Today's commuters are quite different from earlier generations: In those days, you would make your career in Toronto or Montreal or London or New York, but come home to retire in Atlantic Canada. "Like the salmon, Maritimers swim home to die," cracks Sir Graham Day, who fits that traditional pattern—he went from rural Nova Scotia to Montreal to London, England. Now in his 70s, he is home again in Hantsport, Nova Scotia, serving as a corporate director and mentor. But whatever the pattern—road warrior or aging warrior—there is a compelling need to stay connected with home, to the land, the sea, and the down-to-earth lifestyle.

Many pay a huge cost, if not financially, then measured in health and stress. Geoff Flood can manage it better than most because T4G, a national company, has offices in Saint John and Halifax. Besides, much of the technology industry operates on a virtual basis through the magic of a laptop and a Blackberry. Even the extra cost of commuting, $20,000 to $25,000 a year, is not onerous when you can buy a house in Saint John for $200,000 that would cost a million in Toronto. And Toronto has few vistas like the one Flood surveys every morning at his home in the bedroom village of Rothesay, looking out on the wide Kennebecasis Bay. He still owns a small bungalow in the Toronto suburb of Willowdale, with good access both to downtown Toronto and to the airport, where he spends his weekdays. In an ironic reversal of the usual pattern, the Flood family sees the Toronto home as "the camp" for occasional visits, such has shopping trips just before Christmas or a visit to Toronto tourist spots.

Flood admits he is lucky because he has found an easy balance between the two cities, active as he is in company offices on both sides of the divide. He is glad that he can avoid the 5:45 a.m. flight from Saint John to Toronto. He says it is "a national disgrace." If you take that flight, you are basically ruined for the rest of the day, says a friend of Flood's who makes that trip each week. Even David Ganong, a director of Air Canada, is miffed by the lateness of the last flight from Toronto, when about midnight he lands in Saint John and still faces the drive home to St. Stephen. It's a reminder of how hard it is to run a business in a country as big and thinly populated as Canada.

But few Air Canada warriors have maintained the crippling pace of Dean MacDonald, who for three years balanced the job of a senior executive with the Rogers cable organization in Toronto with a home in St. John's, where he spent weekends with his wife and four sons. This self-imposed ordeal began when Cable Atlantic, the Newfoundland company in which he was a part-owner with his friend and premier-to-be Danny Williams, was sold to Rogers Communications in 2000. MacDonald was invited to stay on as a Rogers executive and eventually rose to chief operating officer of the Toronto company's cable arm.

He kept his home outside St. John's, both for his family's sake and to keep a little leverage in his bargaining with the Rogers organization. It was his handy escape hatch. But the toll was punishing. When those weekends in St. John's were finished, he would get up on Monday at 4 a.m. Newfoundland time, to catch the 5 a.m. flight to Toronto. In other words, he would be getting up at 2:30 a.m. Toronto time, and would usually get to bed about midnight that evening. "I'd be one tired guy," recalls MacDonald, who carried on that numbing routine until 2004, when he landed the CEO's job at cable company Persona in St. John's, thus relieving himself of the weekly trek.

He remembers at one point coaching his son's high school basketball team, which would hold games and practices in the middle of the week. On a Wednesday, he would leave Toronto at 1 p.m., and land in St. John's at 5:30, coach a game or manage a practice, then get back on a flight the next morning and be in the office at 9 a.m. Toronto time. Not that he was the only one making that trip. "I saw the same group of guys on the plane every week. There were 10 or 15 that I would run into—they were doing the same thing."

He doesn't totally regret those three crazy years. The reason he did it, he said, was to learn that he could operate in the flash and intensity of a big Toronto corporate job in a publicly traded company. It was his way of answering the question "Can you play in the big leagues?" He points out that Atlantic Canadians have that chip on their shoulders—that embedded self-doubt, the sense that what they do back home in Halifax or St. John's is not really that important or meaningful. "But once you do the Toronto thing, you kinda go 'It's not the brass ring.' You realize that the brass ring is the quality of life and what we have in Newfoundland." He learned a lot in Toronto but he always felt that corporate life was not all it was cracked up to be. "There is a lot more bullshit in Toronto, a lot more sense that the wheels of the corporation seem to be the driver, rather than the wheels of pragmatic decision-makers. It is bigger, more bureaucratic, and in a public company there is the onerous reporting. It makes them move a little slower."

The love of home and family is also what keeps Toronto investment banker Peter Jelley coming back to the Maritimes. He too has found a way to do it, by assembling a growing investment banking practice among the entrepreneurs of Atlantic Canada. Jelley grew up as the son of a high school math teacher in Summerside, Prince Edward Island, went to University of King's College in Halifax, and then to the London School of Economics. He returned to North America to attend Harvard Business School for his MBA, a rare Harvard business grad in the island province. After a stint in New York, he went to Toronto seven years ago to join the investment banking firm First Marathon, which, in a round of industry consolidation, became part of National Bank Financial.

As he tried to make his way in Toronto, he searched his mind for some kind of competitive edge, some market he could tap where people would return his phone calls. He found himself making calls on Atlantic Canadian companies and uncovering a receptive audience. He helped take Bernard Imbeault's restaurant business public through an income trust; he began to do work with George Armoyan.

While he was finally building this financing business, he also found an outlet for his personal entrepreneurial energies. As a kid growing up in Summerside, he had funded his university stints by working at an amusement park in nearby Cavendish, a popular summertime destination for tourists. He became the seasonal park's manager, employing 100 people and making wages that could support his pursuit of various degrees. One day in Toronto, he got a call from his former employer, indicating that the Magic Mountain amusement park in Moncton was up for sale. Jelley was immediately attracted to it, and with help from his old employer and his family, he put together the financing and bought the place.

His brother Mark is now the manager; the family has upgraded standards and management practices, and the place is making very good money. "Financially it has been a very, very good purchase; we have been able to run a lot more efficiently and a lot of that is my brother's work." Meanwhile, 100,000 people a summer are streaming through Magic Mountain, and the Jelley family is thinking about expanding its amusement park portfolio. Back in Toronto, Peter consorts with a bunch of young lawyers and investment bankers from the Maritimes, a handy network for deal-making and maintaining those Atlantic ties.

Jelley is a bit of an anomaly—it is harder to find Prince Edward Islanders among the transplanted commuters from the rest of Canada. It may be the island mentality, which is only slightly modified by a new bridge to the mainland. Perhaps it is because islanders live in a kind of paradise that no sane person would want to leave. The magnetic pull of the island is not irresistible, however. James Palmer comes from a long line of distinguished island lawyers. He graduated from Dalhousie Law 53 years ago and, on the invitation of a classmate, drove straight across the country to Calgary, then a city of 120,000 people. He liked the wide-open spaces and the attitude that "people didn't care who you were, it was *what* you were that mattered." Palmer stayed and built a law practice, although he admits "you miss the water for a while." In time, the proximity of the mountains overcomes any longing for ocean. At 76, he is a confirmed Calgarian, an esteemed corporate lawyer as senior partner of Burnet Duckworth and Palmer, and a rare Liberal power-broker in a city dominated by Conservatives. "I just like the life here," he says. There are lots of ex-Maritimers in Calgary, he says, but after a while they become Albertans. It may be a matter of distance and the lure of an equally powerful physical entity, such as prairie and mountains. Yet some part of James Palmer remains in the Maritimes, where he remains active as a philanthropist and non-profit board member, with strong ties to Dalhousie Law School and to the University of Prince Edward Island.

But there is always a danger of excessive romanticism, of looking at the Maritimes through the rosy lens of nostalgia. In truth, a lot of people have very mixed feelings about their past in the East. Irwin Simon often thinks about his Maritimes roots as he wanders his neighbourhood on the Upper East Side of Manhattan, where he lives with his wife and four children. As he takes his kids to private school, he knows that the annual tuition for each of them is more than his father would make in one year as a grocer in the Cape Breton coal mining town of Glace Bay. Simon is now the most important natural foods executive in the United States, as chief executive and builder of Hain Celestial, a $700-billion (U.S.) business whose brand portfolio includes Celestial Seasonings herbal tea, Terra Chips, Health Valley foods, and the Yves Veggie Cuisine franks that are sold by urban hot dog vendors as a vegetarian alternative.

Looking back on life in Glace Bay, he worries that his children are missing out on the values of a real world, where community and family were more important than money, which was always in short supply in the mining community. But he also has no illusions: It was hard growing up Jewish in a town with only a small community of Jewish families among the area's heavily Scottish-Canadian and Acadian populations. In the 1970s, everything was defined in Glace Bay by whether you were Catholic, Protestant, or something else. "It was absolutely hard being Jewish, it was back to ignorance. I was called a dirty Jew almost every day of the week," Simon says. "I got chased home because I was Jewish and got called names."

This alienation from the core society made the Simon family feel deeply attached to their small Jewish community. They showed people in Glace Bay that they were never ashamed to be Jewish. And Simon expresses no lingering hatred toward those who gave him such a hard time. It was just the way things were, in a time of widespread ignorance about people who were different.

He has come a very long way from growing up in Simon's Grocery on Union Street in Glace Bay. After high school, he took a commerce degree at Saint Mary's University in Halifax, then moved to Toronto to work for the dairy company William Neilsen and its subsidiary Häagen-Daz ice cream. After a few years he joined Häagen-Daz in its New York operations in 1986. "I didn't know a soul. I was scared out of my pants," he says. But he was also very ambitious, eager to build a better life than he had known in hard-scrabble Glace Bay. In the early 1990s, he struck out on his own and bought a Brooklyn kosher-food company and followed it up with a $21-million (U.S.) purchase of the Hain Pure Foods Co. He saw an undeveloped niche in natural foods that quickly widened into a large and growing segment of the food industry. He went on a buying spree that was capped by a $300-million takeover of the funky Celestial Seasonings operations in Boulder, Colorado.

But to do all this, he had to leave Atlantic Canada. "My risk-taking, my exposure to globalization, my exposure to brands, to business, never would have happened if I hadn't moved out of eastern Canada. Could I have done what I did had I stayed in Cape Breton or Nova Scotia? Absolutely not. I might have been in my own business, a store or something, but I would not be running a $700- to $800-million company created from scratch."

For Simon, there is none of that nostalgic rhapsodizing about the Maritimes, and he does not spend time with a bunch of old East Coast buddies, like the Maritime Mafia that hangs together in Toronto. He admits that in credential-obsessed U.S. business circles, it probably hasn't helped him that he has only a bachelor's degree from an obscure East Coast university, not an MBA from Harvard or Stanford.

Simon's realistic assessment of the Maritimes is shared by David Bissett, whose family is from Nova Scotia and who was born in Prince Edward Island, but built a successful investment funds management business in Calgary. Now retired and a major philanthropist in Calgary, he does not get all dewy-eyed thinking about his roots. At one point, through a family friend, he got to know the old Anglo establishment of Halifax, which he says, displayed "a very conservative, very chummy kind of thinking." It was, he said, an inward-looking tribe that only recently has loosened its grip on the city's business mentality. Meanwhile, he thrived in the breezy, risk-taking openness of Alberta.

Similarly, there has been a lot of myth-making built around the Maritime way of managing, which is embodied by operational masterminds such as John Bragg and Wallace McCain. In fact, one of the most dynamic ex-Maritimers, Rod Bryden, the former New Brunswicker who has run a number of businesses from his Ottawa base, has made his name for his financial wizardry, not his ability to operate. He erected intricate financing deals with dizzying tax implications that, at times, only he seemed to understand. Sometimes, they were so complex that he could not pull investors and managers along with him.

That was a major flaw for the visionary Bryden, a farmer's son who became a law professor and federal bureaucrat before going into business. He is the ultimate serial entrepreneur who has owned and exited a range of businesses—computer services giant Systemhouse, the Ottawa Senators hockey team, and medical pioneer World Heart, to name the best-known examples. The pattern is often the same: He builds things up, runs into financial trouble, loses control of them, and then bounces back with another venture. That is a very un-Maritime pattern.

Bryden is the great outlier, the ex-Maritimer who doesn't quite fit the mould. Perhaps that is why he is rarely mentioned as a member of the Maritime Mafia. But in one important way, Bryden does follow the pattern. In summer 2004, he quit as president and CEO of World Heart, a maker of artificial-heart pumps, in the face of angry investors and disastrously disappointing financial results. I managed to catch up with him by telephone as he was cleaning up his office. He declined any comment, except to say he was taking a month at his summer retreat to consider his options. That retreat is on Cape Breton Island, the place where Rod Bryden goes to lick his wounds. Later that year, the Comeback Kid of Canadian business was back again, working with an Ottawa biotechnology company.

Rod Bryden's story shows it is hard to generalize about regions and the kinds of people and managers that they produce. There is no rigid "Atlantic Canada type," but from my conversations with dozens of present and past East Coasters, I can certainly describe a collection of characteristics that apply in many, many cases. Maritime managers do tend to be straight-talking, non-political (in an office-politics sense), and strong in running things. They are creative about finding less expensive solutions that require a bit of improvisation. They often exhibit a rural Canadian lack of pretence and show. They are what they are. In a corporate world beset by greed and ostentation, these are positive qualities. The Maritime style is well suited to a post–Enron era, where there is revulsion toward the image of wealthy CEOs being led away to jail. The Maritime way suggests a simpler time, when a family ran the local mill and all the people in the town worked there. But the Atlantic method should not be mistaken for a lack of sophistication. Lawson Hunter, the corporate lawyer and executive who has dealt with many of the Atlantic clans, observes that "Maritimers are an astute lot, but they like to cultivate this simple image." He warns outsiders not to be taken in by this impersonation of aw-shucks rural innocence in business dealings. "You've got to be careful," Hunter warns.

Indeed, something must be working well, for there are so many success stories among the "up-alongs," the label that applies to Maritimers who have pulled up stakes and moved up along the road (as opposed to the "CFAs," people who have "come from away"). The Atlantic way is travelling very well these days. I met some of these up-alongs at a dinner in Toronto, an event held to honour Wallace McCain as an international businessman. The gala was attended by a microcosm of the group that meets each August at Fox Harb'r: Purdy Crawford gave a speech, Frank McKenna paid tribute to the McCains' drive to global prominence, various Toronto McCains were in attendance.

The Maritime Mafia was out in force, and it was an impressive group. At my table sat the cross-section of the next generation: Tom Eisenhauer, a member of an old Lunenburg fishing family who now heads a private equity firm in Toronto; Jon Barry, a Toronto technology consultant who hails from a good family in Saint John; Danny Graham, Halifax lawyer and then Liberal leader in Nova Scotia; and Paul Zed, then an Ottawa lobbyist but also a former and future MP, who has been married to an Irving.

I kept thinking about how there must be some way to bottle all this energy and brainpower, and ship it home to the Maritimes to run and build companies. But as I talked to more Maritimers and Newfoundlanders, it struck me that Atlantic Canada may actually be enjoying the best of all possible worlds. Here is a cadre of bright well-connected people, living and working in Central and Western Canada and the United States, but absolutely committed to making the East Coast a better place to live. What other region in the country enjoys such devotion from a tight network of people who have penetrated the highest levels of corporate and investment power in the country? That is the Maritime Mafia's great achievement: no longer emigrés, they have taken over the kingdom. Atlantic rules.

TOP 15 SKILLS YOU SHOULD HAVE
IF YOU WORK FOR
AN ATLANTIC CANADIAN BOSS

15. COMMUNICATION.

Appreciate the creative ways in which obscenities can be used in business conversation. You might comment to your boss, "Mr. Rowe, it's wonderful to hear 'bullshit' used as a noun, verb, and adjective in the same sentence."

14. GEOGRAPHICAL DIVERSITY.

It's always useful to trot out your East Coast connections, no matter how tenuous, as in "I seem to recall that my late Aunt Velma came from Canso, and she was always my favourite."

13. CULTURAL SENSITIVITY I.

Remember Newfoundlanders are not Maritimers. They are wilder and crazier than their counterparts from Nova Scotia, New Brunswick, and Prince Edward Island.

12. CULTURAL SENSITIVITY II.

A Newfoundland boss will want to know what you think of Danny Williams. The most prudent response is "I really agree with what he is trying to do, but I don't think taking down

Canadian flags was a good idea." And never ever start a sentence with the words "As my friend Peggy Wente says . . ."

11. OPERATIONAL EXCELLENCE.
When the conversation turns to marketing or finance, your line should be "That stuff is just a lot of Upper Canadian shit. As long as the company runs well, and you keep an eye on the pennies, the rest of that crap will follow."

10. TOLERANCE.
It is useful to denigrate the decision-making skills of Central Canadians, especially the people of Bay Street, as in "Those bullshit artists spend so much time talking bullshit that they bullshit themselves right out of decisions." (Hah, you thought it couldn't be done!)

9. NETWORKING.
Learn to sail, fish for salmon, or run a gi-normous power boat. Talk a lot about the glorious time spent at that lodge in the Miramichi (no matter how grungy the place actually was). Golf is okay, as long as you have played at Fox Harb'r, Highland Links, or some other East Coast course—and talk about it loudly.

8. INTERNATIONAL BUSINESS.
Advertise your global sophistication by mentioning that you've been to Boston twice.

7. SPORTS SAVVY.
Profess your love of Junior A Hockey and your appreciation of Sidney Crosby's skills. Maritime business types, especially family scions, love junior hockey, and throw their cash at franchises in Moncton, Saint John, and St. John's.

6. CONSUMPTION.

Sell the BMW, Lexus, or Miata. Tell everyone you drive a Buick, Chevy, or Ford because "I'm just a simple country girl (or boy)." SUVs are fine, as long as you allude to those "crazy Halifax winters." Downsize to a modest city home, but it's okay to have a palace at Chester or in Bermuda or in Jamaica.

5. SELF-RELIANCE.

When something breaks in the office or factory, don't just buy a replacement. Advertise loudly that you can fix it with a little wire and some spare parts. Even if your solution ends up costing much more than a new part, it will give the impression that you are saving money.

4. AFTER-HOURS.

Find out where the Maritimers hang out in your city. Order overflowing pitchers of Moosehead or Keiths. Become a tiresomely knowledgeable aficionado of oysters, lobsters, or some other delicious aquatic creature.

3. FASHION SENSE.

Casual is in, Armani and Hugo Boss are out. Look as if you just got into the office from a weekend of sailing. But stealing a St. FX ring or pretending you went to St.FX when you did not would be considered a serious offence and could have you fired.

2. TRAINING.

Make sure that you have attended some Atlantic Canada university, even if only for a drunken weekend at Dal visiting your cousin from Etobicoke. It is not necessary to have actually graduated. If fact, it is better to have spent two years there and decided you needed to get out into the "real world."

1. RECRUITMENT.

Hire Maritimers, however slim their relative qualifications. After all, you can simply explain to your Maritime boss that they are "good people." But after that, they are on their own, and they will do well.

WHO'S WHO IN THE EAST COAST MAFIA

THE INNER CIRCLE

▢ ✕ ∅ 🖵 **John Bragg** — Blueberry and cable television tycoon

🖵 $ ⚖ **Purdy Crawford** — Bay Street lawyer and corporate conscience

∅ 🛒 **Richard Currie** — Ex-supermarket boss and telecom chairman

🖵 ⚖ **Sir Graham Day** — Former Thatcher handyman and professional director

🖵 🛒 ⌂ **Ron Joyce** — Doughnut king and golf course builder

✕ 🖵 **Wallace McCain** — Food magnate and key networker

🍁 🖵 **Frank McKenna** — Ambassador to Washington

🖵 🐟 $ **John Risley** — Seafood titan and ubiquitous investor

$ 🏭 ✈ **Ken Rowe** — Aerospace tough guy

🖵 🛒 **David Sobey** — Retail warrior; built the stores

🖵 🛒 $ **Donald Sobey** — Brainy investor; nurtured the wealth

POWER FAMILIES

✗ THE McCAIN GANG

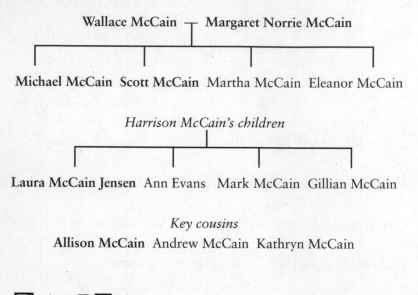

Wallace McCain ── Margaret Norrie McCain

Michael McCain **Scott McCain** Martha McCain Eleanor McCain

Harrison McCain's children

Laura McCain Jensen Ann Evans Mark McCain Gillian McCain

Key cousins
Allison McCain Andrew McCain Kathryn McCain

▣ 🛒 🏃 🏠 ▣ ✗ 🌲 THE IRVING POSSE

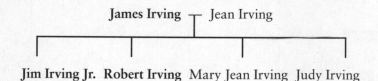

James Irving ── Jean Irving

Jim Irving Jr. **Robert Irving** Mary Jean Irving Judy Irving

Jamie Irving

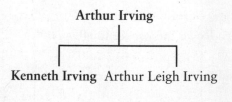

Arthur Irving

Kenneth Irving Arthur Leigh Irving

Jack Irving

John Irving

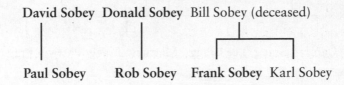

$ 🛒 ⬛ CLAN SOBEY

David Sobey   **Donald Sobey**   Bill Sobey (deceased)

Paul Sobey   **Rob Sobey**   **Frank Sobey**   Karl Sobey

Cousins: Jana Sobey   John Robert Sobey   Jennifer Sinclair   William Sinclair

🐟 🌲 ⬛ $ JODREY GIANTS

George Bishop   **David Hennigar**   John Jodrey

🍺 OLAND BREWED

Derek Oland ── Jacqueline Oland

Andrew Oland   Matthew Oland   **Patrick Oland**   Giles Oland

$ 🏭 ✈ THE ROWE BOAT

Ken Rowe ── Dorothy Rowe

Julie Gossen   **Kirk Rowe**   Stephen Rowe

✗ GANONG SQUAD

David Ganong ── Diane Ganong

Aaron Ganong   **Bryana Ganong**   Nick Ganong

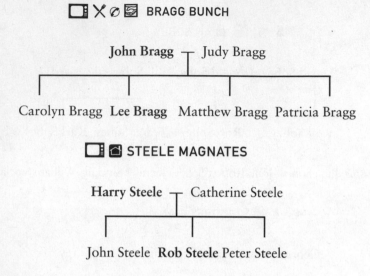

BRAGG BUNCH

John Bragg — Judy Bragg

Carolyn Bragg **Lee Bragg** Matthew Bragg Patricia Bragg

STEELE MAGNATES

Harry Steele — Catherine Steele

John Steele **Rob Steele** Peter Steele

LEGEND

Names in **bold** indicate key players; only major
family players in the business are listed.

- Media
- Food
- Investor
- Law
- Communications
- Networker
- Retail
- Real Estate
- Government
- Fisheries
- Manufacturing
- Aerospace
- Construction
- Oil and Energy
- Forestry and forest products

BEST OF THE REST

KEY CONSIGLIERI
Jim Gogan and Bill McEwan (Sobeys)
Mary Keith and Daniel Goodwin (Irvings)
Stephen Plummer (Rowes)
Dale Morrison (McCains)
Bruce McCubbin (Olands)

TELECOM CONNECTION
Lino Celeste
Jay Forbes
Colin Latham
John MacDonald
John McLennan
Gerry Pond
Stephen Wetmore

NEW BRUNSWICK MOVERS
Bill Barrett
Reuben Cohen
Glen Cooke
Bernard Cyr
Bernard Imbeault
Monique Imbeault
Aldéa Landry
Denis Losier
Jon Manship
Francis McGuire
Paul McSpurren
Tom Simms
Robert Zildjian

TWO FROM P.E.I.
Regis Duffy

Danny Murphy

BLUENOSE BRIGADE
Henry Demone

The Fountain Family

Richard Homburg

Hector Jacques

Steve Lund

Colin MacDonald

Mickey MacDonald

David Mann

Ralph Medjuck

Paul O'Regan

Stephen O'Regan

Steve Parker

Carl Potter

Joe Shannon

Allan Shaw

Robbie Shaw

Hugh Smith

Fred Smithers

Tom Stanfield

Dave Wilson

Ian Wilson

CHESTER IMPORTS
John Hunkin

Tim Moore

Sir Christopher Ondaatje

MEDIA MOGULS
Graham Dennis
Sarah Dennis
Michael Donovan
Charles Keating
Robert Pace

NEW FACES
George Armoyan
Danny Chedrawe
Bernd Christmas
Mani Suissa

LEGAL EAGLES
George Cooper
Rob Dexter
Thomas MacQuarrie
Neil McKelvey
Bill Mingo
Robert Winters

THE TORONTO CROWD
Jon Barry
Mark Binns
Libby Burnham
Rodney Clarke
John Dowd
Tom Eisenhauer
Geoff Flood
Buzz Hargrove
Peter Jelley
Malcolm MacKillop
Al Power
Richard Simms
Annette Verschuren

THE BANKERS
Lise Bastarache
Charles Coffey
Arthur Crockett
Gordon Feeney
Rowland Frazee
Peter Godsoe
Cedric Ritchie

OILPATCH WARRIORS
Grant Bartlett
David Bissett
Lou MacEachern
James Palmer

BRAIN POWERS
Elizabeth Beale
Brian Lee Crowley
Gail Dinter-Gottlieb
Colin Dodds
Wade MacLauchlan
Axel Meisen
Elizabeth Parr-Johnson
Tim O'Neill
Kenneth Ozmon
Dawn Russell
Donald Savoie
Tom Traves

GLOBAL TIES
Kevin Francis
Basil Hargrove
Irwin Simon
Catherine Tait
Cynthia Trudell

OTTAWA SCENE
Rod Bryden
Lawson Hunter
Peter Nicholson
Judith Maxwell
Paul Zed

ST. FX RINGERS
Trudy Eagan
Harris Fricker
Allan J. MacEachen
Brian Mulroney
Lowell Murray
Seamus O'Regan
Sean Riley
Robert Shea
Mark Wallace

NEWFIE BULLETS

Trevor Adey

Rex Anthony

Miller Ayre

Bill Barry

Randy Bell

Frank Coleman

Chris Collingwood

John Crosbie

Rob Crosbie

Chris Griffiths

Albert Hickman

Phil Keeping

Dean MacDonald

Stanley Marshall

Brendan Paddick

Ches Penney

Derrick Rowe

Geoff Stirling

Brian Tobin

Danny Williams

Vic Young

Rod White

Mel and Peter Woodward

OLD AND YOUNG DOBBINS
Basil Dobbin
Brian Dobbin
Craig Dobbin
Derm Dobbin
Mark Dobbin

ARTS AND CRAFTS
David Blackwood
Alex Colville
Brooks Diamond
Cathy Jones
Great Big Sea: Alan Doyle, Sean McCann,
Bob Hallett, Kris MacFarlane, Murray Foster
Rick Mercer
Anne Murray
Christopher Pratt
Mary Pratt
Mary Walsh

INDEX